THE MASTERBRAND MANDATE

The Management Strategy That Unifies Companies and Multiplies Value

LYNN B. UPSHAW

AND

EARL L. TAYLOR, Ph.D.

John Wiley & Sons, Inc.

NEW YORK • CHICHESTER • WEINHEIM • BRISBANE • SINGAPORE • TORONTO

To Jim—My loving brother, my good friend
and
To my wife, Roberta, and daughter, Diana

CONTENTS

PART ONE
Mandate: Build the Customer's Community

PART TWO
The Inside Job: Coach the Customer's Team

PART THREE

The World Outside: Maneuver the Masterbrand

is no simple formula for doing so. Global master-brands are showing how to have the best of both worlds: a focused and enduring meaning across cyberspace and time, along with a resilient and evolving relevance to global, regional, and local brand communities.

Our final chapter summarizes the questions to ask and actions to take when you accept the *master-brand mandate*. You'll also need technology and innovation metrics as leading indicators of your masterbranding capabilities.

ABOUT THE BOOK

One of the most enduring myths in global business today is that brands are solely a *marketing* tool. In the right hands, they are much more: a model for organizing, a structure for selling and profit generation, a focus for achieving, and a template of performance metrics. The very fact that the word *brand* rarely appears in most management texts is a good indication of the latest wave of "marketing myopia" that has led brands to be compartmentalized as specialized weapons of the marketing department.

No one is happier than we that corporate leaders are discovering that brand building and business building are synonymous. Yet, if a company fails to fully leverage its entire organization when building a brand, then that brand will be less than it might have been.

What every company searches for are ways to differentiate its goods and services. Differentiation, however, has become no more than table stakes in today's markets, which require a pervasive internal commitment to brand building to achieve a competitive superiority in the external marketplace. The endproduct of such enterprise-wide commitment is what we call the *masterbrand*.

The difference between branding and masterbrand building is like the difference between memorizing and understanding. Conventional branding is a vital tool, but it is masterbrand building that helped: save Apple from extinction, reinvigorate the foundering IBM, accelerate the Starbucks momentum, and propel the leading Internet businesses like Yahoo! and Amazon.com. If branding is about differentiation, masterbrand building is about value creation. You can take only one of those deliverables to the bank.

We have written this book because we are convinced that companies that continue to market in the conventional way will inevitably lose whatever competitive advantage they may have. In the pages that follow, we will tell you about the "mandate" that we believe company leaders must listen to, and manage within. It is a mandate that may burst forth spontaneously from within a company, or that may be generated by enlightened management, or that may be prompted by an aggressive competitor. It is a mandate that vulcanizes the people of the company and its surrounding community of supporters, that enables leaders and their employee-partners to rally all of their resources around a singular masterbrand, and which powers that masterbrand's central value proposition to the customer.

Over the years, we have had the privilege of advising many outstanding companies, experiences that we bring to bear in this book. These companies stretch across many industries and service many target markets, and include Bayer Corporation, Visa International, Walt Disney, Bell Atlantic, 3Com Corporation, Bank of America, esurance.com, Abilizer (formerly Perksatwork.com), ConAgra, Wellpoint Health Networks, Outrigger Hotels & Resorts, Shell Oil, Noosh, Inc., and others. And, we have conducted extensive secondary research and personal interviews over the past two years which identified how other leading companies have created masterbrands that have made all the difference in the hostile markets in which they compete. These include Lucent Technologies, eBay, Leatherman Tool Group, PepsiCo, Gateway Computer, Rich's Product Corporation, 3M, Enron, IBM, and many others.

We have divided our thoughts into three parts that point toward fundamental imperatives:

- *Part One: Mandate: Build the Customer's Community.* Although the first steps in building a masterbrand will take place within the company, we felt it best to begin with chapters that describe the final objective of the work—namely, the offline and online brand communities that are driven by customer needs. Companies that have built strong masterbrands have done so by creating living brand communities that jointly "own" and nurture the brand. Such communities are peopled by individuals whose collective purpose is to exceed customer expectations.

- *Part Two: The Inside Job: Coach the Customer's Team.* In an age of interconnectivity and "transparent" organizations, the insular company mentality must give way to a new kind of "open architecture" that capitalizes on the blurring of boundaries between companies, customers, strategic partners, and market intermediaries. That will require "coaching" the people of the company on what the masterbrand stands for, and how it must perform, thus leading them to become the most effective possible advocates for their customers.

- *Part Three: The World Outside: Maneuver the Masterbrand.* Masterbrands must be guided into the most leverageable position possible. Just as they may out*source* some aspects of their businesses, masterbrand companies "out-*brand*" competitors by better deploying their brand out among their brand communities, and beyond into the global marketplace. In this final section, we will also discuss how to overcome the inevitable hurdles to change.

Along the way, we will present more in-depth studies of three superior masterbrands that are soundly whipping the competition because their leaders know how to multiply their advantages with the full force of their people, their strategic partners, and their customers. These companies don't just cope with change and accept risk, they use them as competitive weapons. They have achieved their success by democratizing their industries, and by creating powerful brand communities. Those companies are: Sun Microsystems, which has consistently outflanked competitors by creating proprietary systems that can be marketed in open-ended environments; Charles Schwab & Co., which launched marketing innovations that revolutionized financial services; and America Online (now AOL TimeWarner), which has forged the most powerful information and entertainment masterbrand in the world.

Throughout our book, we have also put special emphasis on business-to-business (b2b) and business-to-consumer (b2c) online e-business, because we now know that the dynamics of that particular selling environment are having a profound and permanent impact on all others. It should be no surprise that much of the growth of the Net economy can be directly attributed to online brand building (although even brand building will not offset ebusiness overspending). In the same way, the growth of online communities will guide us in establishing masterbrand communities for all companies that are interested in making the most of their real and perceived equities.

At the end of most chapters, you will find a feature that we call "Managing Your Mandate." It lays out questions that you should be asking and actions you should be taking, if you are serious about transforming your company into a formidable masterbrand.

Finally, we want to point out now—as we will at the end of our book—that readers may be inclined to discount the similarities between their companies and those we use as examples. You may not have the charismatic founder-visionaries that lead Charles Schwab and Sun Microsystems. Your company may not have the capitalization of a Lucent or a Yahoo!, or the cohesive culture of a Nokia or IKEA, or the thriving community of an eBay or an America Online. Nevertheless, whatever your company does own as resources and assets, you can multiply their value many-fold with a strategic and operational focus on your masterbrand.

Understandably, you may resist elevating brand building to a general management mantra, and we certainly do not suggest that it is the only route to success. Yet, when you see a competitor become a powerful masterbrand enterprise—and see that company unify its people and multiply its value—you will come to believe our central message: Brand building should be an enterprise-wide discipline, not simply a marketing tool. That might not be easy for some CEOs and their managers to accept, but when has pioneering better ways to manage ever been easy?

We hope that you enjoy reading our analysis of masterbrand masterpieces as much as we have enjoyed preparing *The Masterbrand Mandate*.

Lynn Upshaw
Marin County, California
upshaw@brandbuilding.com
www.brandbuilding.com

Earl Taylor
Cambridge, Massachusetts
e.taylor@research-int.com

1

Built to Change

Anyone who says businessmen deal only in facts, not fiction, has never read old five-year plans.
—Malcolm Forbes[1]

The global companies that CEOs admire most are known by some of the most recognized brand names on the planet. The U.S. companies that Americans believe have the strongest reputations are referred to by brand names that have become household words. These are not coincidences. Great companies used to just sell great brands; now they have become them.[2]

As it turns out, they have done so just in time. We have raced past the postindustrial age, the information age, the relationship age, and right into the age of continuous evolution. Change, which has become our constant companion, is looking more and more like a stalker. Companies that will succeed in coming years will need to plan their own obsolescence and then discover new and more efficient ways of doing business, or permit their markets to dictate their fates.

Unfortunately, change can sweep away the good with the bad. The faster that companies learn to move, the greater the risk that they will lose their strategic focus, and with it, their value proposition. However, those leaders who build their companies around benefit-driven, overarching brand promises will keep the ship steady and the course true, even as the crew labors to reinvent its purpose with the dawn of each new day.

The Company and the Masterbrand

Recent management books have celebrated the traditional company model, one even calling it "the ultimate creation."[3] While the Ultimate Creator might have some issues with that, there is no question that the company is potentially of greater value to the customer than any product or service that it creates. But if one thing has become clear in global business, it is that the traditional company model can no longer afford to be traditional, especially in the way that it works with the concept of brand.

In simpler times, the boundaries that separated *brand* and *company* were clear: A conventional *brand* was a product or service that was marketed with various promises and meanings. A *company* was a corporate entity that sponsored the marketing of such brands. A *corporate* (or company) *brand* was the external image that was marketed to constituencies and third-party influencers. The marketers were in charge of the brands, and company management concerned itself with the corporate reputation.

Leaders with foresight are now reshaping their entire organizations around company-wide brands that are jointly "owned" by their people and their surrounding "brand communities." We refer to these types of companies and their selling structures as *masterbrands*.[4]

Masterbrands are a company-wide brand force, composed of a central set of associated meanings and benefits, whose scope stretches from the company's strategic core, throughout its people and partners, enveloping its customers, and beyond to its outer perimeter of influence. Masterbrands enact the continuously evolving positioning of a company among its competitors and the character that makes that company uniquely attractive to its constituencies. The masterbrand incorporates the company mission, vision, and values, but translates them into more concrete, leverageable forms.

At IBM, Sun Microsystems, Charles Schwab, 3Com Corporation, Hewlett-Packard, and Lucent Technologies, masterbrand and company are becoming inseparable. The IBM masterbrand is centered on customer service; all of that company's businesses are focused on the customer service mission, and the IBM masterbrand turns that mission into a sellable (highly proprietary) commodity. Sun Microsystems is a masterbrand whose selling power is based on open-ended solutions. Charles Schwab's masterbrand is designed to demystify investing for all Americans. Lucent Technologies, 3M, and Hewlett-Packard are about different aspects of innovation. 3Com Corporation is about simplifying complex networking in the e-business age.

Even so-called holding companies like Enron, diversified corporations such as Sara Lee Corporation, product-focused companies like Procter & Gamble, and historically decentralized companies such as Hewlett-Packard—all are increasingly approaching their enterprise-wide challenges as single brandlike organizations, within which individual product and service brands can be more effectively marketed. In such cases, the building of the company masterbrand is having a profound influence on operations, on selling, on new venture development, and on long-range planning.

Those masterbrands with the greatest potential for positive change now operate within the interdependent brand communities that they serve, whose members include employees, customers, supply chain and alliance partners (some of which are periodically competitors), investors, and other constituencies.

A World of Challenge and Change

A few years ago, the Internet was underestimated to be simply a remarkable communications channel. We now know that it is profoundly transforming our social, political, and especially our business relationships. In this endlessly expanding whirlpool, proprietary product designs are less protectable; innovative distribution systems can be instantly replicated, or bypassed entirely, by second-tier competitors; and spending support advantages disappear overnight when rivals capture $200 million marketing budgets on the first day of an IPO.

Internet e-business is disrupting supply chain management,

redefining resource planning, creating unearthly valuations, and making obsolete whole sections of organizational structure. Analyst William Knoke of the Harvard Capital Group investment firm is among several futurists who predict that companies will respond to this new environment by evolving into an "amoeba form." According to this view, bellwether companies will be "hypermodular," infinitely malleable, altering their form on a dime to fit the business needs of the moment. It will be, Knoke suggests, "like the jellylike blob of cytoplasm seen under the microscope: it's amorphous, changeable, and conforms in shape to its environment; . . . difficult to distinguish where one [company] ends and the next begins."[5]

We are already seeing such organizations that rapidly stretch themselves through merger and acquisition (Cisco Systems), mate with dozens of strategic partners (Microsoft), and suck in sustenance through outsourcing (most U.S. businesses), as they adjust to rapidly shifting environments. As change swirls around and within them, it is of crucial importance that organizations be tethered to a shiftable hub that is at the confluence of what the company is, what its people can do, and what it stands for in the marketplace.

Here are some of the specific challenges ahead that will demand the steadying influence of a masterbrand focus:

The rapid delivery and sheer tonnage of information are suffocating customers, making it difficult for companies to spotlight their value-added benefits. A recent Gallup survey concluded that the average American office worker receives an average of 190 messages a day. Microsoft discovered that typical users of its Outlook software accumulate 1,900 e-mails in their Inbox and Outbox folders before hitting the delete button.[6] Commercial messages are being inserted into every imaginable venue. The glandular growth of the Internet means that online users, who cannot escape commercial messaging as it is, can only watch as their cyberspace becomes peppered with all forms of site sponsorships, banner ads, and interstitials (pop-up messaging). No wonder we hear cries for help like this plea from reporter Janelle Brown of the online magazine, *Salon.com:*

In the course of conceiving this paragraph, I checked my e-mail three times and fired off four responses. I took a phone call, visited a few Web sites—simultaneously, I might add, on two computers—and perused some posts on an online bulletin board. I snuck a peek at the latest news wires, gobbled some take-out Thai food, read a press release. I did this all while switching back and forth between two Internet radio stations, which I listened to through headphones. Some would call this multitasking . . . but for others, it's a sign of the continuing demise of intelligent life on earth.[7]

A cohesive, masterbrand-centered operating strategy gives companies a fighting chance to make an impact in this time of overstimulated, undernourished constituencies, living within an information maelstrom.

In the short term, at least, the centrifugal forces of the Internet are disintermediating valued customer relationships. Disintermediation is the bypassing of traditional selling channels to deal directly with purchasers of products or services—what we used to call the elimination of "the middle man." Not all travel agents, stock brokers, and toy merchants have heard the term, but you can bet that they've felt its sting.

In countless examples, the barriers to competitive entry have fallen faster than anyone had thought possible. Although it is not a new phenomenon, disintermediation has become a prolific art with the emergence of the Internet. Its effect is to undermine the business of victimized companies, requiring that they recast themselves into new kinds of organizations that will rekindle the support of their constituencies including their own people.

Disintermediation does not necessarily mean that we will all be snuggling up to multinational conglomerates in front of a cozy fire, but it does force many companies either to deal directly or to watch someone else do it around them. (See Table 1.1, which differentiates between companies that have been bypassed by distintermediation and those that have bypassed them.)

Ultimately, as we will discuss in later chapters, the Internet will create new and better ways to build value. But those com-

Table 1.1   *Selected Disintermediated Industries*

Industry	Disintermediated Companies	Disintermediating Companies
Books and music	Borders, Tower Records	Amazon.com
Pharmacies	Walgreen's, Rite-Aid	Drugstore.com, PlanetRx
Banking	Citibank, Bank of America	Wingspan, Telebank
Auctions	Christie's, Sotheby's	eBay, Amazon.com
Information	Libraries	Yahoo, Lycos, Go Network
Travel	Carlsen, Rosenbluth	Priceline.com, Travelocity
Brokerages	Merrill Lynch, Paine Webber	E*Trade, Ameritrade
Insurance	New York Life, Allstate	InsWeb, esurance
Supermarketing	Safeway, Kroger	WebVan, Peapod

panies that hope to capitalize on the Net's power should be building a sturdy masterbrand to serve as the articulation of their online and offline competitive advantages.

Companies are gaining competitive advantage by becoming more transparent, and by giving away what they previously thought they "owned." The Internet is also changing the form and value of company assets. Net companies like Yahoo!, Amazon.com, E*Trade, and others are offering free information, products, and services to gain revenue through broader relationships. In essence, they are creating masterbrands that can be owned by their customers and their greater masterbrand community of suppliers, strategic partners, and investors. We will explore these relationships in detail in later chapters.

Merger mania and promiscuous partnering risk blurring company identities, even as they expand influence. Booz, Allen & Hamilton estimates that as much as 18 percent of the total revenue from the United States' largest companies is derived from alliances. Coopers & Lybrand's research reported in 1998 that 66 percent of middle-market U.S. firms had entered into some sort of alliance.[8] The telecommunications, airlines, software, energy, and financial services industries are among many that have embarked on a wide array of co-ventures, alliances, partnerships, and acquisitions.

Is this a good trend? A 1999 KPMG study of 700 cross-border mergers found that 83 percent failed to benefit stockholders.[9] Although such alliances may offer important strategic advantages, the danger is that individual companies and their differentiated masterbrands risk losing their singularity in the marketplace. The more frequently that a company links up with other companies, the greater the need for the creation of a company-wide, brand-based way of doing business, both inside and outside of the organization.

The free-agent mentality among an increasing number of employees is undermining company affiliation. Not that long ago, clear management goals, sufficient compensation, and a positive company culture were all that were needed to retain the bulk of a company's workforce. Today, there are too many opportunities in other places and too much pressure to fill resumes with diverse experiences for employees to stay in one spot for very long. Yet, these people don't just want higher compensation, they want to know that they are contributing to a healthy, growing entity. The rise of team management, knowledge sharing, coaching, and other techniques are efforts to meet this challenge, but alone they fail to create larger-than-life affiliations that most of us need in our lives.

To provide that affiliation, traditional companies can transform their organizations into a living masterbrand that they can use to solidify their community of helpers and supporters. Doing so will maximize a company's opportunity to recruit and hold the best people, regardless of how the economy is faring.

The CEO: Master Builder of the Masterbrand

Given these epochal changes, companies that continue to operate as conventional organizations are at risk of being methodically preempted. In such a reality, the masterbrand becomes an imperative that CEOs cannot afford to simply assign to individual departments or business units. Instead, they personally must work to multiply the leverage of their entire corporate resources by using proven brand-building techniques across the company, and then across its supporting brand community.

The force behind masterbrand building comes in the form of a mandate from the people of the company and its community directly to the CEO. It is anything but just another challenge for marketing specialists. The meaning and impact of masterbrands ribbon through their companies as a whole, and their companies sell through these masterbrands. No person is better qualified to manage that process than the CEO. It does not matter if CEOs have financial planning backgrounds, or if they prefer to spend time with the sales force, or if they are most comfortable with a hard hat on—one of their primary responsibilities is to build the company masterbrand from the moment they take the reins.

If for no other reason, masterbrand building must be considered a company-wide discipline because it has become a corporate financial necessity. In fact, the value of the company-wide masterbrand may have as much or more to do with the ultimate value of the company than any other single factor.

Accountants in the United Kingdom have been battling for years over whether brand valuation can be legitimately included in the financial assessment of the company that sells it. When the latest round of shots died down in 1998, it was generally agreed (at least in the United Kingdom) that certain brand measures were an accurate gauge of a company's once-and-future worth. That set of decisions will soon have a global impact on corporations that are permitted to list their intangible brand values as hard assets. In the interim, brand building is unofficially determining the market value of many companies as you read these words.

The total asset value of some companies is considerably less than their estimated market values, and the difference, or "goodwill," is often largely the incremental worth of their brands. Goodwill is tough to quantify, but it is impossible to deny. The people at Interbrand, the leading experts on brand valuation, calculate that the value of a masterbrand can represent as much as one-half or more of the capitalized value of the company. In Interbrand's estimation, this is true both in companies in which a single brand dominates sales, as well as in those that market multiple product or service brands, which they call *portfolio brands*. (See Table 1.2 for selected list of brand valuations.)

Because the capitalization of a stock is frequently based as much on perception as it is on real-asset worth, a company's perceived value as an investment is frequently determined by the impressions that it makes as a competitive brand in the marketplace. Consequently, when an entire company acts as a single, integrated masterbrand, there are rich rewards to reap. In such cases, the intrinsic value of a brand to a company is not just as a selling tool, but it is also an operating mandate for the organization itself. In marketing warfare terms, the brand is no longer just the weapon, it becomes an extension of the warrior.

This is even more true of Internet companies, because the perceived value of the masterbrand is based solely on expectation of success, rather than on earnings that may not emerge for many quarters into the future. In the most dramatic example, the capi-

Table 1.2 *Company/Brand Valuations*

Brand and Company	1999 Estimated Brand Value (US$ billion)	1998 Brand-Related Revenue (US$ billion)	Brand Value as Multiple of Branded Revenue	Market Capitalization (US$ billion, as of 1/99)	Brand Value as Percentage of Market Capitalization (%)
Individual Brands					
Coca-Cola	83.8	16.9	4.96	142.2	59
Microsoft	56.7	14.5	3.91	271.9	21
Disney	32.3	18.8	1.72	52.6	61
McDonald's	26.2	12.4	2.11	40.9	64
Nokia	20.7	15.5	1.33	46.9	44
Gillette	15.9	4.1	3.83	43.0	37
Portfolio Brands					
Procter & Gamble	49.2	37.2	1.32	95.1	52
Johnson & Johnson	47.6	23.2	2.05	105.2	45
Nestlé	38.8	54.1	.72	38.8	50
Unilever	32.9	45.2	.73	33.9	50

Sources: Interbrand and Citibank.

talization of the Yahoo! portal company (which *is* generally profitable) doubled to $80 billion the first week in December of 1999, when the stock was added to the Standard & Poor's 500 Index. Even taking into account the effects of computerized buying by institutional investors, this unprecedented run-up was driven by the once-and-future value of the Yahoo! masterbrand, much more than by its physical assets, which are minimal. (See Figure 1.1 for a graphic of Yahoo!'s December 1999 stock ascent.) Of course, Yahoo!'s stock price has since fallen back down to Earth, but then, the entire market has experienced extraordinary similar volatility in recent years.

Leaders of masterbrand organizations manage by making several key operating assumptions: First, they recognize that the best way to simultaneously run a company and build its masterbrand is to consider them one and the same. As we will describe in later chapters, operating the company wholly within the context of its masterbrand can greatly multiply its value in the marketplace.

Second, masterbrand leaders use their masterbrands to create opportunities to spotlight and unify their people. In such organizations, employees routinely become *brand ambassadors*, advocates for what the company masterbrand offers its customers. As Hal Rosenbluth, CEO of the successful Rosenbluth International travel firm, has characterized it: "If you focus on the people who work for you, they will focus on the customer."[10] This is a lesson

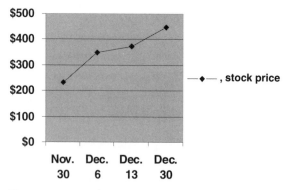

Figure 1.1   *Yahoo!'s 1999 December to remember.*

learned long ago by Herb Kelleher at Southwest Airlines, Fred Smith at FedEx, and investment pioneer Charles Schwab, all of whom are sponsors of superior masterbrands.

These leaders also know that their future depends not only on the quality of whatever end product or service is sold out the door, but also on the long-term relationships that the company as a whole can establish within its brand community. Most important, they understand that a product or service is the manifestation of its masterbrand, which is both the birth mother and the umbilical cord through which the company can establish a lifelong customer connection that yields profitability over time.

Finally, such leaders also acknowledge that brand building must be demonstrated by them personally to the people of their organizations and outwardly to their greater constituencies. Bezos of Amazon.com, Jobs at Apple, Welch at GE, Dell of Dell Computer, Branson of Virgin, Schultz at Starbucks . . . all are masterbrand strategists with CEO titles. In our experience, the most savvy CEOs realize that the masterbrand is their personal ward. Also, CEOs are in the best position to ensure that masterbrand building is embedded throughout the organization, thus fulfilling their fiduciary responsibilities to grow company assets.

Of course, there are some CEOs who continue to view brand building as the sole responsibility of the senior marketing officer. Perhaps feeling uneasy with marketing issues, they steer clear of what they regard as branding decisions. Masterbrand management, however, is not confinable to certain sectors of the business; it is at the core of the business itself. To treat it as anything less seriously limits a CEO's influence over where the organization is going and how quickly it will get there.

Typecasting Masterbrands

One way to distinguish different types of masterbrand companies is according to their brand structures, and the diversity of the businesses in which they compete. For example, what we call *Single-Brand-Dominant* companies primarily (although not exclusively) support only one major brand of products and/or services. Single-brand companies are usually in a better position to establish a unified masterbrand organization. However, as we will demonstrate in upcoming chapters, it is also very possible for a multiple-brand company to establish a company-wide brand organization, and to achieve strong brand-driven business returns, as well. Single-Brand-Dominant organizations may market a diverse array of products and/or services, or a more uniform group.

In contrast, *Multiple-Brand* companies market from several to dozens of different brands, and their leaders are often less inclined to fold those various brands under a single company brand umbrella. These companies must work harder to find commonalities that all divisions or groups can rally around. A good many companies of this type have done so, though, and they often benefit from the reputation of being diverse, yet strategically focused. These companies as well may market within relatively uniform, or very diverse, markets.

Some examples of companies that fall into these categories (see Table 1.3 for masterbrand typology):

- *The Home Depot* (More Uniform, Single-Brand-Dominant). This is one of the most successful retailing organizations in the past half-century. This is a company of managers and workers who are committed to a specific masterbrand model, which has catapulted many of them to financial independence, and which has become a permanent part of the U.S. brandscape (see sidebar).

- *Tricon Global Restaurants* (More Uniform, Multiple Brands). The divested offspring of PepsiCo's once-troubled restaurant division is now a growing $20 billion company of three restau-

Table 1.3   *Examples of Masterbrand Companies*

	Single-Brand-Dominant	Multiple Brands
More uniform businesses	Charles Schwab, Starbucks, The Home Depot, Coca-Cola, Sun Microsystems	Tricon, Johnson & Johnson, America Online, Walt Disney, Gap
More diverse businesses	Motorola, Virgin Group, General Electric, 3M	Sara Lee, Procter & Gamble, Gillette

rant chains (KFC, Taco Bell, Pizza Hut), with an unprecedented sense of unity among its people and franchisees.

- *General Electric* (More Diverse, Single-Brand-Dominant). This is arguably the best-run diversified company in decades. While GE operates several other strong brands (NBC, RCA), it is a single-brand-dominant company whose management has created a renewed belief in the company as brand, successfully positioning itself as a smart investment, a well-disciplined competitor, and a thoughtful employer.

- *Sara Lee* (More Diverse, Multiple Brands). Sara Lee still carries the brand name from its days as a food specialty company. Now, the diversified organization markets such far-flung brands as Hanes hosiery, Coach premium accessories, Douwe Egberts European coffee products, Kiwi shoe polishes, and of course, Sara Lee foods.

Masterbrand success stories are not confined to the Fortune 100. Many exist among small and mid-size companies that have become intrepid competitors through the creation of brand-based communities. In later chapters we will learn more about such masterbrands as:

- *Leatherman Tool Group.* This mid-size manufacturer has built a small but profitable empire with the jaws of a handy pocket tool.

- *Whole Foods Markets.* This specialty foods retailer has built a powerful brand with very unbrand-like techniques.

- *Tom's of Maine.* A societally conscious company that proselytizes its masterbrand in unconventional ways.

- *Outrigger Hotels & Resorts.* The largest hotel chain in the Hawaiian Islands, this is a prime example of a strong masterbrand in the process of being made stronger.

- *The Boelter Companies.* A Midwestern paper supply company whose business has been transformed by an innovative extranet.

THE MASTERBRAND-BUILDING BRAND

Company Chairman Bernie Marcus has a hard time believing that any town can have too many Home Depots. In his words, "Part of the whole philosophy of The Home Depot has been that we were able to create business where business never existed before . . . It was a revolution, a social revolution in the United States that was created by [The] Home Depot and is still continuing." As of this writing, the revolution shows no signs of slowing down. The Atlanta-based retailing behemoth generates more than $40 billion in revenue, a figure that has been increasing annually for many years by 20-plus percent.

Marcus and his colleagues reasoned that there was plenty of room for a retailing brand whose role was to bolster the confidence and skills of do-it-yourselfers so that they did not need to hire contractors to upgrade their homes. In addition, customers could save money doing it—relative to the outrageous costs of contractors and premium prices at local hardware stores. In the process, long-time employees, like their counterparts at Wal-Mart (the biggest retail masterbrand of them all), are not so slowly getting rich on stock incentives, because the company's stock price has vaulted 40-fold in the past decade, splitting 11 times since it went public in 1981.

Other key members of The Home Depot brand community are their vendor-partners who are at the business end of a tough-love relationship with the company. The Home Depot suppliers are expected to perform in a certain proscribed manner, or they are prevented from participating in lucrative contracts. The company gives vendors a very limited time to convince buyers that their material is right for The Home Depot. If it is accepted, that's when the really tough part begins—delivering the enormous supply of whatevers that The Home Depot moves. According to Marcus, "we buy so much that (our vendors) have had to change many of the ways they do business."

The Home Depot is a masterbrand company whose positioning in the marketplace is understood and is committed to by its employees, vendors, customers, and other members of its brand community.

- *Rich Products Corporation.* A family-owned food company in Buffalo, New York, that has made the concept of family a company-wide masterbrand platform.

- *iVillage.* The pioneering women's online community that is forging new ways to convey important information while creating durable customer relationships.

Differences between Masterbrands and Conventional Well-Run Companies

Every senior executive strives to lead a well-run company, and the definitions of *well-run* are long and well documented. What we are discussing here, though, is a particular kind of well-run company, one that magnifies its strengths in the marketplace by planning its strategies and executing its tactics within a brand-based framework. Merrill Lynch, Compaq, and Norelco are all fine organizations, but they appear to be less brand-driven in their company-wide efforts than are Charles Schwab, Sun Microsystems, and Gillette. Both sets of companies can certainly find new and creative ways to make money, but powerful masterbrands will ultimately be able to create proportionately more impact in the marketplace because of the concentrated firepower that they bring to each market.

Strong masterbrands share common characteristics that help explain their success in the marketplace. For example, masterbrands tend to be based on an almost transcendental trust that pervades all of their supporters. Masterbrands are often a product of a powerful interaction between all stakeholders who have a clear understanding about what is being promised to customers and constituencies. That is, the benefits that it provides to its supporters are the focus of the company.

You can see companies gain and lose their sense of a central brand, as well as the effects that those experiences have on their businesses. American Express, Xerox, Kodak, Sears, Kmart, Kellogg's, and AT&T are just a few of the companies that have endured at least one lengthy and difficult period of stalled growth and waning support from inside and outside of their organizations. In all cases, the perception of their central brands suffered significant declines in positive awareness and prestige, sending the organization on a less-than-pleasant roller-coaster ride of volatile identities and valuations. Other factors aside, in each case these companies might have lessened their hard times by more adeptly maneuvering their masterbrands.

Masterbrand organizations enjoy supplemental advantages over their more conventional competition (Table 1.4) in a number of ways:

Customer relationship management comes more naturally to master-brand organizations. Creating and holding onto customer relationships are prices of entry in most markets today. The foundation of such relationships is mutual trust, and the end result has been the offering of more choice, and the transference of more control, to the customer. Not coincidentally, how well a brand performs is often determined by how much trust it has earned by matching or exceeding the expectations of users.

Table 1.4   *Masterbrand versus Conventional Companies*

Business Advantage	Conventional Company Features	Supplemental Masterbrand Company Benefits	Example Masterbrand Companies
Superior business performance	Based on the cumulative performance of individual product/service brands	Driven by the synergistic impact of company-wide brand-building efforts.	Charles Schwab, Lexus, Sun Microsystems
Motivating employees	Company vision and values that are meant to guide employee actions	Specific brand parameters and benefits that are more concrete and practical to work with.	Dell Computer, Tom's of Maine, Whole Earth Foods, Wal-Mart
Superior employee-customer relations	Conventional seller-buyer relationships	Mutually supportive relationships centered on the value proposition of the company-wide brand.	IBM, IKEA, Nordstrom
Formidable competitive barriers to entry	Technology, pricing, distribution defenses, etc.	Enhanced brand equities that further raise barriers to entry.	ESPN, Starbucks, Kinko's
Financial community support (public companies)	Vulnerable to scrutiny and criticism from the investing community	Given additional leeway because of company-wide strategic vision and initiatives.	FedEx, Amazon.com, America Online

It is simpler and easier for employees to experience and rally around a masterbrand than it is for them to grapple with less concrete visions and values. As a consequence, it is also easier for them to take practical actions to build the impact that the masterbrand has in the marketplace. Whether commemorated on plaques at company plants, or canted as a mantra at annual meetings, company visions and missions can provide important guidance. Yet, they are often very tough to relate to the day-to-day realities of the marketplace. The discipline of building masterbrands provides a more solid, reality-grounded handle for employees to grip, for customers to embrace, for strategic partners to complement, and for investors to buy into.

Values-driven companies, such as Tom's of Maine, Ben & Jerry's, and L.L. Bean, have organized their value systems around brands, not just philosophical positions. British Airways was once literally considered the "world's favourite airline," and it lived up to that claim because its vision was made real and tangible in the form of its masterbrand. (As of this writing, British Airways, the company, is struggling, and its historical commitment to brand may be waning—a dilemma that awaits any company that sets high standards for its masterbrand, then fails to live up to them.)

In such instances, employees have been imbued with an urgency of action that was driven by the brands they were actually selling in the marketplace, not simply by the desire to sustain a lofty vision.

Masterbrand companies forge stronger employee-customer relationships that provide sustainable momentum, which may very well grow exponentially. Conventional companies seek business (and relationships) from their customers, using product or service brand promises. Masterbrands offer a broader-based value proposition that is backed up by the full currency of the entire company.

Relationships backed by company-wide commitments helped enable Lou Gerstner to turn IBM around, and both IKEA and Wal-Mart to build retail juggernauts. These victories can at least partly be attributed to the focused, strategic intermingling of employees and customers within a larger brand community, compared with the more conventional "selling at" approaches used in the past to influence constituencies to support standard corporate brands.

Masterbrand companies usually create sturdier barriers against competitive entry, that market latecomers have great difficulty overcoming. Although these advantages initially might be proprietary technologies or strong marketing support, the most enduring competitive advantages are the enduring fortitudes of masterbrand companies. The ESPN network has attracted the "sincerest form of flattery" from CNN/SI sports, Fox Sports, and a spate of local look-alikes. Yet, ESPN's continual replenishing of its masterbrand gives it an edge over latecomers that focus more on attracting new viewers than on cultivating their equities. The same edge slows competitors that seek to compete with Starbucks, Sun Microsystems, and Whole Foods.

Public masterbrand companies often enjoy more positive reviews from Wall Street. Financial analysts tend to favor those companies with a clear and decisive direction that is based on sound brand planning. If the numbers are delivered, analysts will frequently take that as an affirmation of the company's long-term staying power. If earnings or revenue don't come in as expected in a given quarter, the masterbrand company in question may be given a bit more slack, especially if the long-term vision is in place and continues to make sense to financial prognosticators. Importantly, that vision may be more complete, and may appear to be more realizable, within a masterbrand context. Such views won't protect a masterbrand forever, but it has cushioned the fall during dicey times for such giants as Coca-Cola, Hewlett-Packard, and Merck & Company.

Some analysts have even made it their business to learn more about the brand-building discipline, and now they have a working knowledge of such concepts as brand elasticity, identity migration, and brand equity management.

Finally and most important, masterbrands tend to achieve greater leverage in the marketplace and to build upon that leverage by incorporating innovation and change. For example, automobile companies that expected their nameplates alone to add value to their value proposition have been passed on the left by the Lexus and Saturn organizations, which focused all of their organizations' resources in a company-wide form of brand leverage. (See Table 1.4 for masterbrand versus conventional company comparisons.)

Of course, building a company-wide masterbrand does not guarantee success, but it can certainly increase the opportunities to succeed. Nike, Levi Strauss, Apple, Gillette, and IBM have all faltered from time to time within recent memory, and yet they are all superior, brand-driven companies that ultimately recoup their losses and come back with renewed strength.

Is It a Masterbrand If No One Meant to Build a Brand?

One irony of masterbrand building is that its champions didn't necessarily start out to be brand builders. Howard Schultz of Starbucks and Scott McNealy of Sun Microsystems were initially determined to create great companies; only later did their teams invest with the intent to build their brands. Jerry Yang, cofounder of the outrageously successful Yahoo!, once pointed out: "We didn't know it was a brand. It became a brand when real business-people told us it was a brand." (Yang and his partner did have the good sense to hire a CEO who understood the value of the brand.)[11] Howard Mackey, the founder of Whole Foods Markets, even admits to occasionally thinking of his iconoclastic organization as an "anti-brand."

Thus, in masterbrand building, *initial intent* is far less important than *ultimate effect*. Michael Dell built a state-of-the-art company with lightning-quick customizations and Internet-driven direct marketing. The Dell masterbrand was the end product of brilliant operational decisions as much as marketing brilliance. But does that mean that Dell has nothing to teach us about masterbrand marketing? On the contrary, Dell and his people have fostered a major masterbrand, regardless of the founder's original intent.

The business models that these companies devise are strategic building blocks for their masterbrand. Dell's commitment to the direct channel has become what the Dell brand stands for, to the point that it is difficult to find the Dell name/logo without the phrase "Be Direct." Its rival Gateway's foray into retailing (Gateway Country outlets) may have been seen as a distribution decision, but it was also a powerful way to reinforce and extend the masterbrand's reputation of offering customers what they want as individuals, including the desire to touch and feel a PC before they buy it.

The way that these companies are organized (e.g., Sara Lee's brand-driven structure), the way that they seek out and hire new employees (Gap Inc.'s highly competitive recruiting program), and the way that they train their people (Motorola University)—all are strategies, directly or indirectly, that help to reinforce the solidity of their company and masterbrand.

Not to be cavalier about it, but it simply doesn't matter whether the founders and early leaders of these firms set out initially to build brands. On the other hand, future business builders who strategically plan their masterbrands will find it that much easier to gain a competitive advantage over less progressive companies.

Corporate Branding Is Just the Beginning

We should be clear at this point that creating masterbrand companies involves much more than simply supporting a corporate brand, although traditional corporate branding can certainly be a component of the masterbrand-building process. There are several important differences between masterbrand methodologies and the typical corporate branding that is currently in practice. Although corporate branding programs are usually approved by the CEO, they are often not fully integrated throughout the organization. More commonly, management approves the program on an annual basis, the corporate communications people work with their agencies to implement them, and internal and external communications carry the appropriate corporate brand themes.

Although corporate brand efforts often aspire to influence all company constituencies, they frequently are most effective against the financial community and other opinion influencers. It is a tough challenge to convince a company's own people and other stakeholders to really embrace conventional corporate branding efforts. In contrast, masterbrand building is supported, and often sponsored, by employees within the company and throughout the greater brand community because their masterbrands are more concrete in form and function.

So-called corporate reputations are also an important measure of the impact of a company in its various spheres of influence (which is why we mentioned the online survey at the beginning of this chapter). But, again, a company's reputation is only part of the company's outward identity, and that reputation does not measure the full internal and external impact of the firm's commitment to create a brand-driven environment and to employ brand-building disciplines.

To be sure, there are fine examples of successful corporate branding efforts aimed at improving corporate reputations, such as General Electric's long-running "We bring good things to life," Ford's "Quality is Job 1," and Apple's "Think Different" campaigns. But Jack Welch, Jacques Nasser, and Steve Jobs have created much more than memorable corporate branding programs, they have also enabled their companies to operate as unified masterbrands, both internally and throughout their surrounding communities of supporters. Their corporate branding efforts are at the surface of much deeper sea changes.

Brand Building with Digitized Building Blocks

The digitizing of our world is proceeding at an extraordinary pace. Ubiquitous desktop computers, so recently considered a revolutionary force themselves, are now giving ground to network solutions. E-commerce was not even a blip on the retail radar screen in 1997; now, it is expected to account for several trillion dollars early in this decade, most of which will be business-to-business revenue. The role of the brand will be central to the expansion of the commercial sector of the Net, because brands bring two key ingredients that will also be essential to Net travelers: (1) a way of organizing preferences, and (2) a source of confidence and trust in less-than-reassuring virtual environments.

Brands of all types, of course, simplify the purchase decision for business customers and consumers. The clutter and overchoice that are so prevalent on the Net are made considerably less daunting by clear brand preferences that reduce shopper stress (for both consumers and business-to-business buyers) and that provide some insurance against making a bad purchase. When consumers and business customers rely on brands to help them make an investment, they are putting their trust in the reputation of the brand.

Online, trust becomes the oxygen that brands breathe. Trust is mandatory in virtual markets in which prospective buyers cannot touch or fully see what they are buying, in which they will never meet the person or company that is selling it, and in which they are likely to make the purchase using a credit card whose number is being transmitted across the world. In such circumstances, trust mutates quickly into faith. Increasingly, such faith will be created—and kept—by masterbrands that operate as part of larger brand communities.

The issue becomes even more urgent when it is applied to "pure plays" (companies born on the Net) that have become wholly formed brands. Yahoo!, Amazon.com, Priceline, eBay, and E*Trade all quickly built reputations as reliable providers. It was their masterbrands (i.e., brand identities reinforced by outstanding products and services) that led to explosive revenue growth and market capitalization. And now, a parallel stream of established offline corporations has discovered that the Internet can be a dominant force in the building of their companies' identities.

As brands are born and bred at blinding speed on the Internet, most CEOs of online companies have made brand building their personal priorities. Early on, Tim Koogle of Yahoo! saw the critical need to build his company's identity as the preeminent portal brand. Committing to expensive TV and radio spots that built brand identity fast, he created a barrier that was difficult for latecomers to scale. Koogle's brand-building instincts, coupled with his emphasis on building a strong brand community around his portal brand, have made Yahoo! one of the fastest-growing brands in marketing history. It simply wouldn't have happened that way if the CEO had failed to personally tend to the company's masterbrand.

For all of the importance of brand marketing in the past, it was but a foreshadowing of the extraordinary role that trusted masterbrands will play in the online marketplace.

The Masterbrand Mandate

Company-wide brand building serves the same vital purpose that it does at the product and service level: It creates value where there is none, or it greatly enhances what value exists. Just as a product brand can be priced higher than its less developed competitors, so a focused, masterbrand company can acquire greater revenue and earnings from its sales to customers, coax better service from its suppliers, and attract more robust investments from its shareholders.

Above all, a masterbrand company can create a symbiotic community of supporters who can nurture the customer relationships that will form the core of a strong business into the indefinite future. It "takes a village"—or in this case, a community—to help a company stay ahead of its more formidable competition.

In the chapters that follow, we propose that the disciplines of sound brand building can and should be used to help manage a company as a whole, particularly in light of the need for continuous change. We will not be advocating that CEOs wholly replace their general management planning with brand-marketing strategies, but that the two should be merged to make the modern corporation the most efficient possible value machine. We will be pointing out many examples of business leaders who strengthened their companies' masterbrand, yielding an impact well beyond what might have otherwise occurred.

Still, many readers may recognize that their own companies are not at the center of an energized brand community right now, and that such a transformation is not going to happen overnight. For that reason, you may wish to cherry-pick selected features of masterbrand companies that appear to be immediately replicable within your own organization, and then gradually incorporate features that are customized to fit your company's specific needs.

*   *   *

In celebration of the 75th anniversary of the *Harvard Business Review,* its editors asked five distinguished thinkers to ponder the "implications of the present." One of the common elements in several of the resulting essays was the need for internal cultural evolution among business organizations. Peter Senge, chairman of the Society for Organizational Learning, wrote:

> Poised at the millennium, we confront two critical challenges: how to address deep problems for which hierarchical leadership alone is insufficient and how to harness the intelligence and spirit of people at all levels of an organization to continually build and share knowledge.[12]

Why do so many elite companies work so hard to build strong masterbrands and brand communities? The answer is simple and common to all: They refuse to take the unnecessary risk of being preempted by competitors or made obsolete by fluid markets. They fight back with scalable, robust masterbrands.

No category is immune to waning appeal. No market leader can expect share gains or revenue growth to necessarily equate to long-term profitability. No CEO can expect his or her employees to be indefinitely interested in their work, if their work is more of the same. A company is a proven form of commercial organization, but it is not necessarily the strongest template with which to battle the incessant competition and roiling changes that exist in most markets today.

Of course, there are a myriad of decisions and initiatives that must be synchronized to obtain lasting value in the marketplace. Yet, reconfiguring a company into a unified masterbrand enterprise is one key step toward achieving that goal.

PART ONE

Mandate

Build the Customer's Community

Grow the Masterbrand Community

*We think of ourselves as sort of a community-commerce
model . . . a venue where people can be successful
dealing and communicating with one another.*

—Margaret Whitman,
President and CEO, eBay Inc.[1]

B lue Bell brand has become a regional favorite, with plants in
three states that produce more than 100,000 gallons of ice
cream a day. In harmony with their East Texas character, the
people of Blue Bell have worked hard to maintain the brand's
identity as "the little creamery in Brenham." When Blue Bell
expands into new cities, company officials drop in to pay their
respects to the mayor—bringing a sociable gallon or two of ice
cream, and reminding them of their trademarked slogan which
says it all about their product: "We eat all we can, and we sell the
rest." For those folksy Netizens out there, the Blue Bell Web site
reminds visitors:

If you're in our neighborhood, be sure and stop in and say
howdy . . . We don't work on most holidays and we go to church

on Sundays, so the place is shut tight. To be sure we're open before you come, better give us a call at 409.830.2190. If we don't answer, we're not there.

Blue Bell, and better-known masterbrands such as Saturn and Charles Schwab, have all learned to nurture what are called *brand communities*, which may be the single most important extension of brand building since . . . well, the brand extension.

Start at the Heart of Your Company

Why do we keep retelling their stories? The returning of tires to Nordstrom, which doesn't sell tires. The tattooing of the swoosh on the ankles of Nike's sales development field teams, the "Ekins." The tattooing of Harley-Davidson logos on the arms of its customers. The religious-like fervor that compels The Body Shop loyalists to convert friends and loved ones. The corporate Macintosh users who threaten to quit if they are forced to use PCs from the Dark Side. The Saturn dealers who turn recalls into parties. Are we supposed to remake ourselves in their image? Are these paradigms that we are supposed to emulate? Are these perfect companies?

Each of these fine organizations has periodically experienced tough times during the past decade, so we can hardly call them perfect. But their people have also demonstrated an unrelenting commitment to what their enterprise as a masterbrand stands for. Brand commitment—utter and resolute—is at the heart of these firms, and it is what is driven from the inside of their companies and outward into their larger brand communities.

Of course, one could make the case that the employees who are responsible for this outstanding work are just trying to make their companies great, not their brands. But customers don't literally buy companies, they buy products and services provided by companies, the most powerful of which are generally encapsulated in masterbrands. So, while some employees may be hoping to improve the value of their companies in the eyes of customers, it is their companies' masterbrand that is the beneficiary of their labors. Still, masterbrands cannot sell themselves, only committed brand evangelists can do that.

A company's masterbrand, like any brand, is a promise to meet or exceed the expectations of its customers by delivering benefits within a satisfactory context of value. It is a brand's reason for being. This "value proposition" is no different than those crafted for individual product or service brands, except that at the masterbrand level, there are opportunities to drive it (or seed it) throughout the employee force, and outward into the greater brand community, in tandem with customer-directed efforts.

How Masterbrands Are Created

Masterbrands have been created within any number of different circumstances, which can often influence how they operate as they mature.

Some masterbrands are born and bred. This usually happens when the founder(s) instinctively breeds brand into the DNA of the young organization. The Saturn division of General Motors was culturally cocooned from its parent in order to create the best end products from its processes and strategies. The Saturn experience turned out to be a textbook benchmarking of how to establish a masterbrand attitude and process from the very beginning. Such was also the case at Gateway Computer and America Online.

Another group of masterbrands could be called "born again." These are companies that created a franchise through more traditional methods; then, their CEOs realized in midgame that their opportunities could be greatly enhanced by more aggressively focusing on their masterbrand. Examples include IBM, Nokia, and Apple, whose business turnarounds were brand-related; Harley-Davidson, whose renewed focus on the power of its brand in recent years has led to strong new growth; and General Electric, whose renaissance, led by Jack Welsh more than a decade ago, had an equally important unifying effect on both masterbrand and company operations.

Some masterbrand companies are opportunistic. Such companies took organization-wide actions to bolster their brandedness because their leaders saw (or, in some cases, foresaw) great opportunities on the horizon. Here, we include the Marriott hoteliers because the family owners at the time saw the value of driving their brand-oriented messages throughout the organization, even as their portfolio expanded to include the Ritz-Carlton, Fairview Inn, and Courtyard brands. Another would be Intel, a company that stumbled onto its brandedness, largely because of a mathematician whose discovery about the flaws of the Pentium chip helped then-CEO Andy Grove to understand that Intel was knee-deep in the brand business, like it or not.

Finally, some masterbrand companies are especially competition-driven. These are companies that didn't see the value in fully brandifying their organizations until prompted by their rivals. United Parcel Service (UPS) was more of an American icon than a broadly marketed brand, until FedEx challenged them with ubiquitous overnight delivery, and prompted UPS into competing aggressively in the overnight business itself. The ultimate result was a refreshing set of changes at UPS, including the decision to offer a highly successful IPO in the fall of 1999 in order to fund further expansion and countercompetitive initiatives. We would include MasterCard in this group as well (although it is an association owned by bank members, not a corporation), because it has solidified its worldwide masterbrand in the face of continuing pressure from the category leader, Visa International. (See Table 2.1 for a list of masterbrand origins.)

In Search of the Masterbrand

How, then, can companies determine what and where their masterbrands are? We would recommend that management authorize a thorough diagnostic to help the organization get a firm understanding of where the enterprise-wide brand stands at present. The diagnostic may need to be administered by those in the company who are most familiar with the brand-building discipline. However, its results should *not* be heavily influenced by marketing executives, but only by the honest appraisals of all employee-partners and members of the company's greater brand community.

Table 2.1 *Origins of Masterbrands*

Type of Masterbrand	Origin	Example Masterbrands
Born and bred	Founder(s) built as brand-based from inception.	Saturn, Gateway Computer, Virgin, AOL
Born again	Reconfigured and/or repositioned.	Apple, Harley-Davidson, Nokia
Opportunistic	Capitalized on ongoing changes in its industry and/or channels.	Marriott, Charles Schwab, Enron, E*Trade
Competition-driven	Became (more) brand-driven in response to competition.	UPS, MasterCard

While such a diagnostic can be extensive and can delve deeply into many complex subjects, basically it should address several fundamental questions:

Who and/or what are the company's primary sources of growth and profitability, and how should they be prioritized? There are literally dozens of groups that could have an effect on the business opportunities of even a small to mid-size enterprise, let alone a major corporation. These must each be evaluated and ranked, according to their real and potential impact on the company's short- and long-term business.

What are the core value expectations of customers and other contributors to the company's growth? Is the company known as delivering on its promises, or has it been seen as falling short of the mark on too many recent occasions? Are its end products and services considered superior to, at parity with, or inferior to those of its competitors? Are the company's people seen as consistently bringing value to the customer and partner?

What is the full set of core benefit promises offered by the company to its sources of business, in the past, and at the present? How can the fundamental benefits provided by the company be distilled down to a few core statements? These should be stated clearly in the marketing and operational plans of each business unit. If they aren't, that should tell you something about the need of the company to focus on masterbrand issues.

How do the company's benefits and performance stack up against its competition? As we will point out in later chapters, competition may include any and all alternatives, which may be other companies, other individual brands, or the option not to purchase within the market at all.

What are the most critical points of masterbrand contact? There are important "moments of truth" when a company's contact with customers has a significant impact on the business, whereas other contacts are not as critical. What are the major points of contact (it would be unlikely that all could be identified and categorized), and how can they be weighted for importance to the business?

A company's masterbrand is a living record of what has been accomplished, what has been planned and has fallen by the wayside, what has been promised and delivered, and what opportunities exist in the future. An accurate portrait of each of these faces in the mirror is necessary before the masterbrand can expand into its full community.

Expanding into the Brand Community

Online communities are cropping up left and right now that more marketers are understanding the power of self-reinforcing audiences. But, long before the Web emerged, brand communities were being fostered in many industries. Brand communities are strategically interdependent relationship clusters that form the spokes and wheel that surround and support a masterbrand. A brand community is peopled with the employees, customers, shareholders, suppliers and strategic partners, and other stakeholders, all of whom are sustained by a shared commitment to a pervasive masterbrand value proposition.

Rich Products, a family-owned food company that we will discuss in a later chapter, has built its community on superior customer relationships, as facilitated by the cooperative work of its own people, its brokers, suppliers, and its distributors. Outrigger Hotels & Resorts relies on travel agent members of their brand community, who must be excited about the Outrigger properties and even more excited about the power of the brand in the highly competitive Hawaii and South Seas hospitality markets. Outrigger must pay special attention to that segment of its brand community, or it may not have guests to worry about. On the Web, eBay, the online auction house, is a community whose revenue depends *both* upon meeting the access needs of sellers and offering the convenience of carefree buying to bidders.

Companies at the center of masterbrand communities are more successful than their conventional competitors at attracting and retaining customers because they operate within an interdependent selling environment in which participants help create mutually advantageous benefits. As Australian marketing consultant, Michael Kiely, has put it: "Customers thirst for connections, and this desire is building communities around brands. More than loyalty programmes, these 'brand communities' generate real emotion and intense loyalty."[2]

The core strength of a brand community is often a shared heritage or set of goals that transcend and transform its members. Unlike company values or visions, however, the best brand communities are more likely linked by concrete brand benefits that are part of an overall brand proposition. For Charles Schwab, it is the empowerment of its users to make the most of what they have with a minimum of constraints. In the America Online and Sun Microsystems communities, members and developers, respectively, are connected to a continuously evolving network of new experiences. For The Gap and Gateway Computers, it is the opportunity to personalize what customers buy and what they can do with what they buy. (See Table 2.2 for a list of communities and their members.)

The Community Begins and Ends with the Customer

In later chapters, we will be exploring in more depth how to build a masterbrand from the inside out. Before doing so, however, we

Table 2.2   *Selected Brand Communities*

Masterbrand Communities	Key Community Members
Sun Microsystems	Developers, strategic partners, enterprise IT executives
America Online	Subscribers, content companies
Saturn	Employee-partners, customers, dealers, marketing agencies
Apple Computer	End users, developers, sympathetic press
Charles Schwab	Customers, employee-partners, affiliated financial advisors
Harley-Davidson	Retailers, employee teams, owner groups (HOGs)
Dell Computers	Customers, employee teams, suppliers

need to examine the end goal of the masterbrand, namely, the customer relationship, both in traditional channels and online.

Successful brand communities usually include at least five essential constituencies:

1. A core base of *current customers* who remain loyal over time because they are committed to the idea that underlies the masterbrand, in addition to enjoying the benefits of the company's products or services. Customers who are emotionally affiliated with a masterbrand are much more likely to become advocates and ambassadors for the brand within their peer groups (e.g., at Apple and The Body Shop). The customers provide the strategic direction for the masterbrand because their needs must be met first and foremost. All other priorities must take a backseat to those.

2. *Motivated employees* who are committed to doing superior work because they understand the impact of their work on the masterbrand. These employees are generally treated as more than employees, and they feel as if they are an integral part of the brand-building process . . . as well they are (e.g., at Home Depot and L.L Bean).

3. Depending on the industry, the community may include a loyal group of supporting *providers, developers, resellers, marketing communications agencies, and consultants,* who reliably

provide what the enterprise needs to do business because they know that the more they can do to help the masterbrand to succeed, the more likely that they will build their own brands as well (e.g., at Sun Microsystems).

4. An ever-evolving array of *strategic partners*, allies, and informal "friends of the company," that seek to build their own businesses by enhancing the enterprise-wide brand. Ironically, of course, many of these may be direct competitors to the brand community in some markets, but serve as partners or allies in others (e.g., at Motorola).

5. A comparatively faithful group of *investors*, usually via public exchanges, who believe that their investment is secure with a company that understands precisely where it stands and where it is going. There is a difference between conventional investors who could care less what they invest in, as long as it makes money, and those who tend to stick with a company with a clear brand understanding, even in tough times. Masterbrands tend to attract more of the latter group, all other things being equal (e.g., at Intel).

Each brand community has its own set of relationships that make it unique. How the masterbrand company nurtures the participants in its community helps form the proprietary advantage that it has over other brands. For that reason, it's not uncommon for companies to be torn between their need to service the customer and their desire to cater to the needs of other key members of the community.

Dell Computer has created a masterbrand community with the help of a cadre of top-rate suppliers who understand what it means to the company and brand to have just-in-time deliveries arrive as scheduled. In addition to traditional supplier-motivating techniques (promotions, awards, financial incentives), Dell also established valuechain.dell.com, an extranet for suppliers only that displays a "supplier report card" as further encouragement to perform. The company also uses the site to share best practices among supplier companies. These are reinforcements of the entire enterprise, and of its masterbrand, in that they help to build the identity of the Dell brand as accepting nothing but the best from its suppliers, in order to deliver nothing but the best to its customers.

How can companies determine where they should put their greatest efforts within their communities? They need to ask: What will best serve the customer? Because, while customers are only one segment of the community, they are the *point* of the community. All decisions about how to configure and serve the community come down to what will best serve the customer. So, in our earlier examples, Rich Products nurtures its relationships with employees, suppliers, and distributors *in order to better serve its customers*. eBay's bidders and sellers are all customers, so no more attention can be given to one than another. Outrigger may depend on travel agents, but the travel agents will find out soon enough if the guests do not enjoy their stay.

No matter how populated and complex a brand community may become, it is no more than an apparatus to serve the customer's needs and, thereby, to build value for the masterbrand. Brand community building is also a far more effective device for building momentum behind the brand than conventional branding disciplines alone, which often do not make full use of enterprise-wide supports. (See Figure 2.1 for the masterbrand community dynamic.)

How Customers Own the Community . . . and Why You Want to Give It to Them

Since adman David Ogilvy first defined a brand as "a consumer's idea of a product," it has become conventional wisdom that the customer owns the brand. That is, since the brand is the customer's *idea* of the product, service, or company, it resides in the mind of the customer. Unfortunately, too many managers consider the brand to be *theirs*—theirs to position in the marketplace (Sears lost its lead in retailing by failing to reposition itself within customers' minds); theirs to innovate at the time or place of their own choosing (Acura lost valuable share by failing to innovate at key points in its brand development); theirs to increase prices when more profit is needed (Kellogg's paid dearly for its arbitrary price hikes in the mid-1990s).

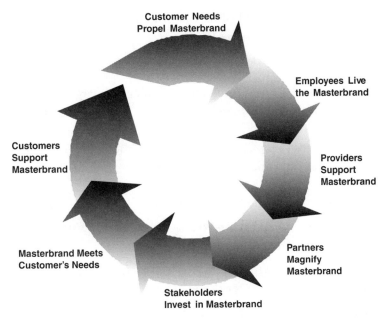

Figure 2.1   *The masterbrand community dynamic.*

A brand only exists to the extent that it is appropriated by its customers; that is, it becomes part of their way of viewing the world. In the same sense, a masterbrand company helps that appropriation to happen. Paradoxically, legal owners of brands only realize their full value if they are offered to customers to be owned by them as well. The value of a brand grows proportionately as its ownership is shared.

What does it really mean, though, to say that customers own brands, and what is it exactly that customers own? When a brand makes a promise, it creates certain reciprocal expectations and obligations. For example, any car must fulfill the customer's *functional* need for mobility. Above and beyond that, a Lexus promises to meet the customer's *emotional* or *nonfunctional* needs for status, prestige, and so on. If a brand not only makes but *becomes* such a promise to the customer, then the customer can and should feel entitled to hold the brand to its promise. If this expectation is *not* fulfilled, the customer will likely feel disappointed, or even betrayed. Such was the case with the Yugo and the Cadillac Cimmaron, the IBM PCjr. and Motorola's Iridium, McDonald's Arch Deluxe and Anheuser-Busch's LA beer.

If the brand as promise creates reciprocal obligations, it also creates benefits for *both* the company and the customer. For the company, a strong brand means premium price, higher margins, greater return on investments or assets, increased customer retention, usage and cross-selling, receptivity to brand extensions, and greater forgiveness of customer service failures.[3] For the customer, strong brands and the companies that market them mean the following:

- Simplifying the purchase decision: "AT&T. The right choice."

- Making it easy for customers to like the product: "With a name like Smuckers, it *has* to be good."

- Providing assurance/reassurance of consistency: "When it absolutely, positively has to get there."

- Creating a sense of security: "Drive safely."

- Enhancing a customer's sense of self-image: "Just do it."

As the rise of the Internet and virtual communities illustrates, a masterbrand community exists in and through a shared sense of belonging, through collaborative efforts and a feeling of joint ownership by its members. The stronger the sense of community centered on a masterbrand, the more the feelings of connectedness and relationship are multiplied.

A very important extension of this reciprocal relationship is creating affiliation, sometimes by giving something away. A number of years ago, researcher Judith Langer reported that customers literally love some brands and enjoy being part of brand clubs that "provide an element of continuity in their lives." In addition to playing the practical role of simplifying purchase decisions or the emotional role of helping customers to express themselves, brands play a social role, acting as "badges" that identify and align customers with certain groups or movements. Even if we do leave home without them, we are known by the brands we keep—and such membership definitely has its privileges, as American Express cardholders, Macintosh users, and Mercedes drivers can attest (if you can get them to admit it).

In the Internet era, we are also seeing hopeful brand communities literally trying to buy their customers' loyalty, in much the same way that packaged-goods marketers must buy their way onto grocery store shelves with the infamous slotting allowances. Online, everything from cash incentives to air miles are used to lure triers onto sites and to keep them coming back. Thus, the growing number of sites devoted to nothing but giving something away, such as Webstakes.com and Freegiveaways.com. The idea is to develop a habit that requires periodic "virtual fixes." It is, however, for brand or brand community, a slippery slope on which many a brand has lost its shirt, without so much as a single truly loyal customer to show for it.

In contrast, positive loyalty dynamics are multiplied in a true brand community. When customers can sense the power of the brands to which they are loyal, this power is easily transferred to the company, and it is more easily shared among members of a brand community. The airline that delivers you promptly and safely to your destination on trip after trip has earned some degree of loyalty, although that loyalty may be tested by fare pricing and flight schedules. That's why those who like the flight attendants on a particular airline are very disappointed to learn that the ticket counter personnel are not necessarily as friendly. But when the ticket counter people *are* friendly, customers begin to believe that the entire company is really there to make their travel more pleasant. Those customers may then pass along a recommendation to a friend, and the beginning of a brand community may be in the offing. Welcome to the neighborhood.

In multiple-brand companies, this sense of belonging can also be attached to the company behind the brand in favor, but it may be a less direct process. When Nestlé's scores a hit with a new product, the consumer is not likely to applaud the company for its efforts. On the other hand, the next new product that Nestlé's introduces may have a better chance of success with that consumer. And this connection may grow over time into a loyalty to the Nestlé (i.e., its brand) and, eventually, to the company that produces all of the Nestlé's products that the household is enjoying.

In short, customers own your brand because they can legitimately lay claim to the promises it makes to them. You *want* customers to own your brand, because only by benefiting them—functionally and emotionally—will the brand benefit, and thus enable the company to create a strong brand community.

Leatherman Tool Group: The Customer's Community

Tim Leatherman is a soft-spoken mechanical engineer who is more comfortable walking through a plant than acting like a typical CEO. He is, nonetheless, proud to be the founder and CEO of Leatherman Tool Group of Portland, Oregon, and a purveyor of enterprise-wide brand commitment.

Back in 1975, Leatherman was taking a low-budget tour of Europe with his wife when their rented Fiat repeatedly broke down. Having just acquired a degree in mechanical engineering, Tim figured he could make any repairs needed, but his trusty scouting knife wasn't up to the job. Upon his return to the United States, Leatherman went in search of a versatile, compact multipurpose tool. When he found that none existed, he figured it was time to invent one. For the next three years, he worked out of his brother-in-law's garage (Tim didn't have one) and his parent's basement (he didn't have one of them, either). He kept trying to design a knife with a built-in pair of pliers. What he didn't know until many designs later was that the world was really waiting for a pair of pliers with a knife built in.

Tim and his partner, Steve Berliner, were turned down by every retailer and catalog company they visited for eight long years. Finally, after nearly giving up on his dream, Leatherman received his first order for what would come to be known as the Original Leatherman Pocket Survival Tool (PST). Since that day in 1983, the company has sold more than 22 million tools to nearly 10 million owners worldwide. Revenue has doubled in the past five years and now tops $100 million annually. "It was," Tim Leatherman once told a reporter, "an overnight success after eight years of trying."[4]

Beyond the story of a local boy who made good, the Leatherman success is also about infusing a company's employees, suppliers, and customers with a total commitment to producing what Leatherman calls "high quality, compact, multi-purpose tools," and the brand that represents them. Without that commitment, the Leatherman tool would have fallen by the wayside long before now. The Leatherman brand community is driven by its simple set of values: "Winning relationships with customers, employees, suppliers, and community."

For the past generation, all new Leatherman employees are handed a personally engraved set of Leatherman tools when they join the firm. Tim Leatherman continues this practice because it is a constant reminder of what the employee should be striving to accomplish in his or her job. "If they want to know how they're doing," Tim Leatherman likes to say, "they just have to pull out their own tools to check the quality." The tools that employees carry on their belts have become the common language of the company.

Customers of the Leatherman company include consumers, who often consider themselves to be part of the Leatherman "club," with an affiliation that is bought into with the purchase of the tool. These folks are more likely than most to write an e-mail or snail-mail endorsement of the product, and they are encouraged on the Leatherman Web site to tell a "Tool Tale" (see the sidebar). Retail channel customers are important community members as well, and they are visited regularly and solicited for their opinions about the design and features of the product. Both groups are researched annually to learn about how their views may have changed.

The Leatherman formula has been repeated by many successful entrepreneurs throughout the world, often without the principals consciously thinking about brand building in the marketing sense. Nevertheless, brand building it is, and those companies that are operating with something less than the Leatherman commitment have an opportunity to learn from this masterbrand.[5]

How a Brand Community Can Manage a Masterbrand

Masterbrands exist in and through the communities that create them. However, this joint ownership of a brand between a company and its constituencies means that a brand transcends a community at any particular point in time. The occasional nostalgia for certain brands evocative of simpler times is one illustration of this. So, too, are the acts of the faithful—those who, having been

"TOOL TALES": CUSTOMERS PROSELYTIZING A MASTERBRAND

Part of the Leatherman brand lore are true-life stories of how its tools have saved property and lives. The stories have been featured in major print advertising campaigns and are recounted in recordings to those who call the company while they are being connected to their party. The stories, each of which has been authenticated, are a good example of how customers can contribute to a healthy community by proselytizing the brand. Here are some samples:

- A firefighter in Panama City, Florida, was called to the scene of an accident where a truck had plunged into 12 feet of water, with a terrified driver inside. According to the account, he dove into the water, "reached for the Leatherman Tool that is always at my side," cut away the driver's thick seat belt, and pulled her to safety.

- A private pilot was descending in his plane to 12,000 feet over the Alaska mountain range when he realized his landing gear was stuck and the backup system had failed. While his copilot flew the plane, the hero pulled out his Leatherman Tool, pried open the instrument panel, fished out the broken cable, and yanked with all his might until the gear came down and locked. The customer "gave my Leatherman Tool the next day off."

- Then, there was the fisherman from Syracuse, New York, who was landing a feisty Chinook salmon in the Strait of Juan de Fuca when he managed to whip a large hook deep into his brother's stomach . . . a hook that was also attached to 35 pounds of flailing fish. The fisherman grabbed his trusty Leatherman Tool and performed external stomach surgery on the spot. The Leatherman ad concluded, "[my brother] is no worse for wear . . . As for the salmon, let's just say he's caught his last fisherman." (See Figure 2.2.)

converted, become "missionaries" to others. But, what happens when the brand goes astray in the eyes of its followers, when the brand covenant is strained, or even broken?

During his stint as Apple's official "chief evangelist," religious tolerance was not Guy Kawasaki's forte. Echoing the sentiments

Figure 2.2 *Leatherman Tool Group advertising focuses on real-life stories from the community's customers.*

found in the famous 1984 Macintosh commercial, Kawasaki insisted that the issue is "not Mac vs. Windows; it's choice vs. totalitarianism."[6] Scott Kelby, *Mac Today* editor and publisher, added his own observation: "When you meet a Mac user, you find out the computer isn't just a tool. It's like their buddy. It's their friend. It's another reason why we get touchy when someone speaks badly about it. It's like someone saying your girlfriend is ugly." That loyalty to the Macintosh, of course, was extended to its masterbrand, Apple, and then outward to its community, which never gave up hoping for Apple's recovery. When the iMac was introduced a few years later, it reawakened the community's fading passion and drove the masterbrand right back into business.

Yet, the community created by a brand can be a very fragile structure. Even as the Apple franchise was being restored and rejuvenated, the company managed to enrage once-and-future customers by announcing in October 1999 that it was going to retroactively raise the prices on some of its hardware, even hardware that had been ordered and paid for. The uproar, especially among the Apple faithful who had counted on the firm to be honest and straightforward with them, ultimately forced the company to back down and rescind the order.

The saga of Snapple Natural Beverages has been told as a brand legend, but it is really about a masterbrand community. In 1997, *Beverage World* magazine declared Snapple the "drink of the decade," three years before the decade ended, but with the title came large amounts of angst. At its peak in 1993, Snapple sold about 75 million cases nationally. In 1994, it was sold to Quaker for $1.7 billion, but under Quaker's ownership, sales fell precipitously to 45 million cases in 1996. The brand began to lose focus, customers, and money. Ultimately, Snapple's loyal fans and admirers wouldn't stand for a change in *their* brand. A "Bring Back Wendy" campaign was launched by a Colorado radio station, and it rapidly gained momentum. In 1997, Quaker sold Snapple to Triarc, Inc., for $300 million and took a $1.4 billion write-off, which ultimately cost more than one executive his job.

Triarc knew they had a winner (they received a $400 million offer for the brand within months of their $300 million acquisition), but they also knew they needed to take immediate action to restore Snapple's market vitality. In this particular community, the distributors held the key to any comeback. The Triarc senior executives hit the road to convince them that the brand was back with that ol' magic . . . literally. In their road show, each Triarc Beverages executive performed a magic trick for the distributor audiences, and CEO Michael Weinstein made a giant bottle appear that filled with money when he waved a Snapple hankie in front of it. But in its most popular trick, Triarc also brought back another important part of the community with a small but fervent ticker tape parade down Manhattan's Fifth Avenue. As was reported at the time, "Wendy is back—and with marketing savvy any CEO would kill for: a passion for the product and a rapport with the consumers buying it."[7]

The Snapple brand community simply wouldn't let the beverage or the brand die a cold death in the 7-Eleven cooler. Snapple is back now, with an array of new products and advertising, and it is pumping along at an annual revenue rate exceeding $600 million, thanks to those who would not let its brand community go under.

Halfway around the world from Triarc headquarters in Manhattan, a hotelier brand is going through some significant changes of its own, moving from a banner-branded organization to what management refers to as a "two-brands, one-company strategy." With 27 properties and more than 13,000 rooms and suites throughout the Pacific Islands, Outrigger Hotels & Resorts is the largest chain in the Hawaiian Islands and is one of the fastest-growing hotel companies in the region. A closely held firm that is still family-owned, Outrigger built its business in the Islands thanks to a decades-long relationship with airlines, vacation packagers, and travel agents.

For 35 years, the company marketed all of its properties under the Outrigger brand, but the extremely wide range in pricing and accommodations quality was stretching the elasticity of the Outrigger identity.

In mid-1999, management made the decision to open up new properties on other Pacific islands such as Tahiti, Bora Bora, and Fiji. It was then that Senior Vice President of Marketing Rob Solomon decided that the time had come for Outrigger to be what he called a one-company, two-brands organization. Solomon and his colleagues rebranded lower-end properties as "Ohana by Outrigger," and they reserved the mainline Outrigger brand for only their more premium hotels and resorts. Although this change was welcomed throughout the company as a smart marketing move, it has required reeducating much of the staff about the need for, and the implications of, the branding renovation. A key segment of the Outrigger masterbrand community was not so sure that this was a good plan.

Marketing and HR executives carefully orchestrated the change to enable the launch of the new brand, without losing the support of loyal employees who did not want to see the Outrigger name removed from their properties. Through a long series of employee meetings, the executives explained their reasoning and the key decisions behind the change, and they candidly answered questions about intent and effect. They also made sure to fully communicate the planned reorganization well before any prospective guests saw the advertising for the change. The same careful prelaunch sessions were held with travel agents and vacation packagers, who are also key members of the Outrigger masterbrand community.

Importantly, the company retained the Outrigger masterbrand *Ke 'Ano Wa'a* employee program that bridged over the two brand names and provided some needed continuity to employee-partners. *Ke 'Ano Wa'a* (pronounced kay-ah-no-va-a) roughly translates to: "Working as a family in harmony with our culture and environment." *Ke 'Ano Wa'a* is the set of beliefs and operating guidelines that make Outrigger a special kind of masterbrand company. By carefully orchestrating the key changes in the Outrigger masterbrand, the community retained the loyalty and enthusiasm of its people, which can be seen in the friendly greetings that each guest receives from Outrigger employee-partners.[8] (See the sidebar.)

Driving the Brand through the Building and out the Door

An important part of what Lou Gerstner accomplished at IBM was to ensure that its brand management achieved the same

THE OUTRIGGER *KE 'ANO WA'A* COMMUNITY

The Outrigger *Ke 'Ano Wa'a* culture is introduced to each new employee in an orientation to the company's approach to welcoming guests and making them feel at home in the Islands culture. The cornerstone values of Outrigger are *Aloha* (treating a guest as you would like to be treated—with love, compassion, and dignity) and *Ohana* (we are all one family). They are introduced to guests within the *Ke 'Ano Wa'a* culture, which includes several key concepts:

- *Ho 'okipa* (hospitality) and *Kina'ole* (without flaw) form the foundation of *Ke 'Ano Wa'a*.

- *Ho 'okipa* acknowledges the interactive relationships between a host, a guest, and the place visited, and that the host has the responsibility to manage that relationship. *Ho 'okipa training* begins with a new Outrigger employee's training in Islands history, culture, arts, sciences, and human values.

- *Kina'ole* as a guide to achieving higher standards of *Ho 'okipa*, resulting in greater guest satisfaction. *Kina'ole* is designed to promote a caring environment that fosters a feeling of personal accountability among employees for the guests' experience at an Outrigger property.

Ke 'Ano Wa'a is Outrigger's corporate culture, but it is also a key part of the company's success at creating a loyal following of guests who return again and again to its hotels and resorts.[9]

Source: Company reports

attention as the company reorganization. In fact, Gerstner understood that the two had to undergo inseparable metamorphoses. Led by IBM's Vice President of Corporate Marketing, Abby Kohnstamm, the IBM marketing programs became more focused. Global advertising was consolidated with a single agency, Ogilvy & Mather Worldwide. Marketing communications of all types carried the "Solutions for a small planet" theme. When the masterbrand committed to online problem solving, the company as a whole fell in line behind the "e-business solutions" theme and methodology.

In 1998, management at Hewlett-Packard, historically one of the steadiest growth machines in Silicon Valley, began a complete reevaluation of the company and its organization. After a comeback from earnings dips in the early 1990s, the company had been responding well to new opportunities, then stagnated as aggressive competition, a lack of innovation, and the Asian financial crisis all took their toll. The conclusion reached by CEO Lewis Platt and the board: The company should be split up, and new management should be brought in.

Hewlett-Packard began its spin-off of its core components, chemical analysis, medical, and even its core test-and-measurement businesses. The spin-offs represented more than 15 percent of its 1998 revenue. Carly Fiorina, formerly of Lucent, was named CEO of the new H-P, which would remain primarily as a computer product and services company. According to former CEO Platt, the old H-P's famous decentralization was still the right approach, but it needed to be executed more completely.

Apparently, his successor did not agree. Ms. Fiorina had been in place for fewer than six months in the fall of 1999 when she announced a shocking change for the determinedly decentralized organization: H-P would mount a $200 million worldwide advertising campaign. That work, and all company communications, would thereafter carry a new logo that replaced the words "Hewlett-Packard" with the single descriptor (and internal imperative) "Invent," which was a reminder of the Bill Hewlett–and–David Packard entrepreneurial spirit that had built the company. As the *Wall Street Journal* reported at the time, "the campaign is not so much a marketing gambit as a way of helping transform H-P from a collection of largely autonomous businesses into a cohesive whole."[10]

Fiorina's other moves included tying executive compensation to the progress of the company as a whole, rather than to individual unit performance, and redirecting the duties of two top executives toward resuscitating the H-P masterbrand in the eyes of its key customers. Thus, Hewlett-Packard's 100-plus product lines became, for the first time, centrally coordinated and fully integrated, in much the same way that IBM had done five years before.

All in all, this was an astonishing admission that H-P was not succeeding as a decentralized company, and that it should instead be capitalizing on its enormous leverage as a single masterbrand community.

A third example of a brand community in a state of productive transition is 3Com Corporation, the $6 billion (revenue) enterprise and consumer networking hardware company, and the parent of the popular Palm Pilot line of products. In early 2000, the company chose to spin off its Palm division and to offer its stock for public sale, in order to concentrate on 3Com's primary business of networking. The company embarked on an extensive top-to-bottom restaging of its masterbrand throughout its brand community.

The restaging process had just begun when this book was going to press, but coauthor Lynn Upshaw is assisting 3Com in employing every possible internal and external communications channel to establish a new playing field for the 3Com brand, including extensive employee, reseller, strategic partner, investor, and multi-level customer programs.

Every company, no matter what size or in what industry, has a potentially powerful masterbrand community waiting to be leveraged. The idea of integrating the work of employees and suppliers in order to better serve the customer is hardly new. If, however, that work is to deliver maximum impact in the marketplace, it should be driven by the clearly established principles of a living masterbrand, whose performance advantages and unique values permeate the relationship between the community's members.

MANAGING YOUR MANDATE

A brand community transcends any single member, including the legal owner of the masterbrand itself. Building a brand community is more like an old-fashioned barn raising than a feat of social engineering. In that sense, you need to coordinate volunteer help in a common undertaking that creates mutually rewarding experiences for the members of the brand community, rather than draw up detailed blueprints or attempt to script every action.

(Continued)

Questions You Should Be Asking   Begin by addressing a series of questions about your readiness to plan a brand community, starting with a hard look at your company's aptitude for brand building. This would be an interrogative that assesses how much work would need to be done to construct a working brand community. Consider this:

How important is brand building to your company's overall mission? Do all the key players use the same definition for the term *brand?* Is brand building considered central to the welfare of your organization, or is it seen as one of several important sectors of the business? Or, is it a relatively small factor in the scheme of things, regarded as a specialized staff function that is clearly secondary to the more important operational roles?

Is it clear what your company-wide masterbrand is, in the context of your company's current business, and anticipated brand community? What is the essence of the masterbrand, your company's core competencies, values, and disciplines? What proprietary benefits does it offer each of your supporter groups? Why is it superior to alternatives? What does it mean for your entire company to be lived as a single brand?

What is the value proposition that underlies your brand community? If you manage a service company, are there specific service performance standards that can become proprietary competitive advantages for the masterbrand? Is your company faster? More focused? Does it offer a better value? Is your company more consistent? More efficient? Does your company in any other way demonstrate the superiority of the company-wide brand? Can the masterbrand community measurably enhance that advantage and, if so, how? If you cannot build your community on proprietary superiorities, can you preempt competition by "owning" features that they could have, but chose not to focus on?

Is your top management team and your board likely to support the development of a brand community? Obviously, key company leaders understand the importance of good relationships with customers, distributors, developers, and so on, to the business. But what we are talking about here is the strategically planned, meticulously executed nurturing of these constituencies. If your managing team is generally enthusiastic about the prospect of building a brand community, then planning should proceed at least to the stage of laying out the steps and commitment that are needed to complete the transition.

Do you have a leader in hand who (1) is qualified to plan and execute a community development process; (2) who can give up his or her current position, at least temporarily, to lead the process; and (3) who has the respect and trust of the company's people, management, and key members of the community-to-be (i.e., vendors, partners, customers, investors)? A task of this magnitude must be directed by such a leader, or it will surely fall short of its goal. Do not pursue this effort if such a leader is not available for full-time assignment for at least 6 to 12 months.

What do your "relationship barometers" say about how closely your people are linked to the members of your brand community? How well are your people connected to your customers and strategic partners? Do your people consider other members of the community to be full partners of the organization, or do they regard them as third parties that are to be serviced? How effectively do you bring to life their understanding of customers and constituents with regularly updated profiles? How often do your people get to meet with the customer? If meeting the customer is part of your business, do they ever meet with the customer in nonbusiness situations?

How personally committed to your brand are your core customers? How close do your suppliers feel to your company? Have your strategic partners embraced your masterbrand's stance in the marketplace, and do they understand how their company will benefit from a strong position for your masterbrand? Or, are they solely concerned with the short-term benefits of the deal that you have struck with them?

You should be able to literally map out who your real and potential partners may be in the brand community, and the degree to which each is committed to the enterprise.

Which sectors in your brand community should receive your greatest attention? Are you in the consumer service business, and thus are your employees your greatest point of leverage in terms of making your company-wide brand all it can be? Or, are you in a business-to-business service, where continuously interacting with customers is the most effective way to guarantee success? Or, are

(Continued)

you in a rapidly evolving technology business in which your strategic partners may hold the key to long-term growth, and yet your partner portfolio must grow and evolve as rapidly as your technologies?

Whatever your organization, the customer always comes first, but you must prioritize how much time you give your other constituencies, or the masterbrand enterprise could become diffused and lose momentum.

Actions You Should Be Taking   Once these and similar questions have been asked and accurately answered, your company may be ready to begin building its brand community. Although each building process depends on the specific needs of each individual company, we can recommend some initial actions to be taken to start your organization down the right track.

If your company has already created a multidisciplinary team to spearhead brand-driven initiatives, make use of that team to direct the community development process. The team should report directly to the CEO, and the CEO should be a participating, or at least ex officio, member of the planning group. If such a group has not been organized, recruit individuals who show an interest in the brand community concept, an understanding of the power of brand building in general, and a strong knowledge of the company and its customers. In general terms, the group should be charged with the following:

- Crafting a realistic, up-front timeline that is strictly adhered to and that is carefully managed online via the company intranet by a qualified member of the brand community planning team.
- Establishing a research and reporting process, both within the planning group itself and to key decision makers within the company.
- Developing a set of achievable business objectives, measurable metrics, preliminary strategies, and a first-cut budget. Once this phase is completed, the group should seek senior management guidance and approval.

Review existing quantitative and qualitative research surrounding the key dynamics of the state of the market, your company's development strengths and shortcomings, and the health and dynamism to date of your masterbrand and offspring brands. This could include the following:

- Market status and trending, including the short- and long-term prospects for growth in the market, and the likely sources of that growth.
- Customer marketing research that might indicate the most profitable and loyal segments, the key drivers of change and brand choice, the benefit attribute ratings, the company's and competitors' advantages and points of vulnerability (including brand image and equity), and the favored purchase channels.
- Qualitative or anecdotal research about your company's relationships with vendors, allied partners, and supporting constituencies (e.g., software developers, health care consultants, trade journal reviewers).

Reach a consensus on key strategic issues that will form the DNA of your brand community—most notably, a clear and relevant value proposition to its constituencies, supported by a compelling positioning and proof points. This is the basis for long-term relationship building, and it must be present in order to foster a strong brand community.

For example, if you are a business services company, are you known throughout the industry for a single, compelling benefit (or set of benefits) that you provide your customers (e.g., minimum down-time response, customized enterprise solutions)? Or, if you are a consumer offline retailer or e-commerce company, do you have a clear brand promise that is closely associated with your brand? What can prospective community members find here that they can find nowhere else? How will they recognize your brand community as their own—one that they cannot only identify with but also contribute to? Are these views held *at least* as strongly within your company as outside of it?

Compare and match the strategic opportunities in the marketplace with the strategic and logistical capabilities of your enterprise and its potential brand community.

- Create a prototypical community model, projecting who will be the members of your particular community. A community supporting a consumer services company might include: the existing and prospective customers, individuals, or organizations that might influence purchase decisions; company suppliers whose cooperation is needed to provide the highest-quality,

(Continued)

real-time support for your services; and key employees who are most likely to interact with, and have an impact on, the community as benefits are delivered to customers.

- Develop a community SWOT analysis (strengths, weaknesses, opportunities, threats), using the information obtained in the exploratory stage described earlier, which focuses on market events and trends, community capabilities as a whole, and the specific capabilities of your company.
- Compare and contrast the needs of the market with the capabilities of your company and its community, creating an opportunity assessment using as much empirical data as is available and applicable.

Initiate your brand community building process, employing one or more of the following:

- Using the analyses discussed above, conduct a series of exploratory exercises with employees that include activities such as offsite ideation sessions to identify current and potential points of contact and leverage with existing and prospective brand community members (customers, trade allies, distribution channels, etc.). When forming and conducting such sessions, break down functional silos and involve employees across your organization. In a true brand community, employees should feel as if they are on the front line, projecting the positive brand attitudes that attract community members and earn their trust. Employees need to feel a part of, and contribute to, the process of creating a brand community in every possible manner.
- Based on the results of these discussions, create permanent "listening posts" and discussion forums that become part of the backbone of your community communications and research functions. These can include: customer advisory panels; site visits; employee exchanges; users' reunions and the like which require and encourage employees and customers to "rub elbows," both on and off the job.
- Follow a similar approach with other representatives of the future brand community, such as suppliers, alliance partners, and so on. And don't forget to include your marketing communications agencies, which could have a significant impact on the attractiveness of your community to potential cus-

tomers. In some cases, special arrangements with these companies' respective managements will have to be made to conduct such research and follow-up work.

Prioritize which groups within the brand community are most important to the health of your enterprise-wide brand, and make decisions accordingly. It's tempting to believe that all of the groups in a brand community are contributing to sales, and thus, they all need equal portions of time and support. But there is never enough time and support to go around, so prioritizing is vital. Also, remember that the customer must ultimately come first for any masterbrand, but more attention in the short term may need to be paid to gatekeepers or influencers, in order to provide your customers with what they want to buy.

Create an environment in which contributors to your brand community are encouraged to be creative, yet disciplined about how they demonstrate their commitment to what the masterbrand stands for. Not everyone in a brand community can, or should, participate in every such activity, but that such activities are ongoing will inspire all members with a sense of the brand community's legitimacy and mission. Brand communities are resilient to the degree that they change in creative directions, yet within mutually defined limits.

- *Consider carefully those aspects of your masterbrand that customers want to—and can meaningfully—own.* Identify the specific aspects of heritage, trust, and aspiration that set your brand and its community apart from others. Give members tangible evidence that they own these aspects of your brand. As with any true community that is greater than the sum of its parts, a brand community grows and changes incrementally and organically. Like a healthy organism, a healthy brand community changes and adapts to changing circumstances, while remaining true to its purpose and kind.

- *Create opportunities for customers to adapt and apply the masterbrand and its value proposition in their own lives—and to share this with others, customers and employees alike.* Part of this process is facilitating all members of the community to be brand "missionaries," willing to proactively evangelize about

(Continued)

the brand, even if that simply means giving off-the-cuff testimonials to friends and coworkers. Members of your brand community should be motivated boosters of the masterbrand—but in thoughtful ways with sound rationale, not as mindless cheerleaders.

Set specific and realizable goals and limits for your community. Members want and expect a certain degree of stability and comfort from their association, but not at the risk of allowing the brand community to become moribund and ultimately irrelevant to their changing needs. Consequently, you must not only tolerate but actively seek out constructive criticism. Test the limits of your brand community, and encourage customers to do the same. If the fundamental trust and credibility are there, you both will survive the experience—and even be stronger for the occasional misstep.

- *Establish specific mechanisms for feedback and dialogue.* Be clear about your strategic focus, but be open to surprises as well. As your brand community grows, it will become increasingly self-defining.

- *The masterbrand thrives in a brand community by its openness and "transparency" to members.* This is less a matter of wearing your heart on your sleeve than it is of demonstrating (not merely verbalizing) the brand promise in every action, large and small. Rather than rigidly dictating every action, masterbrand companies inculcate a sense of brand throughout the community, allowing employees and customers to creatively manage the creation and delivery of value.

Finally, consider conducting periodic off-site workshops with representatives from all sectors of your brand community to discuss how well the enterprise is developing. Community representatives should include members of the customer panels, partner alliance companies, vendors, communications agency partners, appropriate company staff, and other brand supporters. These should be facilitated, carefully structured meetings in which specific information and sharing objectives are set and adhered to. The goal of the meetings should be to review the status and health of your brand community, to reevaluate the strategic direction that the community is taking, and to discuss what future events or trends might have an effect on the brand in the marketplace.

*　　*　　*

No factor is more critical to the growing of strong brand communities than the eruptive spread of online communications and commerce. What began as an interesting experiment in electronic information exchanges will likely be the most important cultural and commercial movement of our young century. Our next chapter reveals how the masterbrand community will reach its full potential on the Internet and other online channels.

CHAPTER

3

Interactivate the Brand.comm

Toro's Electronic Community is content, it's community, and it's commerce . . . The extranet has become critical to keeping our distributors and dealers viable in this new marketplace while at the same time keeping our customers happy in a direct relationship.
—Cindi Love, Director of Customer Service Systems,
The Toro Company[1]

I n the fall of 1999, three little-noticed events in quick succession validated the obvious: The Internet really *has* changed everything:

- On October 28, habitually conservative Federal Reserve Chairman Alan Greenspan gave a speech in Boca Raton, Florida. In what may prove to be a watershed moment, Greenspan heartily endorsed the emerging technology-driven economy, which he said was creating a "virtuous cycle" of burgeoning productivity with little inflation. To veteran Fed watchers, Mohammed had moved to the mountain.

- On November 27, President Clinton, in his regular Saturday radio address, encouraged U.S. citizens to shop on the Internet. Not since the Great Depression has a U.S. president so specifically encouraged commerce. If you listened carefully, you could almost hear the e-tailers humming.

- On December 1, owners of the Saint Louis Galleria, an upscale mall in Richmond Heights, Missouri, announced that they would accept the inevitable. Mall management had banned its 175 tenants from conducting any commerce on the Internet. The resulting firestorm of objections from tenants and debilitating publicity from the rest of the world cowed the owners into submission and signaled that commerce without the *e* is unthinkable, not to mention un-American.

For the last 400 years, give or take a decade, the world economy has grown when geographic expansion took place. In the twenty-first century, the new frontier for emerging businesses will largely exist on the Internet. It may be difficult to predict what direction this world within a world will take, but we are certain that it will be masterbrand communities that reap its greatest commercial rewards.

How the Net Is *Becoming* Business

The Internet has exceeded everyone's expectations largely because it has altered fundamental economic relationships. It has changed the way that consumers shop for and purchase an enormous range of goods and services. It is now in the process of reinventing supply chains in dozens of industries by making it easier and less expensive to directly connect the seller with the buyer, causing a domino effect among distributors, resellers, and assorted service brokers.

While business fundamentals still apply, this new kind of economic dogfighting is forcing all players to rethink how they make money. No new communications channel—up to and including telephones and television—has had anywhere near this much economic impact in so short a time. When the revolution becomes truly global, it will shake the planet to its steamy core.

In 1994, a small group of us were touting the World Wide Web and its breakthrough HTML code as the next *big thing*. We really didn't know what we meant, but it smelled like a winner. None of us—with the possible exception of Steve Case at AOL—really understood how short of the mark we were, and even Case seemed to be looking from the outside in.

According to a University of Texas study, the total value in 1999 of all businesses that were associated with the Internet was U.S. $301 billion—making it the 18th largest economic environment in the world (just behind Switzerland). That figure will easily reach into the multiple trillions of dollars before this new century is five years old. Two-thirds of this value is hardware and software infrastructure, applications, and intermediaries. The remainder is the value of online retail sales. Having grown 175 percent in just three years and employing 1.2 million workers, the Internet now rivals established sectors such as energy, automobiles, and telecommunications—each of which took decades to reach a comparable size. (See the sidebar.) And, while Internet-based interactivity has been hailed as the "ultimate triumph of consumerism," its future potential is even greater for business-to-business commerce.[2]

As we'll see in this chapter, emerging e-corporations are pioneering ways to interactivate their brands and to forge ever stronger online ties with their brand communities. The online experience has something to teach all companies, whether they are planning to jump immediately into e-branding or bide their time on the sidelines. In any case, the explosive growth of e-business and e-commerce sets the stage for the ultimate triumph of brand building as a central discipline of business management.

In the coming age of Internet-empowered customers, *all* marketing will necessarily be permission-based, the direct marketing concept that calls for first asking prospects if they want a product or service, then delivering it. Increasingly, we will rely on customers themselves to provide the information we need to meet their needs and manage our businesses. Enticing customers to come forward and volunteer such information on a semiregular basis will require creating a brand community to which they want to belong. The Internet and related interactive technologies offer

SUNRISE, SUNSET: WHEN DID YOU GET TO BE SO TALL?

Tracking the size and growth of the Internet may be the only job that makes cosmology look easy. Here are some stabs at the monster that won't stop growing, and won't sit still long enough to allow anyone to determine how big it is in real time. Much of the following data is obviously outdated as you read this, but we hope that they will provide some perspective, if not precision. (Sources in parentheses are based on January–September 1999 data.)*

- Time to reach the first 1 million domain names: four years. Time to reach from 4 million to 5 million domain names: three months. (Network Solutions)

- Seventy percent of Web traffic goes to 4,500 sites. (Alexa Internet)

- Number of pages on the Web: 800 million, only 16 percent of which are covered by the best search engine. (NEC Research Institute)

- Global Web population projections: 142 million in 1998, 196 million in 1999, 502 million in 2003. (International Data Corp.)

- Americans represent an estimated 44 percent of Web users; 177 million Americans will be online by 2003. (International Data Corp.)

- Global e-commerce spending projections: $50 billion in 1998, $111 billion in 1999, $1.3 trillion in 2003. (International Data Corp.)

- Business-to-business sales online will grow from $131 billion in 1999 to $1.5 trillion in 2003. (Forrester Research)

- CEOs who believe that the Net will have major impact on the global marketplace within three years: 92 percent. (Booz-Allen Hamilton and *The Economist*)

*As reported in Maryann Jones Thompson, "Tracking the Internet economy: 100 numbers you need to know," *The Industry Standard*, 13 September 1999.

the ultimate tools for building such a community, but they are only that—tools. Without a clear plan and the guiding discipline of brand building, we risk misusing these tools and falling far short of our objectives.

Whether you plan to use the Internet to literally interactivate your brand, there are important lessons to be learned from those who have already done so.

For the masterbrand builder, the ultimate promise of the Internet is not mass customization or customer self-service; it is the opportunity to interactivate your masterbrand and to transform it into an online brand community, or what we refer to as a *brand.comm.*[3] Companies that accomplish this feat radically change the dynamics of value creation and the relationships between their organizations and their customers.

Cyberspace, like nature, abhors a vacuum. One person's disintermediation is another's opportunity for reintermediation. In both retail and business-to-business markets, brand communities are being knitted together in ever more intricate and resilient value chains of companies, partners, customers, and intermediaries. Increasingly, a brand.comm is known by the companies it keeps. Such companies are also becoming, at the insistence of their customers, transparent organizations. The Internet leaves a company no place—or time—to hide from customers, allies, and competitors; it also means there's no *need* to do so. Rather, as numerous companies large and small are beginning to discover, you can use the Internet to interactivate your masterbrand within a blessedly glasslike house.

Marketing That Doesn't Look like Marketing

The Boelter Companies began as a family business supplying paper goods to Milwaukee-area taverns. Today, Eric Boelter, vice president of sales and marketing, manages an inventory of over 9,000 items, selling $60 million a year to some 2,000 hotels, restaurants, and food services across the country. His best customers, such as the Hyatt Regency and Drake hotels in Chicago, were interested in replacing his 360-page paper catalog with customized price lists and access to their own ordering history.

Boelter is one of the estimated 8 million small businesses with Internet access (half of all such businesses, and growing daily).[4] A password-protected extranet (a secure Web site that is accessible to key upstream suppliers and downstream customers) now enables Boelter's customers to place and track orders. Importantly, they need only make a few clicks to review past purchasing patterns and to resubmit standing orders. Although he doesn't call it "My Boelter," this is essentially the same strategy of personalization that is adopted by online behemoths such as Amazon.com, AOL, and Yahoo! to make their brand community members literally feel at home. As Eric Boelter modestly explains: "We aren't using [our extranet] as a marketing tool. We're just trying to make it a service for customers who are serious about using it."[5]

Of course, the best marketing is marketing that doesn't *look* like marketing. That is often the case when members of a brand community interact to create value as they extend the masterbrand in new and creative ways. By using an extranet to interactivate his brand community, Eric Boelter has moved from being merely a vendor of supplies to a preferred segment of his customers' own management resources. The commitment from this family-owned business to serve is the foundation of its nascent brand community. The Internet is merely the tool that makes it possible to extend this sense of community service to new customers in new ways. Like many other small businesses quick to capitalize on the promise of the Internet, Boelter is on its way to becoming a brand.comm.

Creating a Win-Win for the Brand.comm

The Internet challenges a lot of conventional business wisdom and is forcing strategists to rewrite the rules of competition and cooperation. Not the least of these is the conventional assumption that manufacturers and distributors are engaged in a zero-sum game like poker—that is, one party's winnings are at the expense of the other. Instead, it is increasingly apparent that the Internet creates new and creative win-win relationships among customers, companies, strategic partners, and even competitors (witness the strange-bedfellows alliances announced almost daily among high-tech, communications, and other companies that were once thought to be deadly enemies). Realizing this potential, however, requires the understanding and discipline to manage your brand.comm in ways that actively mesh with the needs of other community members.

The Toro Company dominates the domestic market for lawn care and snowblower equipment. The specialized needs of golf courses and country clubs make them some of Toro's steadiest and most profitable customers. Although company management felt it had to get closer to these charter members of its brand community, it did not want to compromise the two-tier distribution channel that had helped it become the $1.1 billion U.S. market leader. A mindless charge into e-commerce might wrench relationships with the dealers who were also key members of the Toro brand community.

Toro's answer was to create its own brand.comm, the Toro Electronic Community, a bi-level Web site where both customers and dealers can tap the Toro resources. The open sector of the Web site allows customers to obtain general information about products and check their account data. The secured sector functions as an extranet that links Toro with its supplier and dealer partners to exchange information, place and track orders, and comment on product designs. The Toro Electronic Community has been an essential part of maintaining and growing a brand community that benefits Toro, its customers, and its distributors. Rather than wave a red flag at its dealers and distributors, Toro has harnessed the power of the Internet to strengthen, extend, and supplement its traditional channels.

In the same way, General Electric sought to interactivate its appliance brand through its Direct Connection extranet-based program, and it was careful not to alienate its traditional distribution channel of independent dealers. In fact, by offering online information and support to its independent dealers, GE was able to help them maintain a more complete, but less costly virtual inventory. Dealers now agree to maintain a specific, limited number of lines and display models and to ensure that GE products account for 50 percent of sales. In exchange, GE promises quick delivery to customers without tying up the retailer's capital in inventory.

An added benefit is that GE can track actual sales, rather than inventory, and thus adjust to changing market conditions more rapidly and accurately. What could have been the mechanism of disintermediation has, instead, served to strengthen GE's ties with the dealers that make up an important part of its brand community.

Managers at Michelin North America also decided that interactivating their brand community would yield mutual benefits that could outweigh the purported advantages of disintermediation. Its Bib Net extranet (named after the famed Michelin "tire man," Bibendum) links the world's largest tire manufacturer to virtually all of its U.S. independent distributors. Corporate planners at Michelin wisely sought out dealer input on the design of Bib Net, thus ensuring that it would be used by even the most low tech of its distributors. As one observes: "They gave us carte blanche to design the system the way we wanted. I was very impressed. A lot of companies would just tell us what they had done for us."

Perhaps the greatest benefit for Michelin is that, in the words of another distributor, the way it implemented its extranet "shows that Michelin is dedicating itself to changing its reputation among dealers by becoming more dealer-friendly."[6] That's one way of putting it; another is to say that Michelin has created a successful brand.comm.

The (Second) Loneliest Job in the World

The success of a brand is often more dependent on postsale servicing and performance than on presale reputation. Balancing the two parts of the same reputation can be tricky business, and a brand's identity can sometimes be damaged from the strain between the two. By carefully guiding the information and relationship management of key members of a brand community, the masterbrand can sometimes turn potential damage into significant gain.

Hyundai Motor America provides a valuable example of interactivating a masterbrand to save it from the consequences of its own success. Throughout much of the 1990s, Hyundai had a poor reputation for quality in the American auto market. More recently, internal research indicated that actual and perceived quality of its auto parts had improved dramatically. Unfortunately, Hyundai owners now had less reason to visit the company's authorized dealers and parts suppliers. This meant that dealers had fewer opportunities to provide after-purchase service and to sell Hyundai parts. Instead, service tended to be performed by local garages that were not part of Hyundai's distribution network.

Like Maytag, Hyundai was in danger of giving its repair people "the loneliest job in the world." The result could have been that Hyundai would not be able to achieve the critical mass to create and sustain a brand community of dedicated intermediaries and loyal customers. If customers weren't coming to Hyundai, Hyundai would have to go to them . . . in this case, through the customers' chosen intermediaries—local garages.

The solution was the Hyundai Enterprise Internet Commerce System—an extranet that links dealers, distributors, consumers, and independent auto repair shops. Customers and intermediaries can find parts, place and track orders, and get information about specific repairs. Orders are routed to Hyundai dealers who, in turn, price them at wholesale or retail, depending on whether the car owner is dealing directly with them or through a local garage. In another win-win scenario, Hyundai sells more parts (+10 percent annually), and car owners get the service they want from their chosen intermediary. By addressing customers' concerns about the availability of postwarranty parts and service, Hyundai is also strengthening ties to its brand community.

New Rules for New Forms of Brand Contact

As the Boelter, Toro, GE, Michelin, and Hyundai examples illustrate, moving online to interactivate your company as a brand.comm is a preemptive way to create more productive relationships with members of your masterbrand's community. However, this means changing business processes to fit the Internet and related information technologies—not merely grafting these technologies onto existing practices.

Intranets and extranets can be inexpensive ways to communicate with employee-partners, customers, and distributors. But more important, such interactive technologies enable companies to link all of these parties in a symbiotic value chain, fully leveraging the collective intelligence of the brand community. However, this realigning of existing relationships and integrating new intermediaries into the brand community requires the focus and discipline of specialized brand.comm management.

The experience of Levi Strauss & Company illustrates both the potential and the pitfalls of brand.comm managing. Levi's was one of the first manufacturers to go online (in 1994) in an effort to sell direct to its customers. By not undercutting offline retailers' prices, Levi's planned to cash in its brand equity directly with customers, pocketing the difference in the form of increased profits.

The November 1998 relaunch of its Web site received technology awards and kudos. The sophisticated site was designed to function as a "jeans advisor," allowing customers a 360-degree preview of how their customized clothes would fit and look. Whereas the traditional selling experience culminates in a purchase that becomes the end of the relationship, Levi's hope was to use its Web site to initiate and maintain a direct relationship with its customers. Online contact would allow Levi's to notify customers of promotions and to facilitate reordering. By stitching together a value chain that enabled customers to tailor their own fashions, Levi's also sought to create an ongoing, virtual focus group that would help it understand how to mass-market its off-the-shelf jeans. In short, it would pull its customers snugly into the brand.comm.

Less than a year later, Levi's announced that it would cease selling online after Christmas 1999. Although it planned to occasionally offer special products through its Levi's and Docker's Web sites, the flagship site would mainly support the company's marketing and branding initiatives. Although its Web site helped customers' jeans fit better, stand-alone e-commerce wasn't a good fit for Levi's. The company realized that it lacked the deep pockets that were needed to compete online and decided to shift its e-commerce to its existing retailers. (That was also a smart move to avoid unnecessary channel conflicts at a time when the company needed to strengthen its relationships with retailers).

On the other hand, the Levi's experience of using intranets and extranets to link employee-partners and intermediaries reportedly has been very successful. As early as 1997, the company began to set up an intranet to link all of its 37,000 employees in 46 countries worldwide. It deliberately opted for a free-range system that allowed employee-partners to develop their own Web sites around different geographies and functions. Levi's wanted employees to be free to use text, sound, and video to exchange information about products and problems, thus building closer ties to each other and to customers.

In keeping with its operating philosophy, the system deliberately had no "air-traffic controller," although there were guidelines imposed by a global intranet editor. As a spokesperson noted at the time: "We operate on a devolved structure. It's part of our company culture, which is not autocratic but which seeks to involve everybody in what we do, and which is led by creativity."[7]

A couple of years later, Levi Strauss was using the Internet to interactivate its brand in a quite different, though complementary way. Levi's developed a concept shop program—a "store within a store"—to market its Slates line of men's clothing. It needed to ensure consistency in the look and feel of the Slates sites in its retail outlets. It also wanted to monitor their financial performance. The company thus created an extranet that was accessible to service providers, such as architects, fixture manufacturers, and store installation teams, who were responsible for setting up and maintaining these sites. Among other things, the extranet allowed architects to post computer-assisted design (CAD) visual store plans online rather than producing and shipping expensive hard copies—saving $10,000 a year in overnight delivery costs alone. More important, the extranet enabled managers to monitor compliance with setup and promotions and to link the sales performance for each shop to the cost of maintaining that shop.

As Levi Strauss discovered, the greater potential of the Internet for some companies may be in creating a brand community of customers and intermediaries that builds upon, rather than bypasses, existing relationships for the sake of e-commerce.

What's Good for the Customer Is Even Better for Employees

Progressive companies have been quick to exploit the potential of intranets and extranets to link far-flung sales and service employees with each other and with the intermediaries and customers—internal and external—that make up their brand communities. In an example of inside influencing outside, Procter & Gamble acknowledged that their employees' enthusiasm for intranets helped drive the company-wide decision to embrace interactive marketing. The company encourages creativity and diversity in its attempts to interactivate its brands. However, P&G also strives to maintain a "sharing network" that lets it rapidly develop and reapply knowledge and avoid merely "digitizing bad habits."[8]

Similarly, Hewlett-Packard uses its Electronic Sales Partner (ESP) intranet to support its sales reps with product data, competitive intelligence, and advice on effective pitches. More than one-half of the almost $2 million spent to create and launch ESP over a two-year period went to training employee-partners to use it, and 60 percent of ongoing expenses are used to keep it up-to-date. Although some insiders fear the stifling effects of a centrally managed intranet, HP hopes to channel early grassroots enthusiasm to support sales and customer service across the entire organization. With the renewed efforts to integrate the traditionally decentralized company (see Chapter 2), the company's intranet will play a key role in focusing its business units and employee-partners on the company-wide masterbrand.

Today's interactive technologies render moot many of the past debates about centralization and control versus decentralization and creativity. The Internet as a whole, the Web, intranets, and extranets all create—for different groups and for different purposes—communication links and information flows that are necessarily open and largely self-managed. This does not necessarily mean that focus becomes a casualty, but the discipline of masterbrand building is required to manage the use of these tools toward their greatest potential.

Far from threatening to disintermediate customers from brands and distributors from producers, interactive technologies can only be fully effective where such ties exist. The essence of the Internet is about openness, transparency, and the free exchange of ideas. It is not surprising, then, that companies built around the Internet and associated interactive technologies are increasingly being designed and managed as *transparent organizations*. In what follows, we'll see what it means to live in this latest version of the glass house—and why a transparent organization is best off as a brand-centered organization.

There's No Place to Hide in a Transparent Organization

From one perspective, the transparent organization is the culmination of the age-old desire to manage any enterprise of life with near-perfect information. In our view, the principles of masterbrand building should guide the design, implementation, and management of tomorrow's transparent organization because it will optimize what a company can be.

The transparent organization is the opposite of the legendary "mushroom" approach to managing customer and employee relationships (i.e., keeping employees in the dark . . . among other things). This is illustrated in its purest form in the online auction. When large numbers of buyers and sellers are brought together with complete information and practically unlimited choices, the price of almost any product or service is inexorably driven downward toward producers' costs. No longer can temporary disparities of information and choice be converted into higher profits. Only truly *value-added* features of the product or service can sustain higher-than-commodity margins.

Similarly, internal management practices that create value for, and trust among, employee-partners can motivate them to be loyal, contributing members of a brand community. Given the transparency of online information about today's labor markets and career alternatives, employee satisfaction and retention will depend on equally transparent and proactive policies and incentives. As cyberspace expands and Internet time contracts, transparent organizations will more frequently become *learning organizations*, rewarding employee-partners' productivity and customer loyalty in highly visible ways.

It is not just that the Internet and other information services have made transparent organizations *possible*; rather, these developments have made transparent organizations *necessary*. With this necessity comes the need for a new, more comprehensive vision of masterbrand building that applies not only to the company, but to the entire value chain that constitutes a brand community. New skills are needed to create and manage brand communities that will draw customers and intermediaries into relationships with a company.

As the term suggests, the transparent organization cannot trick or coerce—but rather must attract and persuade—its employees, customers, and partners. As all marketing and management become permission based, building the masterbrand can become the rallying point and central discipline for transparent organizations.

Interactivating the Masterbrand's Relationship with Customers

When a masterbrand improves its supply chain management, it's not simply squeezing out costs and increasing shareholder value. Increasingly, the online interactivity that is required by efficient supply chain management is creating new links between the company, its intermediaries, and their mutual customers. As the locus of value creation shifts from production to distribution, masterbrand companies are recognizing that their greatest assets are the relationships that they have forged within their brand communities. Managing these assets—that is, managing the masterbrand within its brand community—is thus seen as a top priority.

A Coopers and Lybrand study of customer-care best practices among 60 diverse companies found that six "superstars" were particularly effective in applying techniques of supply chain management to customer relationship management (CRM). These companies employed intranets, computer-telephony integration (CTI), data warehousing, and other enabling technologies to collect, integrate, disseminate, and thus leverage information throughout the organization—online, continuously, and in real time.[9] Importantly, from the customer's perspective, such an integrated approach to account management enhances not only the *speed* of customer service, but also its *responsiveness* and especially its *accountability*. The latter improvements are critical to creating the customer-perceived positive brand attitudes that drive loyalty to the masterbrand and create a strong brand community.

The United States Automobile Association (USAA) offers one example of a brand community that is built, in part, around an interactive customer relationship management (CRM) system. Each week, USAA's ECHO (Every Contact Has Opportunity) collects more than 2,000 customer comments through telephone reps handling everything from routine inquiries to complaints. The latter generate banner messages on designated account reps' computer screens that continue flashing until the problems have been addressed. USAA is convinced that such information-driven, feedback-engineered customer care generates trust and commitment, making this approach the wave of the future. The company's annual renewal rate of 98 percent would suggest that its customers agree.

Webline Communications is one of a new breed of companies that is founded on the notion that the Internet should complement, not supplant, traditional customer service. Cofounder Pasha Roberts was no stranger to the Internet's potential—his father, Larry, had helped develop its forerunner, the ARPANET, in the 1960s. When Roberts and his partner, Firdaus Bhathena, won MIT's 1996 $50,000 Entrepreneurship Competition, they were able to refine their idea for a "teleweb" service. Using Webline's technology, a live customer service or sales representative can actually control customers' Web browsers and guide them by phone through a product demonstration or other use of the Web site that they might not be willing or able to attempt on their own. As more (and less sophisticated) users go online, Webline Communications is making the process a little less intimidating for some.

Turning the Organization Inside Out to Serve Customers

As important as it is to capture, interpret, disseminate, and act on inbound customer-generated information, the transparent organization also has to project itself to customers and strategic partners alike through these same technologies. For upstream suppliers and downstream distributors and customers, extranets are the brand extendors of intranets.

Many companies claim to "bend over backwards" to serve their customers; Osram Sylvania surpasses them by turning itself "inside out" to serve its customers. The company keeps its inventory of more than 5,000 lighting products flowing smoothly through 28 plants and 8 distribution centers in part by using an extranet to make its operations transparent to its strategic partners. The company recruits its suppliers and distributors into an interactive inventory management process, in effect ceding to external customers the control of certain aspects of its own internal operations. Like other transparent organizations, the management at Osram Sylvania understands that interactivating your masterbrand means erasing old distinctions between *inside* and *outside*.

As we have seen, in a true brand community, supply chain management and marketing become one and the same. Federal Express has taken this insight to its logical conclusion: It now sees itself as a strategic provider of e-commerce, logistics, and other supply chain services. What began as a sophisticated way to monitor and manage performance in its core business of package delivery, has now *become* part of its core business. FedEx has become one of the better examples of a brand.comm, transforming supply chain management into customer relations management—and, ultimately, into customer self-management as part of the FedEx brand community.

The Rise of Virtual Companies

The explosive growth of pure-play e-commerce has created the need for a whole new breed of companies that provide a range of logistics and fulfillment services. Online sales of toys has skyrocketed from $1 million in 1997 to $60 million in 1998, to $500 million by the end of 1999. To keep up with the growth of its potential market, Toysmart turned to one such logistics support company—Yantra Corporation of Acton, Massachusetts—to become a part of its supply chain and contribute to its brand community. Lacking the logistics experience of an L.L. Bean or the deep pockets of an Amazon.com (which is building its own system from scratch), Toysmart realized that, as CEO David Lord puts it, "You can't do it all by yourself anymore."[10]

Begun as an offshoot of a local educational supply company in 1997 with 10 employees, toysmart.com launched a $20 million ad campaign in the last quarter of 1999 with the tag line "Click on your child's potential." Because the company's brand community is built around this promise of bringing only educational toys to discriminating parents, customer service and timely and accurate order fulfillment are critical to its sense of brand community and customer intimacy. One in three purchasers revisits the company's Web site to check on the status of his or her order, and returning an incorrect order can cost the company $25. (Unfortunately, that was not enough, as Toysmart.com became a casualty of the e-commerce shakeout of the spring of 2000.)

Logistics support companies such as Yantra are the natural counterparts and complements of virtual companies—whose only assets are the brand-based relationships they have with distributors and customers. The Internet and other interactive technologies allow the literal disintegration of the traditional company into its component functions, such as production, distribution, and marketing. As each type of company becomes increasingly specialized and efficient at doing what it does best, the brand community emerges as the natural unit of analysis and management, encompassing all elements of the distributed value creation process that once resided within a single company. That community has definite value that is based on functional capabilities, but it has much more value as a key contributor to a healthy brand community.

Ultimately, the transparent organization's reason for being is to serve customers—often by helping them serve themselves. Its transparency is the antithesis of customer ignorance. The interactive enabling technologies that make the transparent organization possible and necessary empower the customer to compare and make informed choices. Thus, by serving the customer better, the transparent organization better serves itself. That partly explains, for instance, why two-thirds of sales at Amazon.com are from repeat customers.

Putting Transparency to the Taste Test

A final example of the viability of transparent organizations comes from a recent study that was sponsored by the Marketing Science Institute. This study found that the more customers learned about product quality and pricing, the more likely they were to take the plunge. Among online wine buyers, price sensitivity decreased as quality, usable information was made available to online customers. Another way of putting this is that consumers put a value on—and were prepared to pay for—such information. The authors concluded that "the challenge facing electronic retailers is not how to prevent comparison, but how to use emerging electronic venues to provide consumers with better information about product quality."

There seems to be little doubt today about the value of creating organizations that are *internally* transparent. Virtually all Fortune 500 companies now operate robust intranets. In one study, 80 percent of companies surveyed had an average positive return on investment (ROI) for an overall average of 38 percent, ranging from 21 percent for year-2000 initiatives to as high as 53 percent for inventory management and 68 percent for database access.[11] Intranets assisting customer service can yield as much as a 47 percent ROI. As impressive and important as these "hard" figures are, they understate intangible benefits—including the ripple effect of even modest increases in productivity within knowledge-based organizations.

More broadly, improvements in supply chain management, which rely heavily on intranets and other interactive technologies, can show large and immediate savings. Initiatives at Tenneco Automotive increased inventory turns by 25 percent. Nike quickly improved order fill rates by 40 percent and saw revenues increase 27 percent. Ford was able to reduce delivery time to one-fifth of the former time needed—from 72 to only 15 days. A study by Ernst & Young claims that resulting improvements in cash flow can boost a company's stock value by 20 percent. In another indication of its growing importance, a study by Advanced Manufacturing Research in Boston expected the market for supply chain management software to be nearly $2 billion in 1999, growing to $13 billion by 2002.[12]

All of this is evidence that transparency, particularly when employed in the building of masterbrand communities, can mean as much to the bottom line as it does to the strength of the masterbrand itself.

MANAGING YOUR MANDATE

From virtual companies to stealth manufacturers, transparent organizations have grown apace with the expansion of the Internet. This is clearly no accident. Indeed, the fundamental imperative of the Internet is transparency and the freedom that this brings—from its open architecture and protocols to open online discussions that are hosted by volunteers to the explosion of free services, including Internet access itself.

Like Mephistopheles in the story of Faust, the Internet destroys in order to create anew. Disintermediation is merely its initial, destructive phase, paving the way for creative reintermediation of the masterbrand with its customers and partners (both old and new). Increasingly, the Internet not only *enables* you to manage your company as a brand.comm, it *obliges* you to do so. Increasingly, this means managing your company as a transparent organization, where customers and intermediaries can see right through you. If they like what they see, they'll want to be part of your brand community. If not, they'll soon find alternatives—some of them only a mouse click or two away. Although that might cause some loss of business, it is a continuous stimulus to the organization to stay on the top of its game.

Questions You Should Be Asking   There are some principles that you can observe—and questions that you can ask—as you seek the best way to weave your brand.comm together with its other many owners. Some questions we recommend you consider are the following:

Is marketing still something you try to do to, *rather than do* with, *your customers?* The best marketing may not look like marketing in the traditional sense. Throughout history, the role of market intermediaries has been to know and to serve the customers so well that the customers "sell" themselves. The Internet is merely the latest medium for doing this. Even though the distinction between e-service and e-commerce may be helpful for some purposes, there is a real sense in which the two converge when your masterbrand becomes a brand.comm. With the brand community as the natural locus of

(Continued)

value creation, customers who serve themselves . . . sell them-selves . . . and will keep coming back for more. What are you doing to motivate, train, and reward this new sales force?

Do you still "service," rather than serve, your customers—or, worse yet, do you force them to "service" themselves? Do you use the Internet to push customers away from more costly "real" customer service, or do you use it to pull them toward a mutually beneficial interaction with your brand.comm? A transparent organization must be built around interactive CRM that helps it learn from its success and mistakes, quickly converting the experience of a few into benefits for the many, employees and customers alike. Internet-assisted customer service isn't just about minimizing costs, but also maximizing such learning across the organization and its wider brand community. Is this a central part of your competitive strategy?

Are marketing and customer service still relegated to functions, depart-ments, or groups of outward-facing employees, or are they literally wired into every aspect of your transparent organization? Are you using an intranet merely to save paper on company newsletters, or are you actively managing it as the essential tool of masterbrand building that it is, informing and involving employees within the context of the masterbrand value proposition? Even in a transpar-ent organization, not every employee will be literally visible and accessible to customers and intermediaries. All employees should, however, be encouraged and trained to think and act *as if* they were visible and accessible.

An intranet can be a powerful tool for doing this, by making your organization transparent to itself. It's been said that a fish doesn't know that it swims in water. When employees are com-fortable working and growing in a transparent organization, they'll instinctively live the brand—for each other and for the rest of your brand community. Their first question won't be: Is this my job? but rather, How does this reflect on our brand community? They'll want to be seen by the company they keep and that keeps them. They'll emerge as the creative nucleus of your brand.comm.

How extensive and accurate are your customer databases? Relationships require information, and if your information about customers is sketchy or outdated, you will be wasting your time to mount a major strategic effort with flawed data. (In our experience, database management of customer information is the single most-talked-about and least-acted-upon sector in most companies.) Your online community simply cannot operate as well without strategically planned, meticulously executed and maintained databases.

How well are you measuring not only the "trailing indicators" of improved financial performance, but also the cost and time savings that are created by your use of the Internet? These are the leading indicators of your ultimate competitive and financial success as a brand.comm. Can you identify—and do you reward—those who are responsible? Companies with greater Internet savvy appear to have higher returns on invested capital, in part because much of that investment is in employees who are ready for Internet prime time. Harnessing and managing this potential anarchic talent, however, requires both the appeal and running room that are created by a true brand community and the adaptable discipline of masterbrand building.

Are you still using only traditional market research to "segment" and "target" your customers? If so, then it may be *you,* instead of your customer, who's in the cross-hairs. It isn't just a matter of moving from shotgun to rifle to laser-targeted marketing at "segments of one." In today's cybermarkets, even those elusive ones can flip to zeros in a nanosecond. Customers refuse to stay in the box, no matter how carefully you've constructed it. Chances are your customers themselves don't know what they want until they're about to get it (maybe for free). It's a safe bet that your organization can't do the job alone.

Rather, it takes a brand community to first help define the need, and then to leverage the resources of a range of employees, customers, and intermediaries to meet that need (better, cheaper, and faster). Rather than trying to stay one step ahead of your customers or keep them exclusively for yourself, you need to march in step *with* them as equal members of your brand community. You and your teams should be asking: How can we shift our focus from outdated market intelligence to creating an intelligent marketplace where brand community members do our marketing homework with us (increasingly, from home)?

Are you employing the Internet and other communications technologies only to strengthen one-way or exclusive relationships with selected cus-

(*Continued*)

tomers and suppliers? Or, are you (also) creating online ecosystems that link you to multiple potential customers and intermediaries?* Are you actively sought out by potential customers, as well as by other organizations that want to partner with you? (Does your better mousetrap catch mice *and* attract cheese salespersons?)

Do you still view relations with customers and intermediaries as a zero-sum game (their gains being your losses), or do you operate within a brand community that collectively creates and equitably distributes value for all members? Are you willing to bend over backward *and* turn inside out to serve your customers and other brand community members? Are you using the Internet merely as one more channel to promote your proprietary brand, or have you begun to create and interactivate a masterbrand that can be owned collectively by a true brand community, whether online or off? Have you made your brand community the focus of your strategic planning and the natural unit by which you assess competitive threats and opportunities?

Do you have an active, explicit commitment to, and strategy for, creating value not only for customers but also for the suppliers and intermediaries who are part of your brand community? Are you as open to converting competitors into allies as you are in beating them at their own (old) game? Have you created an extranet capability that allows you to protect proprietary information behind a sturdy firewall, but still permits allies/competitors to interact productively with the organization? Do all members of your brand community know and live the brand promise that aligns them in their values and actions, allowing them to create value through and for each other?

Actions You Should Be Taking   When you have answered these and related questions to your own satisfaction, there are actions you can take to begin to make your brand.comm a reality. Although trying to "cookbook" an online brand community is a recipe for disaster, you're likely to find that some of the following actions will end up on your to-do list.

*For more on the concept of ecosystems applied to business strategy, see James F. Moore, *The Death of Competition: Leadership & Strategy in the Age of Business Ecosystems* (New York: HarperCollins, 1996).

Assemble one or more cross-functional teams to reverse-engineer the internal links in your value chain to see how they might be reassembled and deployed as masterbrand assets. A masterbrand has to be sold on itself before it can sell others and create a brand community. Here are some of the ways you might begin to grow the seed crystals of your transparent organization into a brand.comm.

• Identify all current and potential points of contact between employees and your customers, intermediaries, and trade allies. Don't limit yourself to points of contact that are related primarily to marketing and sales, fulfillment, or customer service. Look for informal and unofficial ones, as well.

• Determine the ways that these contacts project impressions of your organization—outward to potential customers and intermediaries and inward to employees.

• Select a manageable few such points of contact to assess their potential to become masterbrand leverage points.

• Avoid digitizing bad habits (i.e., turning a boring internal newsletter or parts catalog into their online equivalents). Brochureware destroys fine minds.

• Analyze the ways that customers and others can or could use your extranet and other windows into your transparent organization. Can they see your masterbrand at work and want to join in? Or will they end up merely window shopping? Can they do so without divulging their proprietary information, or learning yours?

Implement truly interactive CRM and marketing—whether you're online or not. Analyze your moment-of-truth encounters with customers and determine truthfully whether you are managing these as problems for customer service reps to dispose of as quickly and as cheaply as possible, or as opportunities to create a true sense of brand community.

Use the data capture, transfer, and navigation capabilities of the Internet and communication technologies to coordinate decentralized, dispersed CRM. Do not automate traditional centralized customer service call center "sweatshops." Move customer service out to the customers; don't just expect them to dial up and do it themselves.

(Continued)

As you develop metrics with which to measure the Internet's impact on your organization, and as you begin to hire, train, and reward employees who can move these metrics, make sure you are measuring the right things. The most important value of the Internet is not in saving time and money doing traditional marketing and customer service, but rather in creating "critical mass" within a brand community, fueling a value chain reaction. An online brand community, or brand.comm, is to marketing and customer service what hypertext is to conventional information storage and retrieval. Make sure that you're utilizing the Internet's full potential to link the hot buttons of your brand community (and let them create their own), not merely replacing ink and paper with electrons and video display terminals. By all means, develop measures of the cost and time savings that you can produce by using the Internet, but don't stop there.

Finally, reconsider how you reward employees, given the new realities of the Internet age. To find, hire, and hold the kind of employees you need, you can use the creation of a brand.comm as, in some measure, its own reward. Don't just offer financial incentives to identify and implement cost savings; "pay" employees the respect and recognition they deserve as good brand community builders. That means, among other things, ensuring that they are always made aware of masterbrand and community-wide victories.

*   *   *

As the Internet's scope and influence grow, there is enormous pressure on companies in all markets to participate, either as a purveyor of information or as a purveyor of goods and services. Our next chapter describes how the most advanced companies are using the Net to help their masterbrands create trust and relationships in an environment that is potentially much more treacherous than the world of bricks and mortar.

Extend the Online Community

The Internet doubles in traffic every 100 days.
There's nothing in the world except bacteria that
grows that fast.

—George J. Kelley, Morgan Stanley Dean Witter analyst[1]

A s we have just seen, information sharing via intranets and extranets that may have begun simply as a matter of convenience can—with proper guidance—evolve into a strategic partnership between parties up and down the entire value chain, forging the bonds of a true brand community. Product demos or trials (particularly of software and information services) can be easily and inexpensively conducted and monitored. Online seminars and chat groups can encourage customized brand experience and familiarity.

These developments can be extended outward from e-business supply chain management to actual e-commerce and the creation of full-fledged brand communities. From this perspective, customer self-service can be seen not as an *alternative*—but rather as the necessary *prelude*—to value-added service by the company. Although problems can still occur, a company increases its chance

83

of garnering loyalty when customer service means neighbor help-ing neighbor within a living brand community.

Mass customization via customer self-service is thus a logical extension of so-called permission-based marketing. The customer's input to the value creation process is the information that is needed to customize a product or service. Increasingly, producers must rely on customer self-service—and voluntary self-disclosure—to obtain this critical input. Integrating the customer into the value chain is not just a matter of information or logistics management via inter-active technologies. Unless, and until, the customer is persuaded to participate, there is no (or insufficient) information to manage. Customers rightly resist attempts to get around this bottleneck by obtaining information about them without their knowledge or consent.

Ultimately, then, leveraging the full potential of interactive information and logistics management technologies requires the creation of brand communities that are based on trust and respect among coequal partners. Online or off, managing your company as a brand.comm means keeping this vision in focus and applying it in everything you do.

Customers Are Always Right (Especially When They Help Themselves)

Just when it looked like it was going to take over the commercial world, disintermediation may soon be preempted. What the Inter-net and other interactive technologies are beginning to offer is a chance for customers to *become their own intermediaries*. Although search costs can be greatly reduced, the geometric growth of choices and information sources can also greatly complicate "direct" online purchasing of products and services.

Though old channels and intermediaries may be bypassed, the detour is not without its own costs. Some buyers will revel in the wealth of new choices that are offered via the Internet; others will beat a hasty retreat to the nearest trusted brand. Going online and interactivating your brand gives customers the best of both worlds. Maintaining the discipline of masterbrand building, however, is needed to harness the power of interactive technologies, for customers to help themselves, when and where they want to do so.

Virtually all online e-commerce sites include some degree of personalization. The reason is simple: Such customizations are estimated to increase new customers by nearly one half—and profits even more so. Even with customized site costs in the multiple millions, customization often pays for itself within a year. The popular Internet portal Excite claims that visitors who use customization features of its Web site come back five times as often and view twice as many pages as do others. Compact disc retailers, such as Music Boulevard (now part of CDNOW), report that customized recommendations result in purchase rates of from 10 to 30 percent, 10 times the average for the rest of the site.

Amazon.com founder Jeff Bezos has explained that personalization is fundamental to the community concept: "(Personalization of e-commerce sites) is like retreating to the time when you have small-town merchants who got to know you . . . You get the economies of mass merchandising and the individuality of 100-years-ago merchandising."[2] What Bezos calls "collaborative filtering" occurs as shoppers navigate through Amazon.com's Web site, which refines its recommendations and choices based on previous visits—thus encouraging them to return again and again. Eventually, Amazon.com hopes to make that once-in-a-thousand encounter with a life-changing book become more like once-in-a-hundred. (For his effort and impact, Jeff Bezos was named by *Time* magazine as its 1999 "Man of the Year," a tribute to the intrepid entrepreneur and his extraordinary ability to construct a superior masterbrand, although its shareholder value has been suppressed by profit delays.)

Starbucks has developed a way for its customers to contribute to the brand community, both offline and online. The company co-publishes (with Time, Inc.) a magazine called *Joe*, which carries articles and features on jazz, poetry, fiction, and other cultural potpourri that you'd expect to find in a coffeehouse. The offline magazine is sold at the Starbucks outlets and is available in part online. The publication also encourages customer interaction and research response, further weaving them into the community of the Starbucks masterbrand.

Although Internet skeptics claim it's nuts, to soup companies such as Campbell's and Lipton, Web sites are also a cost-effective way to promote and customerize individual food products. In doing so, each leverages its masterbrand to create an incipient online brand.comm that can enhance customer loyalty, increase usage, and support future brand extensions. The April 1997 relaunch of campbellsoup.com was promoted online, on product packaging, and on TV. In just a few months, the content-rich Web site attracted over 1 million visitors. Many were repeat visitors, averaging 18 minutes each (three times the industry average.) More to the point, Campbell's also noted a spike in sales of featured products.

According to a Lipton researcher, its Recipe Secrets Web site "brings back the old days of shopping, where the corner grocer used to know your food preferences." Predicting that as much as 15 percent of grocery sales will be over the Internet by 2008, Unilever has begun to explore business relationships with online retailers such as the home grocery shopping and delivery service, Peapod.

What retailers are learning to do is integrate the customer directly into the value chain. These companies are applying downstream the same practices of information and logistics management that are commonly applied to upstream suppliers. As this process extends through the entire value chain, however, the operative discipline must shift from supply chain logistics to masterbrand management.

Changing the Meaning of *Brand*

Brands are the embodiment of trust, but the Internet puts an unprecedented strain on that tie that binds. One reason is that it plays the role of the Great Equalizer. When a prospective customer tries to compare brands on the Web, for example, it's much more difficult than in real space to determine which is larger and more legitimate than the next. That's partly because the entire concept of *legitimate* is continuously changing. Who would have thought that a virtual mall would accumulate a stock value of more than $25 billion, or that an Internet portal would be valued higher than $100 billion? If a retail brand has a bigger store, or a packaged-goods brand has more shelf facings, or a business service brand has more trucks, those cues help us decide where to invest our hard-earned cash. On the Net, in contrast, any small-time entrepreneur can appear to be as big as IBM. Caveat emptor, in the extreme.

The biggest offline brands are usually the ones that pay for all those prime-time commercials and Times Square megaboards. On the Web, however, the difference between impressive, less expensive, and more expensive sites is relatively small compared with the real world. Web site size, for example, may have nothing to do with site productivity, revenue generation, or value to the customer. As for marketing spending, it is estimated that Merrill Lynch and Fidelity spend between $50 million and $75 million each in offline advertising. E*Trade and Ameritrade were expected to spend hundreds of millions of dollars in 2000.[3] So, who's the upstart and who's the entrenched incumbent?

One thing that the Net and the offline world share is the effect of fulfillment and customer service on brand reputation. Failing to receive an order on time or encountering a crabby customer service agent will kill a brand deader than dead for that particular customer, and it doesn't matter if he or she is kept waiting online or on the line. No new channel will change that dynamic, although it may be tougher to get the customer back in the online environment, given easy access to so many competitive alternatives.

In fact, the Holiday season of 1999 taught many a ".com" that fulfillment is *the* name of the game, or the game is over. The struggling Toys "R" Us chain had one such nightmarish experience. The company had a minimal online presence until November of 1999, when it decided to jump headfirst into the pool by mailing out 62 million catalogs, encouraging shoppers to shop at its Web site. A few days before Christmas, Toys "R" Us announced that it could no longer promise to deliver orders on time, and it offered angry parents a $100 gift certificate that could only be redeemed at—you guessed it—its offline stores.

Even old-line offline branders, like Procter & Gamble, finally recognized the power of the Net. In 1994, then P&G Chairman, Ed Artzt, had challenged advertisers to develop ways to exploit interactive technology. Reflecting on this charge a few years later, P&G's Vice President of Global Marketing, Denis Beausejour, noted one striking irony—nowhere in his speech had Artzt mentioned the Internet![4] Instead, P&G and many others had focused on the (thus far empty) promise of interactive TV. P&G, however, doesn't do anything in a small way, and by 1999, the company had tripled the number of brands it was interactivating online and had created more than 200 interactive commercial messages. *Advertising Age* named P&G its Interactive Marketer of the Year for 1999, and the marketing world got the message: The Internet had emerged as a mainstream, universally accessible, environment for brand building.

Following suit, U.K.-based Unilever expects to interactivate over 100 of its brands on AOL sites by 2001, and it has established an interactive brand center in New York. These moves are particularly significant because traditional packaged-goods marketers had always assumed that their slim per-unit margins would not permit a full commitment to an unproven channel until the economics could be worked out in their favor.

Part of the reason for P&G's change of mind was based on what Beausejour observed as the interactivity afforded by the Internet, which was "dramatically changing the meaning of what a brand is." In the past, customers learned about a brand through conventional media, promotions, or word of mouth, and then they used the product or service. Although expectations shaped customers' evaluations of actual usage, there was a real sense in which brand familiarity and the actual occasion of product or service usage were distinct phases of the overall experience. Beausejour calls this the "atomic" meaning of *brand*.

By contrast, interactivating a brand online has the potential to more fully integrate all aspects of the total brand experience. (For some categories, the online experience *is* the brand.) As a result, P&G has begun to develop augmented products such as Dryel, which allows consumers to do their own dry cleaning, assisted as needed by a dedicated Web site.

What Seems to Work in E-Commerce . . . for Now

Offline brands have historically sold *at* the customer. In a true brand community, the customer is as much a seller as a buyer, in the sense that purchasers can become advocates for the brand and sell it within the community. This becomes a mutually beneficial interaction between the customer and the brand that runs under, around, and through the marketing dynamic.

E-commerce has accelerated all of this at a rate that no one considered possible even a few years ago. As of this writing, there appear to be some guidelines that have proven effective for successful e-business and e-commerce companies, at least to date. Here is our list of must-haves if you hope to build a formidable brand.comm:

- Site customization (tailoring to an individual's needs) and personalization (recognizing and modifying according to an individual customer's identity) are now commonplace and are enhanced frequently once customer databases are compiled and profiling is established. A variety of stat-digital techniques are used to personalize to, and to profile customers, including clustering (eToys.com), collaborative filtering (Amazon.com), psychoprofiling (Lycos.com), and artificial intelligence (E*Trade.com).

- 24/7/365 service must be provided, ideally in a combination of online and live. It seems to be particularly important that live representatives be available as a backup to an online default (esurance, Lands' End Live).

- Superior fulfillment is required, because the Internet is one channel that seems to imply that all things are possible—another thing you can thank Amazon.com for.

- E-commerce sites cannot survive long without establishing relevant, brand-reinforcing partnerships, joint ventures, and alliances (AOL, MSN).

- E-commerce sites must have reliable, scalable, server farm support or they risk trust erosion if users can't count on uninterrupted service (New York Times On The Web).

- Simple-to-navigate site architecture is a must when you expect people to buy goods and services from your site (Drugstore.com, Dell).

- Strong branding components, such as the brand name, graphic system, strategic selling line, and so forth, must be well coordinated to reinforce the brand at crucial points in the online experience (Saturn.com, Levi.com).

- Substantial "stickiness" to encourage multiple usage and long-term loyalty, via attractive content and/or promotional incentives (CBS.Marketwatch, PCMall).

- Creative CRM is also a required skill set, largely because an e-commerce brand's site is the open door to long-term relationships that could generate considerable lifetime value. This requires strategically sound and tactically fresh approaches to managing ongoing customer relationships (Schwab.com).

- Give it away before someone takes it away. This method of attracting usage is a throwback to traditional promotional incentives, as well as the free information heritage of the Internet's ancestor, the ARPANET (Free.com).

- Of course, a strong sense of community must be built into the site if the e-commerce brand hopes to expand its influence over time. If designed well, a sense of community environment can upgrade the brand from one-dimensional customer relationships into multidimensional seller-buyer-buyer "brand triangles" (e.g., eBay, iVillage).[5]

It Takes a Brand.comm

In Chapter 2, we explored how brands exist only in and through the mutual efforts of the companies that own them in the legal sense, and the masterbrand communities of customers that give them life. Interactivating your brand is as simple—and as difficult—as using the Internet and other information technologies to drive this process to new levels of customer intimacy and brand experience. Like any community, a brand community exists in a specific time and space. Increasingly, that time is real time and eBay is an exceptional brand community that grew up almost overnight. Riding a wave of IPO and Net excitement, eBay has grown from an obscure corner of the Web to become a major force in e-commerce. As of this writing, the web site (see Fig. 4.1) is carrying several million items, generating several billion dollars in gross auction sales, capitalization in the $20 billion range, and a P/E ratio hovering at 7,000, depending on how the NASDAQ fares. Run by marketing heavyweights such as CEO Margaret Whitman (formerly of P&G and Hasbro) and COO Brian Swette (PepsiCo), e-Bay has successfully defended its auction turf against Amazon.com.

Whitman is clear about the eBay vision: ". . . we think of ourselves as sort of a community-commerce model. And what we've basically done is put in place a venue where people can be successful dealing and communicating with one another."*

According to Swette, one of the keys to eBay's success is the nurturing of its most important community members—individuals and small businesses—that are "core sellers," participating in the most auctions and accounting for a disproportionate share of eBay brokering commissions. The job of some eBay employees is to conduct quantitative research about these key customers, but also to just "hang with" them, to understand why they like the auction format, and what features and services will keep them coming back for more. eBay's goal is to "bring back some humanity to the buying and selling process . . . to try to bring Main Street back into the equation." In this way, eBay is creating a warm and welcoming community, devoted as much to getting to know its sellers as to providing a place for them to sell.

However, eBay also experienced several server failures during 1999. Management is obviously very concerned about the effect of such breakdowns on the sales process, but also on its community. Reliability is a cornerstone of any successful commercial community; community, after all, is as much about trust as is brand building.

In the final analysis, eBay is an experiential brand, and it is the job of its community managers to ensure that its virtual "inhabitants," on both the buying and the selling sides, have a positive experience that will bring them back for more.[†]

*Lynn Upshaw with Robert Liljenwald, Interview with Margaret Whitman, *eBrand Letter*.
[†]Based on an interview with Brian Swette, senior vice president—marketing, eBay, Inc., 3 June 1999.

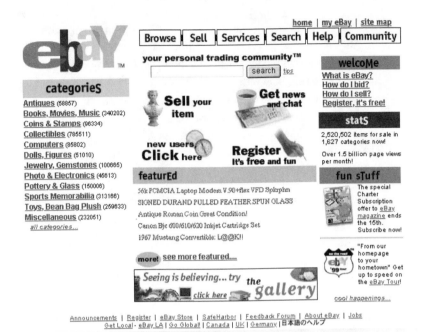

Figure 4.1   *The eBay home page serves as the rallying stage for its successful masterbrand community.*

that space is cyberspace, which offers your company an opportunity to build an online brand community.

Online interactivation is merely the latest and greatest means to fulfill your promise to your brand community. As we have seen, however, this has to be a collaborative process of freely interacting individuals. Building your brand.comm on the Internet begins by creating a virtual place where this can happen—a place where your customers will want to be.

CEO Candice Carpenter launched iVillage.com: The Women's Network in September 1995. From the beginning, Carpenter and cofounders Nancy Evans and Robert Levitan saw iVillage.com more as a place where upscale, younger women could meet and exchange information than as an online publication. More recently, iVillage.com has creatively partnered with other companies to expand their vision. Charles Schwab, for example, offers women an iVillage.com bridge site, called The Investor Center, as part of its Armchair Millionaire online community. According to Schwab Vice President Alexandra Roddy, market research had shown that women were underserved by existing financial services media, and were also more active and loyal online buyers. "Men are hunters, and women are gatherers," according to Roddy. "Women consult more sources of information, talk to people, turn to experts. An interactive community lends itself to that."[6]

By August 1999, iVillage.com had leveraged "integrated sponsorships" with Kimberly-Clark, AT&T, and Ford, as well as key alliances with AOL and Amazon.com, to create a consortium of 17 related Web sites, attracting 5 million visitors and more than 100 million page views a month—making it 27th among all Web properties. Between mid-1998 and mid-1999, registered membership grew from less than 400,000 to over 2 million. The company has fueled this growth by establishing numerous topical links to navigation channels and e-mail services. It also invites prospective customers to sign up for any of its 50-plus newsletters (which have a combined weekly circulation of over 5 million).

In addition to providing women with a place to develop and practice their financial management skills, iVillage.com's affiliated Web sites cover topics ranging from work to parenting to fitness and beauty. For example, a network of volunteers (shades of AOL) help maintain a pregnancy circle. By entering her due date, each member of the circle gets a personalized calendar of daily events she is likely to experience. Participating community members exchange information, advice, and support—and the online interaction is structured to gently steer them toward products and services they may need during and after their pregnancies.

In March of 1999, iVillage.com went public. Its initial offering price of $24 per share zoomed to nearly $96, before ending the day at just over $80. Unfortunately, iVillage.com is an example of a strong brand community that has fallen victim to the volatility of the finacial markets. At this writing, its stock has fallen well below its IPO level, and the company has yet to make a profit. iVillage.com embodies the fundamental principle of all true brand communities: It is the cocreation of its members, working with the resources that are provided by the company and, in turn, producing the resources that are necessary for further development.

As a final footnote on community, you know that a concept is becoming important when companies are created just to manage it. Participate.com is a former extranet consulting firm that markets itself as a manager of online communities, an expert at holding onto customers on Web sites. Clients of its outsourced extranet services include Ace Hardware, AT&T Worldnet, and Arthur Andersen. In September of 1999, the firm raised $15 million of VC money that is betting on the importance of Web community building that will help cultivate customer loyalty, as well as monitor customers' views to help guide future marketing efforts.

Yahoo!: If You Let Them Build It, They Will Come (and Stay)

The real value of what has been called *customerization* does not lie solely in the "fit" between product and customer. The real benefit of letting some customers serve themselves may be in freeing up scarce resources to better serve others at a lower total cost. A study by Booz Allen Hamilton estimated that insurance companies doing business over the Internet can save approximately 60 to 70 percent compared with the cost of providing conventional service over the lifetime of a customer.[7] Federal Express estimates that as much as 40 percent of the hits on its Web site would have otherwise been calls to its 800 number, saving the company many million of dollars each year.

Although we might covet customers with the demographic profile of iVillage.com's well-heeled investors, most votes for the online brand communities to beat are for America Online and Yahoo!. We'll be exploring America Online in a later chapter, but let's take a brief look here at the Yahoo! brand community.

Unlike Amazon.com, Yahoo! was one of the original big Net brands that began making money relatively early on. One reason is that Yahoo! didn't just create a brand through aggressive advertising and promotion, it crafted a brand.comm by literally giving away its services. As industry analyst Jonathan Littman put it: "Yahoo is business proof that—at first, anyway—it's often better to give than to receive."[8] Stanford graduate students in electrical engineering, cofounders David Filo and Jerry Yang had the tech-

ESURANCE: THE STRATEGIC BIRTH OF A ".COM"

The unprecedented publicity surrounding the founding of online .coms has sometimes obscured the need to rely on the fundamentals of classic marketing operating strategies. The online auto insurance company called esurance was officially launched on the Web in late 1999 (see Figure 4.2), but its masterbrand was born several months earlier, on October 20, in a hotel near the San Francisco International Airport. It was there that J. D. Weir, the company's then vice president of marketing, convened a group of 50 advertising, interactive, and public relations executives, marketing consultants, and marketing staff, to discuss how esurance was going to be positioned in the wild and wooly online marketplace.

Weir, a veteran of Procter & Gamble, knew that the best start for any start-up required a carefully crafted masterbrand, marketed in the most integrated way possible. At that first planning meeting, Weir encouraged his teams to critique and absorb the end product of months of hard research and strategic planning, which would boldly position esurance as "Better Than Insurance." As he did so, Weir also asked his staff and agencies to work together under a series of principles:

Principle 1. We are open and act as an integrated team.

Principle 2. We present one unified brand image across all elements of the marketing mix.

Principle 3. All parties practice a results orientation.

Principle 4. There are no bad questions, and we seek proactive input.

Principle 5. We all seek the best idea, regardless of the source.

There have been many changes at esurance since its inception, as there have at similar Internet companies. Yet, esurance and its broader community of supporters continue to operate with a single, unified understanding of what the brand stands for, and how they must work hand in hand to guarantee its long-term success.

Figure 4.2 *The esurance brand.comm is based on carefully crafted strategic planning.*

nical know-how and credentials to make Jerry's Guide to the World Wide Web the ultimate Web site for every fellow geek and techno-nerd. They also had the good sense *not* to do that.

As Unix programmers, Filo and Yang were familiar with the acronym YACC—"Yet Another Compiler Compiler." A burst of late-night creativity familiar to many graduate students saw the birth of YAHOO—"Yet Another Hierarchical Officious Ora-cle"—a name that Filo and Yang admit also fits their public per-sonas. More important, the odd mix of self-deprecating humor and in-your-face attitude created a brand tone that set the stage for what would become "cool" on the Net. (Added a few months later, the exclamation point now seems to be a foreshadowing of how Wall Street would react to the idea.) By sharing the wealth and linking freely to numerous other Web sites, Yahoo! became anything but yet another compiler of places to visit on the Web. Precisely by *not* trying to be the be-all and end-all for its users, Yahoo! became one of the largest and most dynamic online masterbrand communities.

Yahoo! also illustrates how, in a true brand.comm, the community comes first. In the hub of the Yahoo! brand community was a group of Stanford-branded alums including CEO Tim Koogle, VP of brand marketing Karen Edwards, and top lawyer Jim Brock. As Brock recounts the early days, "David and Jerry embraced the community of users. Users provided the URLs. It was an interactive process. They tapped into that power in a way the other navigational tools didn't."[9] From day one, Yahoo! was a community built by—and thus for—its users.

Long before Microsoft began asking its customers "Where do you want to go today?", brand community members were telling Yahoo! that they wanted the potential to go *anywhere*. Exhibiting the sincerest form of flattery of AOL, Yahoo! quickly used partnerships and acquisitions to offer its brand community e-mail, news, chat groups, sports, travel, financial, and other services—all customized via My Yahoo!. Early on the operators of Yahoo! understood that its real asset was its community of users—not simply the online content that it provided them.

Accordingly, rather than developing its own content or co-branding with other providers, Yahoo! decided to become a *content aggregator* for the new medium of the Internet—much as the executive producer emerged in response to the new media of Hollywood movies and TV. Yahoo! pioneered new short-term contracts and arrangements for sharing online ad revenues that provided it both the flexibility and the resources (its gross margin can exceed 80 percent) needed to operate in Internet time and stay one step ahead of the competition.

Putting community first means that a brand.comm must persuade, not force, its customers to go new places. Yahoo! admits that it learned valuable lessons from two ill-fated attempts to extend its brand community in inappropriate ways. Early in 1996, Yahoo! community members resisted the company's attempt to funnel them toward a virtual shopping mall created in conjunction with Visa. A little over a year later, Yahoo! paid off Visa for the failed joint venture and created in its place the Visa Shopping Guide. Rather than creating an online version of the traditional shopping mall, the new service allows community members to research and make purchases within their normal consumption patterns and categories (e.g., tickets, gardening, automobiles, or wines).

Similarly, Yahoo!'s attempt to coproduce a computing channel with publisher Ziff-Davis proved too unwieldy to operate in Internet time. Today, Yahoo! operates the channel, Yahoo! Computers, and Ziff-Davis' *Wired* and other publications provide the content—a Solomonic decision that has pleased both brand community members and stockholders.

While Yahoo!'s long-term success is more certain than ever, the exact direction of its next moves is less sure—which is exactly the way it should be for a nimble brand.comm. In 1998, e-commerce accounted for only about one-quarter of Yahoo!'s revenues, with the rest coming from online advertising. If, as predicted by many analysts, online advertising increasingly moves away from all-purpose portals to Web sites focused on specific topics such as financial services, Yahoo! can expect to retain the lion's share of remaining online ad revenues. Nevertheless, as the popularity of these alternative destinations grows, Yahoo! will also have to continue diversifying services to its own brand community.

And that's exactly what appears to be happening. Among other moves, late in 1999, Yahoo! began an aggressive push into e-commerce, in the expectation that this would become a major source of revenue in years ahead. The company also announced Yahoo! Digital, a service that allows brand community members to download CD-quality sound over the Internet.

The Auction Economy: From "Do It Yourself" to "Price It Yourself"

It started modestly enough. In 1995, Pierre Omidyar, a developer for General Magic, created a Web site that offered an online auction service to link potential buyers. A year later, the auction service had grown large enough for him to devote his full workday to what became known as eBay, which eventually grew to a capitalized worth of more than $25 billion in 1999. At eBay, and at most online auctions, sellers pay a modest fee to put an item on auction, and electronic bidding begins for a set period. eBay collects a commission if the item is sold and that income, combined with relatively low operating expenses, creates that rare bird known as a profitable e-commerce firm.

One of the oddities of the business-to-consumer (b2c) auction communities is the fare they attract. One frazzled mother threatened to put her kids on the auction block if they didn't behave. When she actually listed them on the eBay site, no takers stepped forward, but the kids saw their names on the site and turned into little angels. Mr. Charles "Bud" Obermeyer of North Bend, Washington, claimed that a bidder offered him as much as $2,000 for a blank piece of paper before eBay pulled the plug on the gag (at least Mr. Obermeyer *claimed* it was a gag). And the Yeah, but-who-would-want-it? award goes to the lady who sold "What I found in my couch about an hour ago" for $3.05 (i.e., 79 cents in change, a half-eaten pretzel, a screw, a beaten-up rubber band, a pen top, and chewing gum . . . mercifully, unchewed). "It was my understanding [that the buyer] was going to have the red rubber band professionally restored," the seller reported, apparently with a straight face.[10]

In 1999, an estimated 5 million Web users bought at online auctions. The online bazaars take all forms, including the reverse auction, in which the buyer influences the price through bidding (such as is the case with Priceline.com for airline tickets, hotel rooms, and even mortgages). Then there are the volume discounters, such as Respond.com and Mygeek.com, that permit consumers to make an online bid for large lots of items, then wait to see how prospective sellers respond. The buyer can then choose who gets the sale.

The success of eBay has even lured offline auction houses to the party. Dovebid, an auction house founded in 1937, attracted $12 million in venture capital money in October of 1999 to fund its forays into online bidding. A case, you might say, of reverse auctions via reverse channeling. The model even reaches into the industrial sectors through what are being called *industrial communities;* VerticalNet, Inc., of Horsham, Pennsylvania, offers steel, office products, and other lines on a bid basis.

In a new twist on the auction approach, Dell Computer founder and CEO Michael Dell told *Iconocast* online magazine that his firm is now putting up for sale the cost of entry into the Dell community. When potential partners want to establish a portal presence within the Dell business community—which Dell now claims approaches one-third of the U.S. business market—they have to be ready to ante up a surcharge. As is the case in the rest of the auction economy, the highest bidder gets to come to the Dell dance. Going even further in building its community, Dell established its Direct Commerce Integration model, in which more than 30,000 small and midsize companies maintain pages on the Dell Web site. That site links their customers' purchasing networks to Dell and cuts procurement costs for all parties.

Consultant and author Gary Hamel believes that all of this is more than just an interesting form of e-commerce. Hamel and his colleagues see us as being on the cusp of a broad-based auction economy in which virtually all that consumers and businesses need will be subject to a bidding process. Evidence of that arrived in late 1999, when eBay's German unit, eBayPro.de, announced that it was having success auctioning off entire small and midsize companies. As the company's Andreas Eleftheriadis said at the time, "This could be a big business for us. There's really no limit on what we could sell with this medium."[11]

If so, it will not only reduce prices in many categories of goods and services, but will greatly improve production, distribution, and retailing efficiencies. The ancient pastime of comparison shopping will increase productivity on both sides of the auction block.

Where will a company brand.comm end up in this shopping nirvana? Probably in great shape, if its leaders and managers can carve out some proprietary niches to which the entire company can contribute. For example, an online, auction-based sporting goods manufacturer might concentrate on outdoor gear that is bracket priced according to seasonal weather conditions. Thus, in a good camping year, the firm can start its bidding floor lower than in other years, and it can send signals to prospects that it is more attuned to camping enjoyment factors than its competitors. In the meantime, manufacturing can focus on weather-related conveniences in its designs (tents that breathe in hot weather), and customer service can "weatherize" their conversations with consumers ("It's another beautiful day for camping . . . How can I help you?").

And, as impressive as the b2c auction market has been, it will soon be dwarfed by its b2b counterpart. In late 1999, the fastest growing segment of the Internet was easy to spot: so-called business-to-business exchanges that were virtual backroom shopping malls where businesses could barter discounted pencils and forklifts, all at the click of a mouse. The idea was so popular that the independent exchanges were joined a few months later by global giants that wanted to play the same game, only with their own rules. Big boys like the Big Three automakers, Wal-Mart, Chevron, Sears, and France's Carrefour are rapidly preempting the smaller independents.

On the surface, such exchanges may not appear to have a direct impact on the "front-room" brands of these companies, but look again. Sourcing costs, distribution logistics, sales support, and other key infrastructure issues will be substantively influenced by these exchanges, and that will ultimately impact these companies' abilities to market aggressively. Ford, for one, expects to dramatically streamline its $83 billion purchasing budget, gaining enormous earnings value because of the leverage it will bring to every transaction. "This," commented Ford CEO Jacques Nasser, "is going to change how we think about the business."[12]

More important, the closer these companies dance on business-to-business exchanges, the closer they step to expanding their masterbrand community to include supply-side partners. Said another way, even the most arcane corners of the auction economy will be having a serious impact on the building of masterbrands.

The Value of Mutually Beneficial Interaction

We've heard a lot in recent years about two laws at work in the technology field, both of which are profoundly affecting our daily lives. The first is *Moore's Law*, named after Gordon Moore, the cofounder of Intel, who accurately predicted that the speed of computing will double every 18 months at a constant cost, thus providing greater computing speeds at greater values. Among other things, Moore's Law, which is expected to be accurate for at least another few years, is enabling the democratization of information, permitting more of society's technological have-nots to have the opportunity to drive themselves crazy with computer viruses and error messages.

What may be of even greater importance in the long run is *Metcalf's Law,* named for Robert Metcalf, the principal inventor of Ethernet and the cofounder of 3Com Corporation. Metcalf's Law states that the value of a network rises at the square of the number of the network's participants. The implications of Metcalf's Law for online brand communities and communications networks is staggering, since it may confirm that brand.comms will become the hub of all future online commerce.

A law that may someday be of additional importance (at least to masterbrand leaders), might be called the *Law of Mutually Beneficial Interaction.* Although it is tougher to quantify, this hypothesis could be stated as:

> The value of a brand in the future will be a direct function of the mutually beneficial interaction that is generated between that brand and its greater community.

As we noted in our first chapter, brand valuation firms have been busy in recent years creating assessments of the financial equity in brands. Those assessments take into account such attributes as the quality of the brand's leadership (often defined as the brand's ability to influence its market), its stability of strength over time, its globalness, the impact of its marketing communications, and the security of its legal titles. These evaluations may have to be updated, however, to measure the living relationships that brand.comms in particular create. In the future, we will need to come up with a quantitative measure for the potential of a brand to generate relationship-driven revenue with customers. Although we don't have a specific formula in mind, some key factors in this Law of Mutually Beneficial Interaction might involve masterbrands that:

- *Are positioned in a way that enables them to operate more efficiently in an interactive environment.* For example, repeated use of Wine.com's personalized services may ultimately leave customers with the impression that they have created their own wine shop.

- *Carry brand personality and values that are inviting in a highly repetitive relationship with customers.* To some, Yahoo! may have a more accessible personality as a brand of portal than, for example, the Go Network. America Online has a personality that clearly appeals more to typical Americans than did past generations of Prodigy.

- *Live up to customer assumptions about online brands.* For instance, online buyers assume that eToys, Outpost.com, and Buy.com provide discounted goods and services versus offline competitors. When or if that is not the case, these brands are vulnerable to loyalty erosion.

- *Are inherently relationship driven.* Information sites that visitors check daily (CBSMarketwatch), e-commerce sites that carry staples (WebVan), and community-based sites (iVillage) are most likely to grab and hold audiences because they are tapping into a fundamental trait of the Net. The best of these create larger communities that are self-reinforcing.

An interactive online community is at the convergence of the key forces at work in the U.S. economy today, and where much of the global commerce may be headed. Mastering the intricacies of selling in such an environment will be time consuming and costly, but it will also likely yield far more profitable customer relationships than its offline counterparts.

MANAGING YOUR MANDATE

The Internet and other emerging information technologies present the ultimate challenge and opportunity to interactivate your master-brand and, thus, to realize its full potential to create and sustain a living brand community. Before you consider extending your online operations, your company must determine what its current and potential capabilities are for creating a wider, Internet-assisted brand community.

Questions You Should Be Asking   We recommend that you begin that process by addressing these questions:

If you are not yet participating in a significant way in online marketing or enterprise management, how would you assess your company's commitment to working online? How would you rate your online communications, online brand awareness building, and e-commerce (if appropriate) or e-business implementation, relative to your major competitors? How many examples can you cite of half-hearted attempts at online initiatives within your company? Is there strong pressure from many quarters to make a commitment toward online commerce or business-to-business knowledge sharing or customer relationship management without necessarily understanding the ramifications of such a commitment?

On the other hand, although it might be ideal if your company was one of the leaders in the industry in online communications and marketing, it may be to your advantage if you are slow out of the gate. A lot of mistakes that pioneers made, both inside and outside of your market, have generated valuable lessons to be learned that will benefit your efforts. However, you need to make a realistic assessment of the time and resources that are necessary to catch up with competitors if you have fallen behind.

If your company has already made a significant commitment to online marketing, what steps are being taken to stay ahead of the curve relative to competitive moves and relative to market evolution? Strategists at companies like Amazon.com, Yahoo!, E*Trade, and America Online consider their visible business models to be part of their past (see Chapter 10). Each is stretching to new opportunities that may not fully emerge for three years (a lifetime in the online world). This is at least a two-dimensional issue in that competitors are continually changing on one plane; the playing field itself is not only tilted, it's like playing soccer on top of a geodesic dome, coping with new directions at every step. Successful online companies combine practicality with practical envisioning, to be sure that they will still be relevant when all the rules change (again).

Do you recruit, train, and reward employee-partners for their online skills? Do you reward employee-partners not only for their Internet savvy but, even more important, for their skills as online community builders? Just as the Internet was itself literally made (up) by its users, so, too, will your brand.comm evolve as it moves along, if you have the right sort of people along for the ride.

How inclined toward online activity are the members of your real or potential brand community? If most of your customers have just recently begun using e-mail, you still have an opportunity to be a pioneer in online servicing, at least in their eyes. Conversely, if your vendors or alliance partners are well ahead of your company in online experience, you might consider spending some time with them to learn what progress they have made and to determine how you might work together to initiate, or improve, your online programs.

What is the quality and frequency of dialogues between employees and customers, and between employees and other members of your community, using available online tools? The only situation worse than failing to capitalize on the enormous potential of interactive vehicles is failing to use them to their full potential. What potential brand building channel is not being pursued, or is being pursued only with limited enthusiasm? What effects are those shortcomings having on the business, both current and potential?

Actions You Should Be Taking   Given the previous issues, consider taking the following actions:

Appoint a marketing-led, multidiscipline team to accelerate the creation of a working online masterbrand community. It is important that this

(Continued)

team be led by marketing so that the needs of the masterbrand remain paramount, and to ensure that the customer's needs are equally adhered to. This group, if fully endorsed by management and cooperatively supported by others in your company, may also determine how quickly you can move operations online, and which areas of your company should commit first.

Establish a firm but realistic timetable for your company to have fully integrated your offline and online businesses. From backroom ordering and distribution to customer service and relationship building, your company must capitalize on its online potential, or fall behind at an exponential rate. Consider what strategic alliances might be useful in constructing a fully robust online community. Gauge the masterbrand ramifications to your business if you were *not* to fully engage in an online model compared with the risks involved in changing what may be a successful current operating model.

Launch a full best-practices study to determine the degree to which your company is keeping up with the online capabilities of similar companies. It should not take long to discover what other noncompeting firms are accomplishing online, and how those practices are creating stronger masterbrand companies. If it does not already exist, proclaim yourself the founder of a cross-industry best-practices group, and establish formal dialogue with noncompeting companies that are facing similar challenges.

If your company has successfully created a brand community, search various components of the community to determine which are most likely to respond to fully robust interactive initiatives. Are your distributors willing to invest in online marketing and selling facilities to make your community more efficient? Are your customers willing to go online to expand their information about your products and services, and to participate in brand community–sponsored activities? Sit down with your best thinkers and envision what the ideal brand community would look like if all interactive channels were fully employed; then, use that as your target model.

If your company is not yet at the hub of a healthy online brand community, reach a consensus about how augmenting online capabilities could bring your vision to reality. Frequent, relevant communication is at the core of any thriving brand community. Design creative online communications vehicles that could pull your community members together and help them become more familiar with your masterbrand and its constituencies. Interactivating your masterbrand means engaging your customer in a dialogue. Although this may start out as simply as a product that is supported by an 800 number or a Web site, it has the potential to become an online, virtual relationship.

Get to know and understand the informal information and support networks that customers and other members of your brand community value in their daily lives. Then give them (free of charge, if necessary) the tools to enhance these relationships. In the attention-based economy, these networks are themselves the valuable commodity, not just conduits to move products and services.

Allow, encourage, and assist customers themselves to create opportunities to interact among themselves and with the suppliers and intermediaries that make up your wider brand community. Don't just offer customized home pages or eavesdrop on prospects who browse your Web site, surreptitiously building up a series of one-to-one marketing databases. Similarly, don't just use traditional market research to target customers in (clay) pigeonholes. You help create value by bringing them together, not keeping them apart, and by sharing, not owning, the customer. If you let them come (together), they will build your brand.comm.

Develop measures (qualitative and quantitative) of the density and cohesion of your brand community. Tracking hits on a Web site, using average duration of visits to measure "stickiness," and calculating purchase conversion rates, are steps in the right direction, but better measures can and must be developed.

Be certain that your measures of success line up with and support those of other brand community members. A customer who finds a better solution through your brand community—even if it turns out to be an unmediated transaction with one of your suppliers or a competitor's product—may very well feel more loyal to your brand community as a result. If you are truly providing value to your brand community in other ways, you will prosper not despite, but because of, this. Are you willing, and able, to manage to this strategy?

*   *   *

As more and more customers interact online with your master-brand and with each other, you will reach the critical mass required to set off the value chain reaction that constitutes a dynamic brand community. As brand communities become the natural unit of competition and the locus of customer loyalty, brand building will emerge as the central discipline of business management. In our next chapter, we will focus on the accomplishments of a technology company that has created a successful masterbrand community to help battle a much larger rival.

CHAPTER 5

Masterbrand: Sun Microsystems

*If you want to know where the computer
industry is going, ask Sun.*
—Steven M. Milunovich,
Merrill Lynch & Co. analyst[1]

un Microsystems is an anomaly. It is one of the few major companies to build much of its own hardware (servers), based on its own specs, using its own chips, and using its own computing language. From that angle, Sun is the most closed-ended, self-contained technology company on the planet. Yet, in reality, Sun represents everything that is open ended, interoperable, and sharing, a strategy that is altruistic for the sake of profit.

Open on All Ends

Sun Microsystems (The *Sun* acronym stood for Stanford University Networks) was founded in 1982 by three Stanford grads and a technogenius from cross-Bay rival, University of California at Berkeley. Within six years, the fledgling workstation company had grown to become a publicly traded company with revenues exceeding $1 billion. As of this writing, Sun stands at about $12-plus billion in revenue, with 30,000-plus employees in 150 countries.

In its early years, Sun embarked on what appeared to be a highly risky, profit-preventive strategy, employing the most overused word in marketing: *free*. Cofounder Scott McNealy and his teams planned to build a business by giving things away. Sun was not to follow the proprietary model that had worked so well for "Wintel" and most other companies. Once its protocols were adopted, Sun would make its money by selling servers and workstations that would be best able to run the language they created, as well as by service and support.

Back in the mid-1980s, the company had trademarked the phrase "The Network Is The Computer." Years later, Sun veterans confessed that they really didn't know what the phrase meant back then, they just liked the sound of it. One effort to make it work in the real world was a skunkworks project that began in the late 1980s, led by engineer James Gosling. The team ultimately came up with a new computer language that could create applications that could be run on any computer. At first, it was slated to serve as the operating language for a digital cable environment that was being called interactive television (ITV). This ITV would eventually grow in scale, but not for another generation.

Nevertheless, Sun managers felt certain that they were onto something important. Here, they had a simple language that could be programmed many times faster than the cumbersome C++ type, and it was inherently versatile in keeping with Sun's heritage of open-ended solutions. They definitely had a killer network language, but no network to use it on.

With the emergence of the World Wide Web, though, the people of Sun realized that the Internet was how the computer would become the network. To their delight, the Net was also the perfect network to make full use of the Java language. Sun immediately shifted the direction of its development teams to take full advantage of this exploding phenomenon, long before most companies even noticed that there was one.

McNealy also instinctively understood before most of his peers that we were heading toward a service and experiential economy in which profits were to be harvested from supporting customers who obtained certain products and services at little or no charge. One of the key advantages of such a tack was that Sun could honestly claim that, even though it was competing with some hardware manufacturers in the server and workstation businesses, it was also supporting them in becoming more open and efficient themselves.

As the Internet has become the cornerstone of so many companies, Sun's open-ended approach has become the perfect glove for many working hands. The original ARPANET was launched by engineers and scientists to share information freely so that the community as a whole would prosper. Sun simply applied that principle to the for-profit technology sector. Sun's power grid looks like interoperability and trial-inducing giveaways, supported by an interdependent brand community. CEO Scott McNealy calls it the open-force movement. "Open interfaces," as he puts it, "is what we believe in."[2]

In Sun's view, 95-plus percent of the devices connecting to the Internet are PCs right now, but that figure will plummet to 50 percent or less by the middle of this decade. How will those devices operate interoperably within the Net? Sun is betting that its lead-horse technologies, Java and Jini, will be the answer to that question. In addition, they believe that the "thin client" (meaning a network-based, reduced-capacity terminal versus fully robust PCs) will be the environment of choice because of the absolute necessity for simplicity and free-flowing information channeling. Sun even reversed its previous resistance to the burgeoning Linux OS, and announced in late 1999 that it would be distributing a version of Linux with some of its servers. All of these moves toward open-endedness encourage Sun's developers, channel partners, and end users to employ its technologies. As their work grows, so grows the Sun masterbrand community.

It is not surprising, therefore, that this approach is also quite opposite to the long-standing Microsoft strategy, which was originally based on a closed-end, proprietary system. As Sun grew in prominence, and Scott McNealy became more vocal in his support of open-ended interoperability, the stage was set for a battle royale between the Redmond, Washington, "Goliath" and the "David" (comparatively speaking) from Silicon Valley. The first real stone was slung in 1997 when Sun sued Microsoft for allegedly distorting the Java language to incorporate it into the Windows operating system. (As of this writing, the case is still in the courts.)

McNealy misses no opportunity to preach against the Microsoft giant; no doubt, he felt personally vindicated by Microsoft's legally induced fall from grace. The hand-to-hand combat could come when Microsoft puts its full support behind its NT system and its so-called Next Generation Windows Services.

Taking Control of Its Own Masterbrand

The people of Sun have been called everything from arrogant to empowered. You can probably still find evidence of both within the organization, but as the company has matured, it has lost much of its cockiness and replaced it with a self-assured confidence that its course is the right one. No longer the dismissed fledgling flying on a hope and a prayer, Sun is now a major player among the heavyweights, and its people know that they are erecting a masterbrand that will be remembered as something special in the annals of technology.

While Scott McNealy is not a brand-driven visionary, one of the end results of his work is a masterbrand company. Sun's rebellious, iconoclastic approach has helped solidify its identity as a masterbrand within its own organization, in much the same way that it has at Nike. However, behind that attitude is the internal belief that employees have to make their own success. The still relatively casual structure at Sun permits its people to create informal work teams to accomplish a short-term goal. Yet, Sun also expects its people to figure out how and where they must make their moves, or they are left behind by the more aggressive and adventurous in the building.

Part of that process was formalized in 1996 when the Sun Teams were launched throughout the company, with a stated mission of: "Process Improvement through Teamwork for Customer Loyalty." By 1999, there were more than 300 Sun Teams at work, each with a specific target customer base, and each with a strategy for lowering dissatisfier results. Members of Sun Teams are encouraged to attend a training course on problem solving and process improvement (PSPI), given by Sun University, Sun's internal training organization. The PSPI course creates a consistent process improvement methodology and language across Sun, which is intended to lead to continuous product and service quality improvements and increased customer satisfaction and loyalty.

The importance of Sun Teams is reflected in the company's annual competitions, which are conducted within each division. The best-of-the-best Sun Teams are then invited to present the results of their efforts to Sun's Executive Management Group at a company-wide celebration in San Francisco. The Sun Teams' celebrations provide an opportunity for Sun employees to communicate their contributions to senior Sun management and also for management to show their appreciation. It's a proven device for sustaining a strong sense of the Sun masterbrand.[3]

However, despite the success with Sun Teams, trouble was spotted by late 1997. Sun's customers were unhappy that the company was so decentralized and complained about having to work with different units whose work did not seem well coordinated. The Sun internal structure was reorganized in two phases during 1998, and the result was a significant step forward in turning Sun into a true masterbrand organization.

Before the reorganization, Sun had been divided into *planets* that worked in silos in support of the Java, Jini, Solaris, and other technologies. Each planet had its own sales force, staffs, and even its own logo. COO Ed Zander really didn't want the trauma of reorganizing, but he saw that the various Sun fiefdoms had to go if Brand Sun was ever to emerge as the focal point of the company. Today, the company operates with parallel divisions, but all of its people work for what is called Brand Sun (although some diehards still admit to feeling a stronger loyalty to the Java brand).

Internally, the company's brand is monitored and adjusted as necessary by two brand teams: the Sun Marketing Council and the Brand Council. The brand construct in which they operate is the overall Sun value proposition, which includes the Brand Sun vision, where the brand is today, and the strategic "pillars" [which are the tools and connections that keep it working on a daily basis (i.e., the people, the know-how, and the connections in the industry).]

The two brand teams also make sure that the meaning of the Sun brand is kept fresh and alive. Scott McNealy, an articulate spokesman for the Brand Sun values, regularly transmits his views to Sun employees via WSUN, a Web-based, intranet messaging system with a radio-like format. The company's extensive intranet is also used for that purpose.

Growing the Community

The open-ended and interoperable mission at Sun is both a company value and a selling approach. It serves as the link between the company and its community of constituencies, most notably the militia of developers who are Java loyalists. It was the developers who first capitalized on the opportunity that Java offered, and they now meet annually at a conference called Java One, a convocation and massive cheerleading of the burgeoning Sun community. Attendance at the first Java One in 1997 was about 5,000 developers, and it mushroomed to 20,000 by 1999.

In November 1998, Sun took a huge leap in expanding its masterbrand community when it struck a three-year deal with America Online valued at $4.2 billion. Under the agreement, Sun resells Netscape's electronic commerce software and serves as the primary systems and service provider to AOL, which is committed to buying servers and services through 2002. In exchange, AOL receives more than $350 million in licensing, marketing, and advertising fees from Sun. AOL's big hope is that Sun's ubiquitous network dream is a lot more than a dream, and that it will help make the "AOL Everywhere" slogan much more than a slogan. Sun's assistance, on the other hand, could help AOL to be an even more dominant point of entry to the Net.

Sun has also formalized its community building efforts through a program called Community Sourcing, which the company defines as "(making) the source code for a product publicly available so that developers can download the code free of charge and make changes to it as long as they report back to Sun any bugs they encounter." For this service, Sun charges commercial users a license fee and is only putting a limit on those software portfolios that involve a third-party vendor.[4]

Brand Building the "Church" and "State"

Sun divides its external marketing into what execs call "Church and State." The *Church* side is the company's missionary efforts to create ubiquitous use of the Sun Java language, and the Jini (Java-based) technology. If their technologies are in use everywhere (and even if they are given away at no cost to users), then customers will eventually be inclined to use Sun hardware and services to run that software. It is the selling of such hardware and services that becomes the *State* side of their programs (i.e., providing platforms on which Sun technologies can run and the support to keep them running). Sun generates the vast majority of its revenues and earnings from hardware and services.

Some of Sun's customers also go on to create their own proprietary systems using Sun technology. Sun, for instance, created the Advanced Photo System and gave it away to Kodak, which then developed Advantix (its own version of the technology).

The Internet offered Sun the opportunity to practice its open-end product, service, and brand philosophies, all of which would make it a leader well into this century. That, among other reasons, is why Sun changed its masterbrand theme in 1998 to: "We're the dot in .com", a universal but flexible statement that reinforces Sun's preeminence in network computing.

That same year, the Sun worldwide marketing directors met and were asked to make an impromptu videotape, about "What Does It Mean to Be 'the Dot in .com'?" Some of the intriguing responses included the following:

- ". . . being the dot in .com means changing everything into a network-centric way of thinking . . ."
- "We see a world in the future where everything is connected to the network . . . not just computers, but telephones, televisions, refrigerators . . . and the network will deliver a full set of services."

- "Sun is different because we're not trying to run everybody else's businesses . . ."

For many years, Sun built and sustained momentum for its products in the corporate community almost entirely through public relations. In just one example, Sun developed Java Beans, a technology that permits developers to reuse used code, and Microsoft followed with a similar technology. As it was being introduced at a developers' conference, Sun mailed reporters an invitation to a simultaneous Sun conference, along with bags of coffee beans carrying a decidedly caffeinated question: "Why is Microsoft so jittery?"[5]

Today, Sun also runs a significant schedule of print and broadcast advertising to supplement its grassroots marketing efforts. (See the print ad in Figure 5.1.)

Life with Microsoft . . . or Not

On September 23, 1999, Microsoft announced that it would be introducing a network computing device. The Redmond, Washington, giant acknowledged that software would someday soon be sold as a service package rather than as a boxed product. This was another product of Microsoft's *fast-follower* strategy (i.e., letting companies like Sun pioneer in new areas, then following with its own versions, supported by plenty of marketing money). Microsoft admitted to a growing reliance on its XML protocol, designed to compete with Sun's Java. A Microsoft spokesman told the press, "The vision of the company is about software as a service. This fundamentally changes business models." Never has "fundamentally changes" sounded like such an understatement.[6]

Sun sees much the same vision of specialized messaging, ubiquitous e-mail, and Web access, and hopes to become the primary provider of hardware (for profit) and software and protocol (as shared technologies). All of this would add up to what Scott McNealy calls Webtone, the universally accessible communications link that will be the twenty-first-century equivalent of the telephone dial tone. Such a breakthrough, in Sun's collective

.COM

**By powering
the Net, we're bringing newborn
companies into the world every day. As you may
have noticed, their stock prices are kicking and screaming.**
While a baby might have a mother's eyes or a father's nose,
over half of the world's leading Internet businesses come into
this world with a Sun Microsystems brain. From online bookstores
to brokerage firms to news sources to portals. Consider it a matter
of good breeding. After all, 75% of Internet backbone traffic already
runs on our Net-based technologies, not to mention 15 of the top 20 ISPs.
That's because we help build e-commerce solutions that work. Whether
it's our high-performance systems, universal Java™ software platform,
or robust Solaris™ operating environment, Sun powers business in
the Network Economy. We even have all the services that help
keep your systems up and running. In the end, the most
compelling reason can easily be found any day on
your nearest stock page. Perhaps we should be
passing out cigars. THE NETWORK IS
THE COMPUTER™

We're the dot in .com.™

JAVA ©1999 Sun Microsystems, Inc. All rights reserved. Sun, Sun Microsystems, the Sun Logo, Java, the Java Coffee Cup Logo, Solaris, The Network Is The Computer and We're The Dot In .Com are trademarks or registered trademarks of Sun Microsystems, Inc. in the U.S. and other countries. www.sun.com

Figure 5.1 *The Sun ".com" campaign celebrates the masterbrand's role in the Internet revolution.*

mind, will enable not only more communication, but the restructuring of entire industries, if not all of global commerce.

A few years ago, that stance would have sounded like puffery, but it's becoming more credible by the day, given the extraordinary progress and the investments in Net-driven businesses—not to mention the extraordinary growth of the Sun Microsystems masterbrand.

The Inside Job
Coach the Customer's Team

Coach the Customer's Team

There are days when I'm convinced we're not in the coffee business . . . The business we're in is the business of building relationships with our people.
—Howard Schultz, Chairman & CEO,
Starbucks Coffee[1]

When the future founder of Starbucks was seven years old, his father earned a meager living by retrieving soiled cloth diapers door-to-door, a job that was apparently as miserable as it sounds. One day that he will always remember, Howard Schultz walked to his home in the Brooklyn projects to find his dad lying on the living room sofa, with his broken leg in a cast. With no workman's compensation or any other form of insurance, the family was left to claw its way out of a financial nightmare.

That unforgettable memory led young Schultz to decide that, if he ever ran a company, he would never leave his employees in a similar position. True to his word, when the fledgling Starbucks was still losing money in 1989, Howard Schultz created a generous stock option and health care plan for every employee. Schultz understood that the best companies are committed to supporting their people in every way possible. What he might not have known at the time was that his people would eventually return the favor, in the form of a staunch commitment to the Starbucks company and its formidable masterbrand.

When Money Is Not Enough: Winning the War for Talent

"Show me the money!" was shrieked 14 times in the 1996 hit film, *Jerry McGuire*. By the time the movie had run its course, the world had found a new way to celebrate the almighty buck. Money and ambition will always motivate, of course, but there is only so much that compensation can combat, particularly when it can be matched so easily by other firms.

In 1997, almost one-half of the U.S. CEOs of the largest global companies said that shaping corporate culture and motivating employees took up as much of their time as financial planning.[2] In a 1999 survey by AON Consulting, 52 percent of the worker respondents said they would leave their jobs for a 20 percent pay increase.[3] As if that weren't enough, mergers, acquisitions, career switching, and frenzied job-hopping (often prompted by the vision of ".com" stock options), are all contributing to the free-agency environment in business.

In the face of such siren calls, many corporate employees are simply not as willing to rally to the mission of their corporation, even if that mission has been clearly articulated, which is often not the case. Employees are no longer indifferent about organizational deficiencies, nor are they as willing to tolerate heavy-handed managing and lightweight managers. Thus, the joke that has made the rounds in recent years: Loyalty is when you don't look for a new job on company time.[4]

In 1998, when a division of Sun Microsystems was pressed to reduce expenses because of the Asian financial crisis, the heads of product groups were tempted to convince the remaining employees to take on more work. However, Sun had recently begun a series of candid employee surveys that revealed that some workers were not happy about the workloads as they were. In response, Sun managers shifted deadlines and still made the numbers they had to make. Sun's monthly e-mail polls have identified numerous "performance inhibitors," which have created problems in the past, and which are being headed off at the pass today.

In the winter of 2000, when one of your authors was first asked to provide brand counsel for Internet start-up Abilizer (formerly Perksatwork), he was introduced to a company whose mission was to "transform the global workplace." A tall order, to say the least. The company's plan was a simple one: To help CEOs win the war for talent. In the booming U.S. economy at the time, many companies did not have all the people they needed, and they were finding it extremely difficult to keep the good ones they had. And, even in weaker economic times, CEOs are always struggling to retain superior people.

Abilizer offers corporate employees a browser-driven cornucopia of communication, commerce, content and community channels. These "employee portals" are hosted off-site but fully integrated into corporate intranets. They enable employees to log on at home or work, and to receive an enormous range of company-sponsored services, including educational planning, health/fitness training, employee classifieds, sophisticated family and physical/emotional services, and many others.

But perhaps the most important service that Abilizer is contributing is a sense of community, built around the meaning of the corporation itself. As such tools enable corporate employees to buy, sell, learn, and just communicate within trusted company environments, they are inoculating themselves with important motivations to stay right where they are.

What does all that have to do with masterbrand building? A lot, because it helps to redefine the company in positive terms and gives its brand builders another proof point as they communicate about their masterbrand. For example, Sun found that there was a strong correlation between whether an employee would recommend Sun as a place to work and whether customers would recommend it as a place to do business.

A 1997–1998 study of Fortune 1000 firms revealed that companies that implemented total quality management (TQM) programs and those that implemented downsizing experienced no significant difference in ROIs compared with those that did not undergo such initiatives. However, those companies that emphasized employee involvement in their managing efforts experienced significant ROI gains versus control companies.

There is even more going on here than first meets the eye. In masterbrand examples cited throughout, the companies are making concerted efforts to give their employees a clearer understanding of what their companies stand for as masterbrands in their marketplaces, not just as companies. Those who believe they are valued associates (as opposed to human tools) are more likely to build stronger brand identities at every opportunity they have to meet with prospective customers and constituencies.

It is no surprise, then, that more companies are referring to their employees as *partners* in their enterprise (e.g., Starbucks), *associates* (in the case of Wal-Mart, Rich Products, and Office Depot), *members* (at Haworth Furniture), *coworkers* (at IKEA), and *consultants* (at Kinko's). (As a reminder of the importance of this strategy, where appropriate we will be referring to employees as *employee-partners* throughout the remainder of this book.)

Passion Is Good, Commitment Is Better

In a business world rife with those just "making a living," passion is a rare and wonderful response from employees. In discussing his own company which is filled with passionate people, Charles Schwab & Co. co-CEO David Pottruck has pointed out that passion-driven growth requires contributions from all employees who seek to help costumers.

Passion is certainly helpful if management hopes to inspire coworkers to reach down and give it their best. The only downside is that passion can sometimes burn hot like a bright flame, then flicker out and die, consumed by its own energy, as it did periodically among employees at Kodak, Xerox, Chrysler, and British Airways. Passion may be a useful fire-in-the-belly kind of enthusiasm, but commitment is more like a longer-term contract with greater solidity about what is expected and what will be delivered.

Commitment is almost palpable in those companies with well-defined masterbrands, peopled with zealots who believe that the greatest brand of all is the company itself. For some, the building of commitment must begin slowly by spreading a sustained *sense of brand* throughout the organization. A sense of brand is a shared understanding and active support of a set of promised benefits that a masterbrand consistently delivers to its own people, its customers, and its supporters. A sense of brand is what's spreading right now through companies like Enron, the Houston-based energy company that we discuss in more detail later, and Kinko's, which has been reengineered from a loose confederation of independent outlets into an orchestrated retail masterbrand, led by the tough-minded, former Wal-Mart executive, Joseph Hardin, Jr.[5]

Masterbrand companies drive brand commitment in any number of ways, all of them aimed at establishing strong customer relationships. For example:

Brand commitment can emanate from a founder who builds it into the DNA of a new company. Richard Branson is the famed maverick entrepreneur who has achieved success partly because his people catch his contagious commitment for his businesses. They understand that the Virgin masterbrand stands for unexpectedly delightful service and product quality. That's doubly crucial in the case of the Virgin masterbrand, because Branson's business strategy is to target those industries that have provided substandard customer service. In the case of Virgin Airlines, for instance, that translates into picking up upper-class (business class) passengers at their homes or offices in a limo.

Some of Branson's other marketing techniques (outrageous publicity stunts, gleefully playing the brash David versus his rivals' slow-moving Goliath) have come to be expected by his constituencies and competitors. They are, however, much more than publicity stunts; they enact the Virgin masterbrand personality, and infuse insiders and outsiders alike with a genuine excitement about what Branson brings to any market. Branson's seeming naivete about running headlong into businesses he supposedly doesn't understand only creates that much more impact for his masterbrand when he succeeds.[6]

You can find the same kind of commitment in a completely different brand personality, in the tiny town of Kennebunk, Maine, home of Tom's of Maine. Like their New England neighbors at Ben & Jerry's, this is a company dedicated to making money within the framework of positive social values. The company's burgeoning line of all-natural personal hygiene products has prospered as happily niched players in categories of mass market brands.

Even as his business grew, though, Tom Chappell questioned his commercial success and spent three years in Harvard Divinity School to sort out some issues. Now, Chappell considers his work to be a type of ministry, and is committed to running his business as a blending of mind, spirit, and commerce. His credo: "You don't have to sell your soul to make your numbers." In addition, he puts his money where his spirit is, asking his employees to give two hours per week of their paid time to community causes. Although this may not have a direct effect on customers, it indirectly encourages employees to bring the same type of dedication to their development and packaging of innovative all-natural household products. Tom Chappell has built a very unusual kind of commitment into his masterbrand, but it is every bit as real and effective as the more common profit-driven variety.[7]

Still another example is Ingvar Kamprad, the Swedish father of the world's largest furniture store chain, IKEA. Kamprad, who founded IKEA in 1943 in Stockholm, made it clear in a speech to Swedish bankers in 1976 how he wanted his brand to grow. The speech, which is called the "Furniture Dealer's Testament," and which now serves as the company bible, includes pronouncements such as "Waste of resources is a mortal sin," and "Only while sleeping one makes no mistakes."

At IKEA, no one has titles (everyone is a coworker), no one wears suits, and the atmosphere in the company is said to be casual, almost to the point of loving. It was this sense of openness and freedom that helped transform the Scandinavian tradition of formality within the home to a more relaxed atmosphere. As Kamprad biographer Thomas Sjoeberg puts it, "Working for IKEA is working for a cause. They have an official mission: to make life better for the masses." The IKEA masterbrand lives as fervently in the hearts of coworkers as it does among its 150 million customers who visit 142 stores throughout 29 countries of the world.[8]

There is an understandable temptation to believe that

founders bring a unique commitment to their companies that leaves when they do. So, how does that explain the brand commitment seen throughout General Electric, Johnson & Johnson, or Spencer & Marks? Brand commitment can be rekindled as deftly as it is initially embedded.

Brand commitment can surge from the people of the company and its greater community, once they are rallied to renew that commitment. The Apple saga is about a company that had to look to its own founder and brand heritage to right itself. This is a masterbrand that seemed to be lashed to the back of a runaway missile, from its miraculous conception in the famous Wozniak garage, to its peak as the leading alternative to DOS, to its nadir in 1997 when its stock went begging at $15 a share, to its Lazarus-like recuperation just two years later when earnings erupted and its stock price rose to over $100.

Through it all, the key to reviving the company was tucked next to the essence of the brand: Apple was and is in the business of innovatively empowering its users, many of whom consider themselves more creative than PC users. Apple is not simply providing a technology-driven tool. From the onset, devotees believed in the Apple masterbrand, not just in its unique operating system. If and when that slavish devotion could be tapped, therein would lie the lever with which a savior could revive the unrevivable.

In September of 1997, Steven Jobs returned with a vivid memory of what had built Apple years before, and a clear vision of what was needed to restore its luster. Jobs refocused the company around its roots and updated its capabilities to reflect what Apple must become to justify its existence in a Wintel-dominated world. Jobs didn't do it alone, though. Even before his return, Jon Rubinstein, Apple's hardware guru, began designing the Apple brand spirit into such breakthroughs as the iMac and G3 desktop lines. Jobs and his people then updated an old call to the devoted ("The computer for the rest of us") into a simple imperative for the faithful ("Think Different"). As much as any single insight, Jobs' determination to support the iMac with virtually all of Apple's marketing funds because it symbolized the rising Phoenix was his riskiest and wisest decision of all.

At this writing, Apple stock is trading in the $100 territory, an increase of more than 600 percent during 1998 to 2000, compared with the Dow Jones index appreciation of 47 percent. The company's market valuation has skyrocketed to over $16 billion.

Could Jobs have pulled it off without more product speed and style? Not likely. But, product innovation alone would not necessarily have done the trick, either. What Jobs added was the much-needed leadership of renewed commitment to the rich Apple masterbrand—among employees, developers, resellers, and customers. It's always possible to build a faster machine, but it takes brand commitment to reincarnate faded glory.

At times, market events and competitive pressures dictate the need for greater brand commitment. Enron Corporation was created in 1985 from the merger of two gas-pipeline companies. Cofounder and current CEO, former U.S. Undersecretary for Energy Ken Lay, pushed the new company into gas marketing and into deregulating business-to-business electricity markets. Today, Enron is a $40 billion company (revenue) that hopes to be the leading provider of energy in all markets that have been deregulated or privatized. More to our point here, Enron is also transforming itself into a brand-based organization, even as the twists and turns in energy business are calling for more and more strategic flexibility.

The chance to capture greater shares of energy markets has led Enron to drive brand messaging deep into its organization. Messages about creativity and innovation are sent to employees through their intranet, via T-shirts, in print and television advertising, at employee meetings, in self-training programs, and a wide array of other channels. Innovation is more than an aspiration at Enron, as evidenced by its four consecutive awards as *Fortune* magazine's "Most Innovative U.S. Company" during the mid-1990s.

The company may very well win the award again, because it has recently entered the commodity bandwidth business, a burgeoning sector that sells telecommunications access to business customers. The company's web site handled $27 billion in transactions in its first four months. These moves, and others like them, all reinforce the powerful masterbrand message of best-of-breed innovation.

Enron's leaders were among the first in their industry to internally build an enterprise-wide commitment to an energy resources masterbrand, a commitment that is being translated into end-to-end solutions for their customers. Ironically, when Enron changed its logo several years ago, the hard-liners in its pipeline companies didn't want any part of it, because it meant that they had to turn in their old hard hats and baseball caps. Today, those same workers are the first to order anything that carries the Enron name and symbol. Now, there's something you don't see every day—brand commitment from pipe fitters.[9]

My Masterbrand, My Life

"Living the brand" is an attitude and way of working that was first explored in the United Kingdom. Early proponents pointed out that the strongest brands reflect brand values that are equally recognized, respected, and acted upon by all of those who are involved in the brand relationship. In the marketing of the United Kingdom Wilkinson Sword brand, for example, the company held a series of interactive workshops to discuss how the marketing proposition could be productively distributed throughout the entire organization. That process led to new opportunities for the company's people to help differentiate the firm by how it treats its customers, relative to what Wilkinson stood for in the marketplace—in Wilkinson's case, "A Smartly Designed Company."[10]

The discipline of living the brand has also been demonstrated in some so-called experience brands that extend over banks, hotels, airlines, and retailing service companies. Those types of businesses offer the most frequent opportunities for employees to express the brand in their servicing of customers. In such industries, it is common to experience "moments of truth," in which employees are living representatives of the brand as they interface with customers . . . for better or worse.[11]

One company whose people live what the brand is and wants to be is Amazon.com. By all accounts, the people of Amazon.com are heading in multiple directions at once, but all down the same strategic corridor. People move from job to job so frequently that they rarely have business cards that are up to date. Offices are, at best, temporary quarters until the next assignment is thrust upon them. On one day, a staff member may be creating content for the compact disc site; on another, she may be wrangling items on the auction site. Every Holiday season, most of the staff spends half of their time wrapping packages or picking items out of the distribution warehouses for shipment to a customer. They live a seemingly scattered work life, but it is what Amazon.com must be as a brand: a fast-moving, anything-the-customer-wants kind of world, that mirrors what the masterbrand itself stands for on the Internet.[12]

Experienced marketers, however, are certainly not the only candidates for living the brand. Living the brand actually applies to *all brand contacts*, whether over a retail counter or in developing relationships with supply chain partners. In the United States, the people of Lexus live the brand they have helped build, in every facet of their business. Tom Cordner, creative director at Team One Advertising and the author of Lexus' "Relentless Pursuit of Perfection" theme, once explained it this way: "I think the key to Lexus from the start . . . is that they don't want to be admired for just building great cars, they want to be admired for everything they do."

The same is true of three legendary U.S.-based companies whose people long ago embedded the tenets of their brands deep into their cultures, and vice versa. From their companies' inceptions, the people of Nike, Saturn, and Nordstrom have understood the need to personify their masterbrands in their personal and professional lives. The Nike obsession with serving the performance and emotional needs of athletes is still very much alive. On a bad day, Nordstrom's service is still better than any of its rivals. Saturn workers still believe that they are part of something different and better than what is found in other auto companies. In many cases, the people of these organizations were trained to foster their beliefs, but they would have acquired them without such training. Their well-documented commitment to their companies—and to their masterbrands—is in the air they breathe.

Over in the fast-food business, "Papa" John Schnatter, founder and CEO of the fast-rising Papa John's Pizza chain, practically bleeds brand commitment. Schnatter insists that all of his people swear allegiance to the Papa John's masterbrand by memorizing the company's six Core Values (which, in our view, more closely resemble brand operating guidelines). As Papa John himself puts it: "The Core Values are worthless if you're not going to live them." (See Figure 6.1 for Papa John's Core Values statement.)

Besides the six Core Values, there is also the Ten-Point Perfect Pizza Scale. All pizzas must measure up to this higher plane of pizza, where pieces of the same toppings do not touch, where there are no peaks or valleys along the pizza's border. Nor shall there be, according to the Ten-Point Scale, soup-bowl edges or splotchy coloring on the crust. Schnatter's attention to detail has helped earn Papa John's the title of best U.S. pizza chain in surveys conducted by *Restaurants and Institutions* magazine.

Papa John's is the only one of the four largest pizza chains whose slice of the pie has grown at double-digit rates over the past five years. As of now, the company is generating about $50 million in annual earnings from $800 million in revenue. Papa John's may or may not be the best pizza, but it is likely the best pizza *brand*, at least in terms of purity of the strategic strength and consistency of its internally driven masterbrand.[13]

Brandheart: Turning Company Values into Brand Commitment

Many companies have not been as successful at communicating, and gaining commitment to, a strong set of values—even when those values are incorporated into more action-oriented missions. Yet, when a company is able to link its values with efforts to build its masterbrand, the synergy can yield real competitive advantage. We call it *brandheart*, and it can often serve as a driving force and as an organizational bond, which creates a company-wide masterbrand from what was once just a company.

Focus

We must keep The Main Thing, The Main Thing. We will consistently deliver a traditional Papa John's superior-quality pizza.

Accountability

We do what we say we are going to do when we say we are going to do it. We earn the right to hold others to a higher level of accountability by being accountable to ourselves, our customers, and our business partners.

Superiority

Our customer satisfaction must be consistent, quantifiable, and demonstrable. At Papa John's, we expect excellence—the "best in its class" in everything we do.

PAPA

People Are Priority No. 1 Always (bold theirs). Our Team Members treat one another with dignity and respect.

Attitude

If you think you can or you think you can't—you're right! The difference between winners and losers is a Positive Mental Attitude. Our attitude is a reflection of what we value: successful Team Members must be upbeat, proactive, and passionate about everything they do.

Constant Improvement

We never stop trying to surpass our previous best. We constantly "Raise the Bar." No matter how good we are, we will always get better.

Source: Company report..

Figure 6.1 *Papa John's Core Values.*

During the past several years, the Service Management Interest Group at Harvard Business School has explored the concept of the *service-profit chain,* in an effort to link customer loyalty to revenue and earnings growth. The Group's work indicates that customer satisfaction, which drives loyalty, is the result of superior internal service values (as exemplified by employees). This, in turn, drives superior external service values (as held by customers). In other words, when all the players are operating from the same page, a sense of community exists between the external and internal facets of the company, and growth and profitability are maximized.

Values may be based on a company's historical belief system, such as is the case with Johnson & Johnson's famed Credo. Johnson & Johnson devotes a full day in executive training sessions to discussing the Credo. Every other year, all employees complete a survey about how they and their unit are living up to the Credo. The Credo is a company standard and a set of values, but it is also a strategic roadmap for a great masterbrand in the global marketplace.

One of the most interesting aspects of J&J's masterbrand is the source of its strength. The red Johnson & Johnson script logo is used primarily on baby products and the Band-Aid line, what CEO Ralph Larsen calls, "products that evoke caring and gentleness." The company's caring image is still largely attributed to its reputation as a trusted purveyor of baby products, even though those products now represent less than 10 percent of the corporation's $24 billion annual sales. The people of Johnson & Johnson treat the masterbrand with kid gloves, and with good reason: In a 1999 survey of 10,000 Americans, Johnson & Johnson was declared the most trusted company in the land. In reality, the survey respondents were voting as much for the trust engendered by the J&J masterbrand as for the company itself.[14]

Companies with brandheart have an opportunity to celebrate, yet rechannel feelings of esprit de corps into a strong brand commitment. This commitment intrinsically prompts employees and other stakeholders to participate in the building of the masterbrand business, in addition to emotionally supporting the organization as a company. This support is most obvious in larger companies, but is sometimes even more fervent in midsize companies such as Rich Products Corp. of Buffalo, New York (see the sidebar).

The Masterbrand as a Guide in Tough Times

Sometimes, it's easier to see the merits of living a brand by looking at a company when it is *not* performing at its best. As of this writ-

RICH PRODUCTS: MY FAMILY, MY BRAND

Robert E. Rich, Sr. was a war foods administrator in 1945 when he perfected a soy-based whipped-topping product. Rich secured an appointment with a major Long Island distributor, but when he arrived for the presentation, the product had frozen solid beneath a block of dry ice. Rich borrowed a jackknife and gamely whipped it into a beautiful topping. The frozen-topping industry was born that day in a Long Island office building, or as they like to call it at Rich's, "the miracle cream from the soya bean."

Rich Products Corporation is now a multinational business, and the largest family-owned frozen foods manufacturer in the nation. However, Rich's is not just family owned, it is a masterbrand company based on living and selling the benefits of family. The company's management has successfully balanced its family values focus with an efficient approach to the business they know better than anyone. When new Rich's associates join up, they are immersed in the Rich family values, are immediately considered to be part of the Rich family, and are expected to treat customers as part of the family as well. The company's guiding corporate value: "Caring for customers like only a family can."

The people of Rich's are also considered part of the company's larger marketing process. It is, in the words of the company's senior communications officer, Maureen Hurley, a "classic case of building the brand from the inside out." When customers (or vendors) come into Buffalo, more likely than not, they are driven to and from the airport by Rich's people. One senior executive kept a permanent guest bedroom in his house specifically for visiting customers and vendors who welcomed a hot, home-cooked meal and a family home to rest their wearied heads. Management considers it the marketing department's job to sell products, but everyone's job to be part of the marketing efforts, and to contribute in some way to the brand-building process.

Why would customers care if the Rich's brand is about family? Because they want somebody who knows their business, someone to help them solve problems, and someone to be around for more than a year or two. The entire company operates with the sound, but often forgotten, axiom that people want to do business with people they like and trust. All of this may seem faintly quaint or even old fashioned, but the conviction with which it is taught and learned not only provides Rich Products a point of differentiation versus larger corporate competition, it is a living commitment to a specific brand positioning. And by the way, quaint sells: Rich Products is now a $1.4 billion (revenue) business.*

* Based on interviews with Maureen O. Hurley, Senior Vice President, and Peter Ciotta, Director of Communications Group, Rich Products, June and August 1999.

ing, the stock valuation of The Walt Disney Company has been experiencing a bumpy ride amid an equities megaboom, tripped up by wobbly earnings and mixed business developments. The Disney organization and its offspring brands have undergone extraordinary change during the last decade, and not always with positive results. What was once a film production and theme park company has now been expanded to include a staggering array of ventures, including professional athletics (the Anaheim Mighty Ducks), broadcast news and entertainment (the ABC, ESPN, A&E, and USA networks), luxury travel (the Disney Cruise Line and Castaway Cay), and Internet portals (the Go Network).

Nevertheless, Disney CEO Michael Eisner has a weapon lashed to his belt that will sustain the core of the Disney organization until it can more profitably manage its holdings. Eisner and his people have maintained the founder's zeal for the Disney masterbrand, continuing to drive it through the organization, and out into strategically parallel fields. As one small example, several years ago The Disney Channel hired advertising agency account planners to help determine what the Disney brand meant in the context of broadcasting. Disney, they found, offers families (many of which are in crisis or are dysfunctional altogether) the kind of security and love that they crave. The Disney Channel feeds an emotional need, and in so doing, reinforces it.

Eisner acknowledged the crucial importance of the Disney brand in the company's 1997 annual report:

> . . . our single greatest asset is the same as it was at the very beginning—the Disney name. In a world of limitless choice, the value of a brand that consumers trust is inestimable . . . [And] while Disney may continue to be our *number one* brand, it is no longer our *only* brand (italics his) . . . Just as our company is enhanced overall by [our newly added] brands, these brands benefit from being part of our company.[15]

The Disney masterbrand is the key to the Disney kingdom. Whatever words might be used to describe the Disney brand soul—*fun, family, entertaining, magic*—it is being nurtured in such a way that the stewards of the Disney brand have a strong sense of its content

DISNEY NEVER STOPS POLISHING ITS MASTERBRAND

The essence of the Disney masterbrand is best evidenced at the company's theme parks. Here are some of the guidelines that the Disney hosts follow as they bring their masterbrand to life:

- *"Bump the lamp."* The expression comes from the 1988 Disney film, *Who Framed Roger Rabbit?*, in which star Bob Hoskins bumps a lamp while struggling with the animated title character. Disney animators insisted that the light/shadow from the swinging lamp should be part of the rest of the scene. Such attention to detail added many hours and much stress to the production process, but it maintained the high Disney standards for animation that uphold the meaning of the Disney brand to its own people.

- *Polish the equipment.* Disney camera operators, lighting specialists, and assorted other crew members continuously wax or polish their equipment, far beyond what is necessary to keep the equipment operating smoothly. Disney people are proud of what they do, and it shows even in extra work that will never make a difference to anyone but them.

- *Members serve guests.* Workers at the Disney parks are *cast members*, not employees, because their brand is in the entertainment business. Each cast member is trained to pay attention to *guests* (not customers) as individuals with individual interests. An example: Ask a Disney cast member when one of the famous parades will take place, and they'll tell you when the parade will pass where you are standing, not just when it starts its march down Main Street.

- *Good ideas can come from anyone.* A Disneyland parking lot tram operator suggested that cars be parked in particular spaces in the lots by time of arrival, so when guests inevitably ask for help because they've lost their car, they can easily locate it according to when they arrived at the Park. That attention to detail has saved thousands of hours of guest and host downtime.

- *Know your customers better than they know themselves.* Disney runs continuous quantitative and qualitative research on what its people refer to as the *science of guestology*. For instance, to accurately gauge their value proposition, Disney waits to call past guests until a month after they have visited the Park. By that time, they will have received their credit card bills and can give a more accurate assessment of the value they got for the money they spent.

- *Manage for the "total experience."* The Disney organization is renowned for thinking through the experience that guests have in their Parks, including turning potential problems into solutions. For example, if a family wants to experience a ride that one member of the clan is too young to go on, a cast member will volunteer to watch the young one, and call over a Disney costumed character to entertain the child while the rest of the family enjoys the ride.*

It would be easy to dismiss the Disney culture as unique and unduplicable, but it is no more than a well-defined, carefully managed masterbrand, supported by individuals who are committed to living that brand.

* Based on a report of corporate training taught at The Disney Institute, as published in "What you can learn from the Disney organization," PHC *Profit Report*, 1 April 1999, p. 1.

and inestimable worth. The masterbrand will help buoy the company, until the company returns to its winning ways. (See sidebar.)

Driving the Brand through the Organization

Obtaining commitment to a central brand promise is one thing, driving that commitment across the company is quite another. Each of the key functional processes that makes up a company needs to be involved in the proliferation of the brand commitment. The following illustrates how that commitment plays out in example companies.

SELLING

Kennametal is a $600 million tool-cutting manufacturer that is supplying companies like GM's Saturn. Kennametal employees participate in their customers' planning sessions. They know and identify with their customers' goals and objectives. So much so that, if a competitor's tool can do the job better, Kennametal will buy it and deliver it to the customer. Former salesman and current

Director of Customer Satisfaction, James Heaton, warns that by focusing on price, "the traditional sales force accidentally cuts off communication to the rest of the company." Kennametal's strategy is literally to work together with its customers—even if that means collaborating with the "enemy." Eventually, as a company like Kennametal consistently demonstrates its customer service commitment, the Kennametal masterbrand, both among employees and customers, sets expectations that encourage repetition and promote customer loyalty.

RECRUITING AND HIRING

CEO Jeff Bezos has made it clear that recruiting is one key way to ensure that commitment to his Amazon.com brand will never wane. Recruiting guidelines call for seeking individuals who may be more talented than those who are hiring them. Company interviewers know that they are to push the bar higher at Amazon.com by recruiting stars or stars in the making. Recruits usually have broad backgrounds, are interesting to talk to and be with, and are the kind of people you want to work with long into the night . . . because you will. Recruiting and hiring are, thus, key tools in maintaining the Amazon.com company and the standards of its masterbrand.

TECHNICAL SUPPORT MEETS SALES AND MARKETING

The historians at 3M like to tell the story of how *brand promise* took hold throughout their company. The concept of a brand promise was introduced into 3M in 1994. One of the first attempts to develop a brand promise was around the very successful Post-it® brand for repositionable notes. A cross-functional team of people from sales, marketing, manufacturing, laboratory, customer service, and technical service developed its view of the promise. In that case, the promise was centered around the technical specifications of the product, and the note that would stick "just right" (a nontechnical term that also fit "just right").

A young exec suggested testing the ideas in the marketplace, where they learned that the Post-it® brand promised fast, friendly, repositionable communication and organization tools that got the job done. With that powerful customer understanding, the Post-it® brand promise was communicated throughout the organization globally, and it remains an enterprise-wide charge for all those who work on the brand, no matter what their job may be. In other words, cross-functional teams with technical personnel created and proliferated a brand-marketing template.

JOB HOPPING
Southwest Airlines employees regularly switch jobs to get a more complete appreciation of the company's overall operations. Pilots work as skycaps, reservation agents as administrators. Their famous CEO, Herb Kelleher, enjoys throwing bags in the baggage area or serving peanuts to passengers. Kelleher not only gets a feel for what's happening on the front lines, he is demonstrating what you can learn if you step outside of your job box. Importantly, the people of Southwest also see how their brand is portrayed in various venues, something that makes them that much more committed to the Southwest way of doing things. That's brand commitment they're building, in addition to learning more about their company.

TRAINING
Motorola, Lexus, Johnson & Johnson, General Electric, and other masterbrand companies conduct regular training that instructs and instills company values, along with what their respective brands stand for in the marketplace. This is one of the most effective forms of driving brand commitment through an organization, because it sends clear signals that management and the entire company is determined that all of its people embrace what the company-wide brand means, and where it can migrate in the future.

COMMUNICATING
In countless research studies, *communicating* is listed as the primary challenge in keeping companies working together as a single, unified group. Increasingly, companies are finding innovative ways to keep their people connected to one another, as well as to the happenings of the organization. Within the same week in February 2000, both Ford Motor Company and Delta Airlines announced that they were giving their collective 372,000 employees new PCs and low-cost, unlimited Internet access. This could

fall under the "If You Can't Beat Them . . ." category of organizational management, but it is more likely that it is just two smart management teams that know the value of electronically tying their people together at home, as well as on the job.

Let's take a closer look at efforts to *train* a company's people in masterbrand building, largely by *coaching* them instead.

Coaching Your People How to Build the Masterbrand

Ford Motor Company had great success in the 1980s and early 1990s with the "Quality is Job 1" internal and external corporate campaign. However, Ford's performance fell behind those of its global competitors, and management embarked on an internal reeducation campaign. The program would help restore employee understanding of what the Ford brand meant, in addition to how the company's operations could be improved. Ford found that the links between brand and company performance can be relatively straightforward to teach, whether it is by an outside consultant or an internal trainer. The challenge is in making the commitment to embark on such a program, and showing clearly how relevant and vital the masterbrand is to the everyday work of the employee and the other constituents.

For those organizations that do not have a history in building brand communities, it may be comforting to know that it is a discipline that can be taught and sustained over time. Brand training can be conducted on several levels.

Formal Brand Training

Initially, it is often helpful to bring employee-partners into a group setting to provide them with the basics of brand building, and to demonstrate how brand building is part of their jobs, even if their roles appear to be far removed from marketing. Although some companies avoid classroom settings for their training, most find that it encourages learning from exchanges between the employee-partners.

Fortunately, brand marketing is one of those rare disciplines that can be inherently fun to learn, no matter how little marketing education the employee-partners have had in the past. For example, when teaching at the Bell Atlantic Marketing Leadership Institute, we found that individuals with engineering, finance, and business analysis backgrounds were genuinely excited about the brand-building process. Our experience was repeated at ongoing brand training at Bayer Corporation, 3Com Corporation, and even in a large law firm that was searching for new ways to brand its expertise to potential clients. Although laypersons are not formally trained in marketing, we are all professional consumers, and most of us have a sincere interest in learning more about how and why brands are marketed as they are.

By necessity, the curriculum for such training varies by company, but a typical brand-coaching process includes instructions about the fundamentals of brand building, using examples from other industries with which the participants are familiar, then gradually homing in on what the particular masterbrand is all about. This can be supplemented with observations about how the company brand relates to individual product or service brands within the company, if applicable. The training would then delve into the specific techniques that the company has employed to build its overall branded business over time, and how the individual employee-partner can contribute to that process.

On-the-Job Brand Mentoring

Whatever can be accomplished in a classroom setting, it is only the beginning of a process that blossoms within the workplace itself. If program participants, their peers, and their supervisors have been through similar training or have acquired a strong sense of brand in another way, the individual who is new to the process should be given ample opportunity to be mentored in the tenets of the masterbrand.

There is probably no more successful on-the-job training program than that of Procter & Gamble, often referred to as "the graduate school of Cincinnati." P&G actually trains each individual in the building of *two* brands: (1) the product brand to which the new recruit is assigned, and (2) the Procter & Gamble masterbrand, whose planning rituals, analytical metrics, and internal reporting procedures result in a peerless company-wide brand. In fitting P&G fashion, the company has never publicly admitted that it trains its people in sustaining a company-wide masterbrand but, again, that is the effect, if not the intent.

In some companies, training takes the form of organized mentoring, which may originate from the highest level. For example, Al Zeien, the former CEO of Gillette, knew by name many of his 34,000 employees and he visited every product group in the company on a regular basis. He personally conducted as many as 800 performance reviews annually, and he closely mentored many of the rising stars in the company. Jack Welch, the legendary CEO of General Electric, has personally engaged 15,000 managers and executives in one-on-ones at the GE Training Center on more than 250 occasions in the past 17 years (an experience, it is said, that one is not likely to forget).

Chief Executives like Zeien and Welch understood that the future of their companies depended upon these men and women, and they did not intend to leave that future to chance. Every step of the way, they have taught their people the real meaning of their masterbrands, even as they trained them in the intricacies of sound management.

Continuing Brand Education

The dread of every executive who has ever authorized a corporate training program is that there will be no residual benefit to the time and financial investment. In too many cases, six months (or even six weeks) after the classroom training has been completed, the organization is no better off for the effort.

Here, too, brand training can have an advantage because it deals with something organic that is part of how the company evolves every day, and thus the employee who has just been trained can participate in ongoing masterbrand building. A new television commercial for a company brand, a corporate brochure, or a redesigned Web site, all become living examples of how the masterbrand is evolving. Recently retrained employee-partners can now see these examples as continuing evidence of what the brand means, and of how they can help continue its improvement process.

In addition, brand training is easily adaptable to tools that already exist in the workplace, including videotapes, e-mail, voice mail, intranets and extranets, videoconferencing, and conventional print material. Visits to the external Web sites and internal intranets in such companies as Levi Strauss, Adidas, Visa International, and Virgin Airlines provide employee-partners with daily opportunities to be updated on how their masterbrands are being marketed.

One of the most active and successful brand-training programs is at 3M. Aside from the power of the 3M brands themselves, 3M is also a standout in the degree to which its people have been immersed in brand training. Several thousand 3M employees, from all areas of the company, have undergone brand-building training. The training is completed with the help of the participants' existing managers, and is overseen by corporate brand "evangelists" and divisional brand managers, some of whom are considered to be world-class brand authorities, and are often asked to speak to other companies about the 3M brand experience. That group also publishes white papers regularly, holds forums and workshops, and tracks the progress of the participants.

In a more unorthodox approach to training, Whirlpool experimented in the summer of 1999 with a training format they called "Real Whirled," a combination of team training and ethnographic research. Named after the MTV program that follows six teenage live-ins, the program is designed to train trainers (in this case, the people who teach retail clerks at Sears and other retailers how to sell Whirlpool products).

The company asked eight new hires to live together in a house in St. Joseph, Michigan, in order to experience the rigors of housework, and to learn as a team why Whirlpool products are designed the way they are. Whirlpool executives would drop in unexpectedly for dinner or to inspect the house, putting extra pressure on the recruits to learn how and why the company's products are superior. That experience trained good trainers, but it also embedded components of the Whirlpool masterbrand in individuals who are now walking brand ambassadors, and who are training other ambassadors throughout the Whirlpool brand community. As the company's former national director of sales operations put it, "Trainers *are* the brand. They are Whirlpool. I don't know how we survived before this program."[16]

Managers need to keep these communications in front of employee-partners at all times, regularly illustrating how someone in accounting, operations, or sales, contributes to the building of a company's masterbrand. The more often that link can be demonstrated, the greater commitment from employee-partners a company can expect, and the greater the opportunity for the employee-partners to extend the masterbrand into its greater brand community.

Building Commitment "Virally"

So-called *viral marketing* is a popular selling technique akin to guerilla marketing, frequently used in online settings. Viral marketing starts by seeding a selling idea in strategic places among target audiences, leading to a grassroots spreading of infectious enthusiasm for a branded product or service, and encouraging customers to become missionaries, hopefully converting other prospective buyers.

Examples include Hotmail, which gave away free e-mail service, and added a small commercial message to each e-mail that its users sent. The word about free e-mail spread quickly across the Net, and Hotmail acquired 5 million subscribers in its first year, spending only $500,000 in marketing support. That compared favorably with a $17 million marketing investment by another service that landed only 7 million users. Then, there is the ICQ software by Mirabilis, subsequently acquired by America Online, which enables users to add other users to the e-mail list, thus expanding the recipient list much faster than through traditional recruiting. As of now, it is estimated that AOL's ICQ service reaches 35 million users, and most of that gain with relatively little marketing spending. In the words of AOL exec Ted Leonsis, "The less you do, the more it grows. This is a phenomenon like we've never seen."[17]

What management may be missing, though, is an opportunity to use this tool where it has the most chance for success—namely, *within* the company, among its employees who are even more likely to respond within a more cooperative environment. Viral marketing is an ideal way to encourage employees to share their excitement about what the company-wide brand is up to and what it means to everyone involved. The company intranet, standard e-mail, or more traditional communications channels can all be used to spread a "friendly virus."

At Lucent Technologies, for example, management reinforces the company's role in what they call the *communications revolution*, but it also recognizes that succeeding may be more of an evolutionary process. Using the company's extensive intranet and e-mails, internal magazines, employee-partner town meetings, and information packets for supervisors, the company's corporate communications teams helped accelerate Lucent's transition from an AT&T captive division to a communications and information powerhouse.

This transition was particularly fascinating within Bell Laboratories, the venerable innovation center whose role in the old AT&T company had ebbed and flowed in importance over the years. When Lucent management decided to use the Bell Labs moniker in the company's masterbrand descriptor, it triggered a resurgence of enthusiasm and commitment within the unit itself, even among 30-year veterans. The unit's employee-partners began to think differently, and to move at the speed necessary to stay ahead of the technology curve in today's lightning-quick selling environments. Lucent's Bell Labs had always been innovative (averaging as many as three new patents a day), but because its people now feel part of a larger masterbrand movement, they are creating complex, market-ready products within only a few months, and those products are being sold to satisfied customers, a feat that was unheard of in the old AT&T days.[18]

The powerful masterbrand community is the goal, but the means to that end are often found within the company itself. All businesses are in the service business, and the service is rendered most effectively by employee-partners committed to the masterbrand.

MANAGING YOUR MANDATE

Marketing to internal audiences is no different than what must be done in the marketplace, except that there is a dangerous tendency to believe that those outside the company are more important than those inside, because customers generate the revenue. That, of course, is a fallacy; employee-partners generate the revenue by creating products and services that customers want to buy.

Coaching the customer's team requires a strategically sound, disciplined marketing plan that methodically reinforces the masterbrand from the inside out.

Questions You Should Be Asking   To begin that process, we recommend that you ask the following questions about the company environment. If any of these factors appear to be more hindering than helpful, management needs to select individuals to lead the internal brand-building program who are able to diagnose and resolve these issues in a collaborative way.

How enthusiastic will your employee-partners be about participating in new company-wide initiatives to build a masterbrand? Regardless of your company's size, you likely have a series of *segments* that will be your internal marketing targets, each with its own unique profile. These profiles can have an important influence on the speed and success of company brandification efforts. For example, if a technology company is full of engineers and computer technicians, the concepts of marketing (let alone brand building) may not be common currency. However, if your key group leaders take part in even limited marketing training, brand trainers should be able to help them to understand the basic concepts of brand building, and to learn to apply those concepts to the larger idea of a masterbrand company.

Conversely, are there individuals or groups within your organization who will actively resist creating a strong company-wide brand? If yours is a single-brand company, would some parties see an enterprise-wide brand-building program as a drain on valuable resources, or a distraction from more concrete business building? If your company has multiple brands, would those who are responsible for the brands see a company-wide program as a threat to their individual brands?

Who is best qualified and available to lead your comprehensive internal masterbrand program, and are all the key players genuinely interested in committing to commitment? Who will lead the charge toward a strong brand orientation, and why? What credentials do they bring to the job that will make them credible and persuasive when justifying plans and obtaining needed funding? Are company management and key staff genuinely interested in generating a brand commitment throughout the organization?

   Fortunately, more and more company leaders are aware of the need to cultivate brand building within their companies, including in such far-flung industries as financial services, energy distribution, publishing, and professional services (e.g., law and accounting firms). If key leaders demonstrate a strong desire to acquire and practice the necessary brand-building skills, then the company usually finds a way to make it happen. Without such support, however, an aggressive, enterprise-wide brand-building program is not likely to get off the ground.

Has the history of your internal marketing and communications programs been a positive one in your company, or has there been a legacy of disappointing efforts and results? Were past programs well planned and executed, or were they treated as more of an afterthought ("Let's not forget to show our people what the new advertising campaign is going to look like . . . at least a day or two before it breaks")? How well documented are past programs, and what can be learned from them? How well were the results measured in pre-/postsurveying, and so forth? Who was in charge of those past efforts, and did he or she enlist company-wide support for the work, or run the show with a small staff? Did that planning group report to the CEO, or well down the chain of command?

Is there a communications and operational structure available to support an internal marketing program? Are there existing interdivisional groups that could be employed to encourage the commitment of your employee-partners on the new directions for your master

(Continued)

brand? Are there communications channels that are open and free-flowing, which could be used to create grassroots marketing efforts? Are there individuals who can make creative use of existing house organs, intranets, videoconferences, and other tools to create a lasting, high-impact internal brand-building program? Can you find someone who will be every bit as energized by the challenge of doing world-class internal marketing programs, as those who live to do the more visible external efforts?

Actions You Should Be Taking   Once the preceding questions have been addressed, these are some of the steps we recommend to drive brand commitment through the building.

Conduct internal research among a representative sample of your people to determine their understanding of brands, and how that understanding might be affecting your company-wide approach to brand building. This could include a series of conversations (one-on-ones or focus groups) with key "listening post" employees who have their pulse on what's happening in the organization at various levels. It may involve a full quantitative study with statistically projectible findings, possibly in conjunction with research into other HR or related questions, or as an add-on to quantitative research conducted outside the organization. (However, do *not* tack the brand research onto the end of another survey with a different purpose). Again, this type of research should be conducted prior to, immediately after, and periodically after, the launch of a new internal marketing effort.

Audit your communications channels to determine if their scope and penetration is sufficient to shoulder the burden of a major internal marketing program. Review all types of communications, both formal and informal, offline (house organs, memos, planning documents) and online (e-mail, intranet, extranet) channels. Is there a consistency to how the company is portrayed, and can that be translated into a more brand-oriented set of communications? Are the communications robust enough to rally your people around the masterbrand—not just as their employer—and as a dynamic player in the marketplace of competing brands?

Construct an internal marketing plan that is as productive and cost-effective as the company's external marketing programs. This will be your road map for transforming your organization into a masterbrand. As with an external marketing plan, this should be a living document that is continuously reviewed, discussed, and improved over time. This will require an internal marketing plan that is every bit as rigorous as that which is used externally. If you are not convinced that your external marketing planning is optimum, this is a good opportunity to construct the right kind of planning model for your entire brand community.

As a general guide, we would recommend that the internal marketing plan include the following elements:

- Executive summary
- Internal marketing situation
- Recommended internal marketing plan outline
  1. Marketing objectives
  2. Strategic Brand Platform
  3. Key messaging strategies (targeting, positioning, tonal elements)
  4. Brand training program touching everywhere the masterbrand can be driven through organization (e.g., hiring, training, selling, technical support, etc.)
  5. Specific tactics might include
     a. Internal celebrations of momentous achievements
     b. Internal trade shows with booths and exhibits
     c. Videotapes mailed to employees' homes
     d. Printed collateral, in employee "kits"
     e. Online (e-mail, proprietary communications system, intranet, customer contact via extranet, external Web site)
     f. Viral/guerrilla marketing programs (programmed word of mouth)
- Metrics and measurements
  1. Specific goals and hurdles
  2. Measurement approach

Bolster the masterbrand message by creating as many physical reminders as possible throughout the company. Company stores should be considered a high priority by management and given all the resources necessary to ensure that the masterbrand name and message is worn, carried, eaten and drunk from, and otherwise displayed in as many possible venues. A strategically planned set of posters, intranet graphics, banners, screen savers, desktop

(Continued)

novelties, and so on, should carry the masterbrand name, logo, key phraseology, and, where possible, a brief explanation of what the masterbrand stands for in the marketplace.

Another important "physical" reminder could be a comprehensive community intranet, either created internally, or by an external "employee portal" company.

*   *   *

The way that management treats its coworkers is arguably the greatest single determinant of a firm's success. As Anita Roddick, the founder of The Body Shop once put it: "We have found that when you take care of your customers really well, and make them the focal point, never once forgetting that your first line of customers are your own staff, profitability flows from that."[19]

In our next chapter, we will explore how to organize the company to make brand building a natural end product of the work by the company's employee-partners.

Organize to Brand-Build

The brand must be derived from the purpose
of the organization, or it will just be spin.
—John Mackey, Founder and
CEO, Whole Foods Markets[1]

They call themselves The Orpheus Chamber Orchestra. They have 24 strings and woodwinds, multiple Grammies, and rave reviews from Paris to Hanoi to New York. They have, in short, everything you would expect of an extraordinary orchestra—except a conductor. Orpheus plays beautiful and complex pieces, much of it with tricky tempi and multiphonic harmonies, all without the need of a leader with a baton. Using only subtle head movements and instinctive feel, they have learned to play as one.

In addition to their famous musical gigs, this experiment-turned-phenom regularly visits corporate campuses and business schools to demonstrate the possibilities of what has been called the "ultimate flat, nonhierarchical organization."[2] Without even trying, The Orpheus Chamber Orchestra has come to symbolize the business of the future.

Managing for Customer Focus

Organizations, as the saying goes, would work just fine if it weren't for the people. Human nature has a way of throwing a monkey wrench into the most rational organization chart. What looks good on paper is shredded by politics du jour. What passes the logic test falls flat on its face when fragile egos grade the exam. In a 1998 essay, Peter Drucker commented: "It has been [wrongly] taken for granted that there is one right form of organization."[3] Not only is there not one right form of organization, there may not be *any*. Managers searching for such a Rosetta Stone inevitably discover that they are archaeologists on a dig that yields more mysteries with the lifting of each new rock.

It used to be so clear what managers were to do: You studied the challenge, you pulled together your team, you gave them their marching orders, you monitored their progress, you adjusted as necessary, and you reported on your performance. Furrows on your brows and ice in your veins were good things. Business was war and the competition was trying to take food from your family's mouths. Managing meant leading a team into battle and taking no prisoners. Leading had to do with supporting your people, certainly, but they were *yours*, and it was your job to show them how to do it the right way, which meant your way or the highway. In retrospect, that philosophy sounds like a bad beer commercial. It may have been a good leadership approach at some point, but only from the leader's perspective.

The workplace today is matrixed, team-managed, control-shared, and silo-wary. The manager's job is to transform cooperation into momentum, and disinterest into initiative. Gaining the trust of fellow employees is more important than air itself, and the first signs of trust erosion bring the same kind of havoc that you find on a dysfunctional NBA team. Change is no longer just coped with, it is anticipated and celebrated. Any company that does not seek it out is considered too slow and ugly to care about. Knowledge is king and information is its chancellor. Time is Einsteinian, seeming to slide backward the faster you move. The process is almost as important as the product that shoots out at the other end. Competitors are tomorrow's allies. You don't sell to outsiders anymore, because customers are part of the family . . . and the Board would make them CEOs in a heartbeat if they asked for the job.

Why is it so hard to be customer-centric? Because it is so hard *not* to be process-centric. We often have to concentrate so relentlessly on being productive and efficient in executing our daily tasks that we find it difficult to stay as connected as we should be with the customer. Still, to their everlasting credit, CEOs and their managers relentlessly seek simple, transferable ways to motivate, hoping that their organizations can become more efficient at meeting customer needs.

Amid all this, boundaries and perspectives may be getting blurrier, but focus on the customer must not. If there is one common denominator among all managers in all industries, it is that they must learn, teach, plan for, and practice the Zen of customer focus. With it, all things are possible. Without it, little progress is likely.

We believe that companies can take giants steps forward in achieving customer focus by constructing a masterbrand company. That may not go down well with those who believe that brands are solely the turf of the marketing department, but CEOs and their managers who accurately view masterbrands as company-wide assets will know better.

Masterbrand Building: Somebody's Job or Everybody's Mission?

Marketing should be the primary assignment of a few, but masterbrand building should be the job of all who contribute to the growth of the company. That is understood in some companies more than others. Brand building is at or is near the core of the company's reason for being at McDonald's, Nike, Virgin Group, America Online, and dozens of .coms whose leaders understand that brand equals oxygen. At the opposite end of the spectrum, marketing can be nearly an afterthought in many industrial companies that have not yet discovered how marketing can free them from their historical constraints.

Marketing educator and consultant Philip Kotler has watched many companies evolve through various marketing development stages, which he labels as: *Simple sales departments,* in which less marketing-savvy companies consider traditional sales to be the only real focus, and any marketing duties are outsourced; *separate market-ing departments*, in which marketing has become an important-enough function to merit its own unit under the head of sales; *modern marketing department*, in which a high-level executive man-ages both the sales and marketing functions; and what Kotler tellingly refers to as the *effective marketing company*, in which all of the company becomes responsible for marketing, rather than just the marketing department.[4]

Recognize your company in there somewhere? Is yours an *effec-tive marketing company* or is it more of a vision? Some have sug-gested that the marketing department may no longer be needed, not because it's unimportant, but because brand building is *too* important to leave to a relatively small group of specialists. Every-one in the organization, this school suggests, should literally be involved in marketing.[5]

Our view: All employee-partners should *not* be recruited to be marketers. That's neither practical nor productive. Marketing is like any other discipline that requires years of training and experi-ence. All employee-partners *should*, however, be considered mas-terbrand ambassadors, if not active brand builders. Brand building can be a key point of focus that can motivate an entire company's people, although it should never be served up as a force-fed religion that ultimately alienates more than it converts. The more practical solution is to instill some ownership in the marketing mission and a sense of belonging to the masterbrand value creation process. (See the sidebar for how Nokia does just that.)

3M: Using the Masterbrand Lens

Ideally, employee-partners are organized so that their labors are synchronized and uniformly directed toward the building of the brand. In such cases, marketing and nonmarketing people play a spectrum of roles that are key to creating a productive master-brand.

Minnesota Mining & Manufacturing Company (3M Co.) is a highly diversified manufacturer with $15 billion in revenue. 3M is also a brand-centered organization bonded with a strategic glue as strong as any of its industrial adhesives. Founded in 1902 as a min-

THE NOKIA WAY

Nokia Corporation may be Europe's most stunning example of how masterbrand building unifies companies and multiplies value. Once a weak conglomeration of rubber, wood, and cable companies, Nokia established a firm foothold in the early cellular business in the 1980s. But before the company could reach full stride in its new technology mode, Nokia lost its CEO to suicide and its biggest customer with the fall of the Soviet Union. A few years later, current CEO Jorma Ollila took over and began creating a masterbrand company inside and out.

The people of Nokia think and work in harmony, thanks in part to The Nokia Way, a series of internal meetings that somehow consistently yields just enough centralized direction to enable its people to press forward in a sort of organized creativity. Some of the moves that company leaders have taken to make Nokia a very special masterbrand company:

- They have created products that have universal acceptance, such as cellular phones that adhere to all three major protocol standards, but use the same look and housing around the globe;

- They adopted a corporate culture that is both disciplined, yet creative, and has been called "perhaps the least hierarchical company in the world";

- They studied the great global brands of the world (Nike, Daimler-Benz) and adopted what they call a similar *holistic* approach to manufacturing and marketing (we call it a *masterbrand approach*), which includes using the Nokia brand meaning as a lens when designing, distributing, marketing, and selling a product.

Nokia is now the world's leading supplier of cellular phones, and is in a strong position to compete effectively in a huge spectrum of technology sectors. As ultimate proof of the wisdom of its masterbrand strategy, stockholder value has multiplied +2,300 percent in the last five years.

ing company, 3M now has 40 divisions that manufacture and sell more than 50,000 products. The company invests a relatively high 6 percent of its revenues into research and development, and expects the future to be driven by products and brands that do not exist today. This is validated by a vigorous program called "Pacing Plus," which singles out research projects with the potential to yield huge revenues—to "change the nature of competition," as 3M puts it—and speeds them to market. That program is the most recent in a long line that have contributed to 3M's masterbrand identity as "the innovation company."

The 3M formula for success is based as much on sound brand building as on a corporate mission. At the core of the company's strength is its brand-driven infrastructure, which ensures that innovation is coupled with, if not filtered through, brand-driven decisions. Brand committees have been established within each major division and are guided by corporate brand managers who are more likely to have engineering or scientific backgrounds than marketing. Dean Adams, for example, the corporate executive in charge of overseeing the brand management process at 3M, is a physicist by training. (3M has found that it is much easier to train and instill a technologically proficient person with sound marketing skills, than to teach a marketer how to fuse atoms.)

Managers at 3M, regardless of their job descriptions and educational training, spend a lot of time working on how the 3M masterbrand (what 3M calls its "authority brand") and its "strategic brands" (e.g., Scotch, Post-its) should be positioned in the marketplace. These managers describe brand loyalty as a combination of "product, image, and service." The brand promise consists of two major components: *specialness* (meaning differentiation) and *authority* (trust, leadership, and quality). All of the 3M brands have been described and evaluated according to these three criteria.

The 3M brand structure revolves around a series of brand promises, and they transport those promises across divisions, if necessary, to ensure that the brand stands for the same thing, regardless of the context. The Scotch brand, for example, is sold in both consumer and industrial markets, yet it's positioning promise remains constant: "Scotch brand promises to save time, make the job easier, and eliminate rework." At 3M, what they call their "brand power" creates perceived value, driven by customer satisfaction, that builds brand loyalty and, ultimately, sustainable, profitable growth.

The brandifying of 3M is also very much a management function, especially because the company has adopted its emphasis on a brand asset planning strategy, which puts a financial value on each brand, thus making its contribution to the bottom line as concrete as possible.[6]

The 3M brand stewards keep close tabs on the progress of the authority brand and its strategic brand offspring. Overall brand policies are set by a brand committee, with representatives from throughout the company. Everything that is likely to become a permanent brand component of the 3M, Post-it, or Scotch brands is approved by the committee, which ensures that the new trademark, logo, or strategy is consistent with the approved brand promise. Periodic measurements are taken about the relevance of messaging, as well as the maintenance of differentiation, trust, leadership, quality, familiarity, and share of customer loyalty measures.

In short, 3M is a company that uses its masterbrand as a strategic lens to guide its actions. (See Figure 7.1 for how the lens works in a company.)

Creating a Brand-Centered Infrastructure

Once the best strategic course has been determined, and the opportunities to execute have been optimized, it comes down to

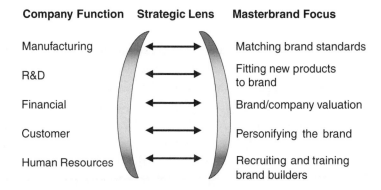

Company Function	Strategic Lens	Masterbrand Focus
Manufacturing	⟷	Matching brand standards
R&D	⟷	Fitting new products to brand
Financial	⟷	Brand/company valuation
Customer	⟷	Personifying the brand
Human Resources	⟷	Recruiting and training brand builders

Figure 7.1 How a strategic lens creates a masterbrand focus.

how well you sell the plan to those who must execute it. It is the job of those in the positions listed hereafter to persuade the apathetic and the skeptical that masterbrands offer everyone in the organization an opportunity to build the company, using an internal marketing program as a persuasion and information tool. That often requires a lean and flexible infrastructure of managers who can hopefully muster a sales force that will evangelize their fellow employee-partners. Predictably, it starts at the top.

The Management Team as Brand Leaders

We discussed in our first chapter the pivotal role that the CEO plays in the development of the masterbrand. However, that is hardly a one-person job. Those who are closest to the CEO must also take an active role in driving the brand through the organization or, as in some cases, cheering from the sidelines when employee-partners grab the ball and run. There are at least six ways that executive management can become involved in the brand-building process, including: (1) incorporating the masterbrand strategy into the most critical planning documents of the organization; (2) building most, if not all, major business initiatives around the precepts of the central masterbrand; (3) participating as voting (but not dominant) members of key brand management committees; (4) personally sponsoring masterbrand initiatives; (5) discussing the goals of the masterbrand regularly with the company's people, strategic and supplier partners, and investors; and (6) incorporating brand-oriented messages into all key communications—written, electronic, and verbal.

The Brand Council

A growing group of companies have created committees or councils that oversee the masterbrand. At Sun Microsystems, the company's branding decisions are reviewed by both a brand council and marketing council, made up of the marketing heads of the various divisions. Similarly, at IBM, 3M, 3Com, Hewlett-Packard, Visa International, and Chase Manhattan, multidisciplined teams are responsible for monitoring the health of the brand, and for ensuring that the organization is fully supporting the chosen strategic brand direction.

If necessary, these groups can also serve as "logo police" to prevent far-flung operations in their companies from inadvertently violating identity guidelines, and they could be asked to review and approve establishing brand metrics and measurement initiatives. However, it is a mistake to allow these functions to become the primary role that a brand council plays. The first and foremost job of council members is to monitor and adjust the strategic *meanings* of the masterbrand and its offspring brands. Do not let more tactical issues interfere with that role.

Brand Champion

The *brand champion* is an individual who is usually at a relatively high level in the organization and who serves as protector of the brand, defender of its funding, spokesperson for its goals, and flagwaver for its cause in management hearings.

In the past, that role involved championing an individual product or service brand within a multibrand company, in which brands compete for time, money, and management attention. However, the company's masterbrand needs its own champion(s), often even more urgently than do individual brands. This company-wide brand champion identifies and articulates the entire organization's role in marketing, and often must fight off attempts to siphon away funds from the masterbrand cause. If the masterbrand champion succeeds, he or she has an exponentially more important impact on the future of the company than a parallel success at the individual brand level.

In companies that we would characterize as inherently brand-driven, such as Nike, Apple, and Ralph Lauren, brand champions are incipient within the original company architecture. At Ralph Lauren, for example, a "brand czar" specifically approves what business units can and cannot do with the brand. In other companies, whose management hopes to become more brand-centric in the future, brand champions are just now being identified and given their charge, such as was announced at Polaroid in 1999.

Brand Coach

Another role that is particularly valuable in a brand-built environment is the *brand coach*. As the brand champion carries the flag in front of management, the brand coach's role is to continuously drive enthusiasm for the brand throughout the organization on a daily basis. The coach's job is to regularly detonate "brand explosions" in the company corridors to maintain focused excitement around the brand. It is the brand coach who might employ ambush or viral marketing on the company's own people to keep brand momentum at its highest possible level. In one form or another, brand coaches can be found at 3M, 3Com, and Lucent Technologies.

Brand Teams and Brand Squads

We believe that there is potentially even greater opportunity to bring the brand to life via what can be called *brand teams* or *brand squads*. These would be small cadres of employee-partners who work with the brand coach and champion to proselytize the brand message among their peers, much as work teams seek to improve operational productivity or manufacturing efficiencies. The Nike "ekins," although created to be sales development teams, also serve as fervent purveyors of brand power. It is through the brand teams that internal viral marketing can be most efficiently deployed. (See Figure 7.2 for brand infrastructure in masterbrand companies.)

Mistakes That Hurt the Masterbrand

A few years ago, a colleague was riding in a taxicab in the outskirts of San Francisco when the driver admitted that he was hopelessly lost. As the cab nosed its way through traffic, the cabby mumbled with some frustration that he had hacked in four other U.S. cities, including Chicago, Cleveland, and Washington, D.C. "But this place," he sighed, "is the worst." San Francisco is, in fact, one of the more difficult U.S. cities to navigate because its layout is the result of helter-skelter growth, unforeseen geographical limitations, and a certain 1906 earthquake and fire that nearly destroyed it during its adolescent years. In much the same way, too many companies have created their organizational structures based on historical accidents, or short-term structural needs. The result is rarely as charming as the City by the Bay.

Figure 7.2   *Brand building within masterbrand companies.*

Human beings being human, we have managed to find a lot of ways to foul up otherwise strong organizations, and that can make it doubly difficult to build an equally strong masterbrand. Although we plan to explore brand-building roadblocks in more detail in our last chapter, let us point out now just a few foibles that can harm the masterbrand:

Mistake No. 1: The Battle of the Budget

You have to get real before you can get aspirational. Power follows authority, and they both follow money. Oddly enough, those with the purse strings are usually seen as "right" more often than those who are left holding the bag. In brand-driven organizations, individuals with the clearest view of what the masterbrand is and where it must go should be the ones with the most budget leverage. Too often, this is not the case, because revenue and profit generation are seen as a line responsibility, and tending to the masterbrand can be a staff function.

Yet, in the dozens of examples we are reviewing in this book, it is clear that those companies that have organizationally focused on the health of their masterbrand have survived and prospered. In most of those cases, the line and staff functions were integrated, and the development of the masterbrand was more than sufficiently funded.

Mistake No. 2: The Tireless Art of Turfing

The care and feeding of a masterbrand is simultaneously an act of single-minded concentration and selfless collaboration. Successful brands—particularly at the company-wide level—are created by team builders who freely share information, insights, and funding. So, what is most likely to stop productive team building in its tracks? Our vote: *turfing* (also known as the torpedoing of productive collaborations for small-minded reasons).

Even in enlightened corporations, individuals are relying less on the company to direct their careers, and so must rely more on their own ingenuity and protective instincts. How many of us have worked for someone who appears to be more concerned with his own career than the company's success, and who somehow fails to see the connection between the two? It's a put-my-oxygen-mask-on-first approach to managing that is disturbing, even as it is predictable.

Yet, when a clearly defined, enthusiastically celebrated masterbrand is the core of the company, it can help blunt the destructive work of turfers because it is clearer to all what can be gained by pulling together. A masterbrand that is everyone's ward is the product of what everyone can accomplish, regardless of what his or her role might be. Restricting actions and thoughts along turf lines can be sadly fatal to company initiatives, but a robust masterbrand can help managers resist such pettiness.

In 1997, Harley-Davidson Motor Company came up with a novel team approach called *circles* that speaks to this issue. The company's functional leaders are assigned to one of three large groups: the Create Demand Circle, Produce Product Circle, and Provide Support Circle. Each circle is a self-contained unit, but works in a highly flexible way to ensure that no balls are dropped in serving the needs of consumers and distributors. No circle has a permanent leader; instead, the role rotates around the group of managers. The circles meet monthly, and the entire group of circles meets quarterly. Representatives from each circle are members of the Strategic Leadership Council, which decides overall strategic policy issues. In this way, the Harley-Davidson teams work in an integrated fashion, but are fully functional at the circle level. Above all, their interaction reinforces the central reason why the circles exist to begin with—namely, to drive the Harley masterbrand.

Mistake No. 3: Flawed Team Building

Some corporate teams have created revolutions in their industries by artfully exporting their end products beyond their team areas. Two examples: (1) the skunkworks team, led by Lee Iacocca in the early 1960s, that created the Ford Mustang, and (2) Sun Microsystems' Jini technology team, led by CTO Bill Joy.

In contrast, the wrong kind of team building can also harm the masterbrand. More than 70 percent of the marketing/brand/product managers who responded to a 1997 survey by *Food & Beverage Marketing* magazine said they spent from a significant amount to most of their time as part of a team.[7] Yet, in the mid-1990s, researchers Richard Whiteley and Diane Hessan found that fewer than 15 percent of large U.S. companies with team efforts achieved their stated goals. They attributed the result to what they called "teamitis," the apparently common habit of undisciplined teams tackling jobs beyond their charge, resulting in administrative and personnel headaches instead of achieving a more modest and useful objective. Hessan and Whiteley also concluded that a company is one big team, and can achieve its goals if it sustains the kind of close collaboration seen most often in start-ups.

Levi Strauss launched an internal experiment in 1993 called the "Customer Service Supply Chain Initiative," with the admirable objective of increasing responsiveness to retailers. The company's 300 employees and consultants who served on the team were given lots of leeway and few cost constraints. The Third Floor Brigade, as they came to be known, succeeded in raising awareness of major problems, but also created divisiveness in their wake as they expanded their charge to include reorganizing the entire company. The Brigade reportedly spent $850 million (70 percent over its original budget). Non-Brigade employees became very unsettled (a good many left the organization altogether), and the time-to-market gap was not substantially reduced. What was reduced, however, was the patience of retailers who found the team's end product to be confusing and counterproductive.

Privately owned Levi Strauss has long been an outstanding brand-driven company, and frequently has successfully introduced some of the best-known fashion brand names around. Even its best efforts, however, have been subverted by unfortunate decision making, including in team building. The Third Floor Brigade worked hard to improve trade relationships for their company, but failed to see how their best efforts could also do harm. To the company's credit, management has learned valuable lessons from their 1993 supply chain initiative and is applying them as they aggressively build a stronger masterbrand community.

Mistake No. 4: Seduction by Success

Many industries have failed to move fast enough because they were using the wrong points of reference. Computer hardware manufacturers were late in discovering that their galloping penetration into consumer markets was turning into a downward chute toward unprofitability. Leading transportation brands have eagerly scooped up new routes offered by government regulators, only to see growth opportunities turn into profit drains. Retailers commonly let the market of the moment slip by them because they rely too heavily on today's tastes.

Banks are an example of an industry that has fallen victim to its closest ally, *inertia*. To this day, inertia is the most frequently cited reason for bank customers to stick with their current checking accounts, traditionally the cornerstone of customer-bank relationships. Ironically, inertia has also mired much of the industry in outdated business models that are rapidly being eroded by disintermediation from a parade of alternative financial solutions. In the process, traditional banks are losing enormous customer household assets to encroaching competition from brokerage firms (Schwab, Ameritrade), technology companies (Intuit, Microsoft), and alternative financial service companies (GE Capital).

If inertia can stymie a half-trillion-dollar industry like banking, it can certainly prevent a single company from migrating to a more productive organizational setup. The happy reality about company-wide masterbrand building is that it prompts participants to constantly reexamine and discard past answers because an outdated brand model is quickly and visibly outflanked by superior competition.

Options That Strengthen Masterbrands

Business history is filled with reengineering efforts that have been aimed at improving performance. Following are five organizational options that various organizations have employed to build or rebuild their companies, and that have had positive effects on their masterbrands.

Option No. 1: Reorganize to Get Closer to the Customer

Arguably, one of the most wrenching reorganizations in recent corporate history took place at Sears in the mid-1990s. The company had experienced a series of poor performance years, culminating in 1992 when the company lost $3.9 billion on sales of $52.3 billion.

The Sears makeover involved a combination of marketing restaging and cultural redirection. The three-year process was personally and organizationally sponsored by CEO Arthur Martinez, who called on the company to become once again, "a compelling place to work, to shop, and to invest." He enlisted the support and assistance of the 100 highest-level executives at the company. At the core of the reengineering model was employee accountability, as measured by customer satisfaction and the overall financial performance of the company and its operating units. Labeled Total Performance Indicators (TPI), it was, and is, an accessible system that involves the employee in the measuring of success and the setting of new goals.

As a guide for the work, consultants created a learning map, a picture of a town or store that led the employees through needed business processes or marketing circumstances (in this case, through the evolving target profiles and market conditions with which the company needed to be most concerned). The team also established Sears University in 1995, which has helped to inculcate the TPI culture.

Simultaneously, Sears marketers and their agencies launched the highly effective "Softer Side of Sears" marketing communications campaign. The effort, initially designed to reattract female shoppers to the chain, was eventually so successful at repositioning the entire store, that it evolved to the "Many Sides of Sears," and was used against all of the company's target audiences. For much of the 1990s, the campaign served as a beacon to both customer and employee-partner that Sears was reclaiming its place as one of America's most bountiful retailing resources.

Sears is a company that overcame onerous organizational, personnel, sales, operational, and marketing issues to breathe new life into its laggardly business. At the cornerstone of the turnaround was the redefining of what the Sears masterbrand meant to its customers, its employees, and its current and potential investors. The many and varied components of the organization had to be retooled, one by one, but the end product of the turnaround team's labors was a renovated masterbrand that was stronger than its predecessors. (As of this writing, Sears is currently undergoing a second phase of reorganization because its management has discovered that the early work is not yet completed, and must be consummated if the company is to reach its ultimate business goals.)

Option No. 2: Converge on the Middle

To foster a brand-building culture throughout an organization, consider a dual emphasis on top-down direction and bottom-up motivating. In this approach, the vision and direction that are communicated through company officers (and hopefully based on the views of the employee-partners) meet the hopes and enthusiasm of the workers in the middle of the organization. The result is a swirling together of goal and action at all levels that infectiously spreads enthusiasm for the brand promise and brand-building programs.

Dilbertisms aside, middle managers with formidable leadership skills are running key teams in virtually every major corporation you can name. Often, middle managers are the repositories of the knowledge and information that serve as the strategic glue for many of the corporate world's most productive revolutions. However, such managers are also feeling the squeeze, particularly in the information services industry, where the younger execs are sometimes better, and usually cheaper. As one middle-aged middle manager poignantly put it, "For my salary, the company could hire two twenty-somethings. I'm good at what I do. But am I better than two people? Even I know that's not true."[8]

To be successful, this type of "brand-converging" approach calls for management to communicate brand-building priorities for the company-wide brand, and for employee-partners to accept and inject their inputs into the brand-building process. It falls to the middle managers, then, to meld the influences of those hierarchically above and below them into a new brand-driven energy force that transforms internal activities and refurbishes relations with customers and other constituencies.

Of course, as organizations become flatter, there will be more integration between former employee-partner layers. An example of this dynamic can be seen at Whole Foods Markets, the leading chain of natural foods stores. (See the sidebar and Figure 7.3.)

Another example of this approach was being launched at 3Com Corp. as this book was going to press. Jan Soderstrom, 3Com's senior vice president of marketing and brand management, is in the process of creating a company-wide brand council, with a series of brand teams reporting to that group, which are represented throughout the organization. All of the brand team members are undergoing special brand training in central location workshops in the United States, the United Kingdom, and Asia Pacific. Simultaneously, the management of 3Com has taken every opportunity to emphasize the critical importance of embracing the new 3Com masterbrand, and employing its strategic tenets throughout the company and its wider community of customers, channel and strategic partners, and investors.

Option No. 3: Replenish the Culture

Johnson & Johnson, Levi Strauss, Kodak, and Hallmark all have extraordinary histories that have spawned extraordinary corporate cultures. Once gained, they must be guarded with care, or the company is forced to start again—a long and painful process. To borrow a phrase, a culture is a terrible thing to waste.

The people of IBM know just how long that process takes. Its turnaround ranks among the most dramatic in the past half-

WHOLE FOODS: TEAMS VERSUS TOTALITARIANISM

John Mackey, founder and CEO of Whole Foods Markets, is not all that sure that he has created a masterbrand. In fact, he admits that he has even thought of his company as an "antibrand." From its founding in 1978 when Mackey borrowed $10,000 from his dad to open a natural-foods store in Austin, Texas, Whole Foods has grown, through acquisition and same-store growth, to more than $1.5 billion in annual revenue.

The company has also approached retailing from a different path. For example, management believes strongly that there shouldn't be management, at least not in the conventional sense. The entire company is organized around decentralized, self-managed teams that do their own recruiting, hiring and firing, evaluations, P&Ls. The teams are based on what's called a shared-faith program, meaning shared power and shared responsibilities lead to shared rewards. The teams compete aggressively with one another to outperform their peers, and their accomplishments stimulate the other teams to work that much harder to exceed goals.

Whole Foods, as an organization, operates with a set of what managers call *processes*, which are considered to be far more important than any organizational structure. They include:

- No employee (including the CEO) makes more than 10 times the average employee salary.

- The books of the company are wide open for any employee to inspect, including the salaries of all other employees.

- Good ideas are spread around liberally through the annual store tours, in which selected stores are on display, thus creating a systematic best-practices program.

- The company encourages statistical comparisons at every turn, to quantify what has been accomplished, and to set goals for future initiatives.

- "Tribal gatherings" are held annually for 400 managers to review and reinstill the company's value proposition.

- Most unusual of all for a strong brand-built company, Mackey and his teams specifically *forbid* consistency. Defying the logic of brand building, the people of Whole Foods believe that, in Mackey's own words, "consistency is a euphemism for totalitarianism."*

Whatever John Mackey calls it, his Whole Foods Markets *is* a masterbrand company, one that has proven the power of nontraditional thinking in a very traditional market. (See Fig. 7.3 for a typical Whole Foods advertising.)

*Michael Hartnett, 1998 Build Brand Value Conference.

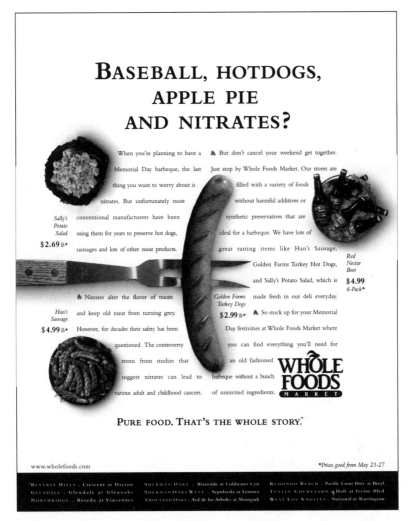

Figure 7.3   *Whole Foods Markets is the preeminent natural foods masterbrand.*

century, and a renewed commitment to the famed masterbrand played a big role in IBM's reincarnation. Lou Gerstner joined IBM on April Fool's Day in 1993 as the first outsider ever to run the legendary company, and the first to be asked to save a struggling behemoth of this size and complexity. The company had suffered through four years of stagnating revenue, profit margins that fell

17 percent in five years, and a market valuation that plummeted $60 billion in seven years.

In addition, the company, which had always been known for pioneering and sharing new technologies, had found itself in the unprofitable position of failing to make those technologies work for its own proprietary purposes. The result, breakthroughs like its reduced instruction-set computing (RISC) technology, made fortunes—but for other companies, such as Sun Microsystems. This was not how IBM had built its once impregnable masterbrand.

Gerstner took what seemed to outsiders as an agonizingly long time to make corrections. Yet, he apparently saw almost immediately that there was an appalling loss of focus on the customer, which historically had been the hallmark of IBM. Methodically, he and his new teams created an environment that he termed *restless self-renewal*, a process of realigning the direction of IBM's employees toward identifying and implementing customer solutions. Lou Gerstner and his teams reinvented an enormous company, and an important part of the reason was a renewed commitment for its extraordinary masterbrand. Gerstner's efforts have been rewarded, among many ways, with a stock price that has increased 10-fold since his arrival, and which has successfully weathered extreme volatility in the U.S. financial markets.

Option No. 4: Divest What Distracts from Building the Brand

One characteristic of brand-built companies is that they ultimately cut away parts of the organization that hold them back from achieving their full potential. Until 1998, PepsiCo had integrated its marketing operations with those of its bottlers, creating an unwieldy management situation. When PepsiCo divested its restaurant operations (Pizza Hut, KFC, and Taco Bell, which formed Tricon Corporation in 1997), followed by its bottling operations, the central marketing job became considerably more focused.

Pepsi-Cola North America now includes four major units: (1) brand management (with responsibility for the integrity of the overall brand and marketing programs), (2) channel management (which was formerly in sales, but now receives the information and coordinated support of marketing directly), (3) marketing initiative development (which translates marketing initiatives into simple sales stories and promotions), and the (4) innovation team (whose job is to bring product and package innovation to the group). Dawn Hudson, Pepsi-Cola North America's senior vice president of strategy and marketing, sees her role as building an esprit de corps based on brand focus and trust.

The successful introductions of Pepsi One, the Pepsi "Joy of Cola" campaign, and the global promotional tie-ins with the release of *Star Wars: The Phantom Menace,* were all examples of well-executed initiatives that are directly attributable to the brand-centered cohesiveness of the Pepsi-Cola organization. Importantly, the Pepsi-Cola team also is careful to treat their own people as customers. Each major new campaign is previewed among employees, and the approaches are explained so that as many Pepsi-Cola people as possible will understand the thinking behind the work.[9]

Option No. 5: Brand Chartering

Consultant and author Chris Macrae and his colleagues at the World Class Branding Network have pioneered investigations into what they call *brand chartering.* Chartering is the creation and updating of *living scripts,* which guide a corporation's efforts to build its brand internally and externally. As Macrae pointed out in his book, *The Brand Chartering Handbook,* ". . . brands have become more than unique selling propositions. They are now also unique organizing purposes around which a company needs to organize all its processes and resources."[10]

Chartering parallels our premise that it is vital for a company to determine how best to run the living brand through the veins of the organization, pumped by management's commitment to sustained interaction between the brand and the employee, and between the employee and the customer. It does this by allowing employees to voice questions and demand answers as to how the brand connects together all the intangible values and strengths within the organization. It also guides the company in creating value within the greater brand community of customers, strategic partners, and other supporters.

A key element of brand chartering is the cross-departmental networking within a company that drives the brand dynamics throughout the organization. Macrae suggests looking for *branding junctions* in organizations, intersection points that provide opportunities for information to be shared and value to be added to the brand-building process. These junctions include points at which teams deal with the brand essence, its heritage, the quality and value that it promises, and the general flow of teamwork.

Although it's not always easy to have much say in what happens in the greater marketplace, there is a marketplace that is at least as important—the one within the walls of the company—that may be very responsive toward a greater focus on masterbrand building. What follows are some suggested questions to ask and actions to consider, that could initiate that process.

MANAGING YOUR MANDATE

Our quote from Whole Foods CEO John Mackey at the top of this chapter gets to the heart of the matter: The core of a company's brand is derived from its purpose as an organization. The purpose of your company is no doubt to serve customers by meeting or exceeding their needs. That's the primary role of marketing, of course, and the same can be said of masterbrand building.

Questions You Should Be Asking   As you evaluate your company's current organization, consider the following questions:

Are individual groups, teams, and divisions within your company working toward a brand-oriented goal, or are brand issues low on their priority lists? Do they see the strengthening of the masterbrand as a vital step toward gaining a stronger foothold in the marketplace, or basically as someone else's problem? Do they see the link between how a company is organized and how a brand is lived by the company's people? If brand building is a natural place for your people to refocus their efforts, then organizational decisions based on brand needs will come easily. If not, you need to consider what it will take to make brand building a logical guiding light for your company.

Are the roles and duties of your brand builders clearly delineated within the organization, and do they extend well beyond the marketing teams? Have the terms *brand champion* or *brand coach* ever been spoken in the halls of your company? If so, have they referred only to those responsible for individual product and service brands, and not the company-wide masterbrand? Is it assumed that those individuals must have marketing backgrounds? Does a brand council exist (i.e., an interdisciplinary group of decision makers from around the company)? Are those roles possible to create, or would they generate resistance from others?

Are middle managers willing and able to meld direction from management and the needs of your workers into a focused brand-building culture? This is asking a lot of such managers, and it requires an understanding of, and a commitment to, the long-term building of the company masterbrand. If this enthusiasm is not latent within the company, it may require an integrated, multilevel effort to rally the troops. On the other hand, a strong leader of a brand movement, backed by management and supported by the rank and file, can bring brand building to life and bring new life to a coasting company.

Have past and present organizational and structural decisions within your company been based on functional or logistical needs? Have company planners ever considered how the organization should be structured according to what would best strengthen the company-wide brand-building efforts? Have such moves been looked at from the perspective of the entire brand community—including customers, of course—but also from the perspective of strategic partners, providers, and other constituencies? Is it possible that the most customer-driven decisions that could be made would be based on the community's total needs, not just those of the customer alone?

Actions You Should Be Taking Consider the following actions as opportunities to involve both the customer and employee in the brand-building organization:

Offer your people an opportunity to "own" a piece of the brand-building action. When prospective employees are being interviewed, they invariably ask about the organization of the work team they will be involved in. How many company recruiters answer that your

(Continued)

company is organized entirely to meet the needs of customers? How many recruiters would *want* to answer that such a priority even takes precedence over the needs of the employee-partners? How many recruiters can answer that building the company-wide brand is one of the most important functions in the organization?

Consider implementing a "convergence" approach to enterprise-wide masterbrand management. Look through the middle managers of your organization and select one or more who are up to the challenge of leading a new focus on brand building. Ensure that at least one is not from the marketing department, but has an aptitude for the work, nonetheless. Assess whether they have the credibility with management and the currency with the rank and file to orchestrate a coming-together of the company on brand-building issues.

If such an individual(s) is (are) available, create a loosely structured set of recommended steps to begin the brand-building process, and seek the opinions of the middle management candidate(s) for the job. Based on their input, along with the views of others you might consult, appoint the convergence manager, and begin constructing a specific brand-building plan that pulls together the guidance and endorsement of management with employees with a more street level view of the marketplace.

Establish a clear set of brand-related roles, duties, and reporting relationships. Create a brand culture by appointing as many people as possible to brand-related roles. Seek to build a lean but effective group of brand leaders who will work cooperatively with one another and with the CEO to ensure that the company-wide brand is well served inside and outside of the organization. Select individuals who have not necessarily been formally trained in brand marketing, but who have an aptitude for the discipline.

Help the customer manage the brand community. With the onset of mainstream customer interactivity and mass customization, customers expect to participate in the marketing directed at them, and that's generally helpful. As long as it does not overly burden us as customers, we want to be cocreators of that which we seek to buy. Brand building is a collaborative process; as a collaborator, customers can provide feedback about the masterbrand, offer suggestions for improving its performance, and develop a greater sense of ownership as a result.

We suggest that you invite customers to help manage your masterbrand, by providing insight about what would make the masterbrand ideal from their standpoint. Some tactical ways to do that might include the following:

- Providing customers with significant savings on their purchases if they participate as members of an ongoing panel. Alternatively, offer to give them the first opportunity to try "beta" products or innovative new services, in exchange for periodically providing the company with guidance. Expose them to strategic planning options (simplified as necessary) to give them an opportunity to comment on the direction that the masterbrand is taking. This is a chance to hear how customers view the company, and what roles they believe the company should ideally play in their lives.

- Invite rotating groups of suppliers and partner groups (e.g., software developers) to look at marketing concepts, especially those that might involve these partners.

- Create online and offline newsletters that keep these groups involved in ongoing company events, and that provide them with an easy, interactive channel to suggest new and better ways to market to your brand community.

- Establish online surveying (with appropriate incentives) to ensure that there is a continuous stream of new responses to ongoing company initiatives.

Active participation by your customer offers sellers a better opportunity to build relationships that radically increase brand involvement and that often lead to expanded lifetime value.

*   *   *

In our next chapter, we take a closer look at one of the superior masterbrand communities in financial services, or any kind of services, for that matter. Charles Schwab & Company is an example of how an enterprise-wide approach to masterbrand building can be successfully implemented.

Masterbrand:
Charles Schwab & Co.

*One of the things we like about Schwab is they recog-
nize early what the customer is interested in. We
view them as perpetually next year's model.*
—Michael J. Freudenstein, J.P. Morgan & Co.[1]

An internal e-mail from within a leading New York brokerage
firm leaked to the press in September 1999. The e-mail read:

> If we are going to be Financial Consultants to wealthy and suc-
> cessful individuals and businesses, then we don't have time to
> provide personal services to the poor.[2]

This was no doubt a well-meaning sentiment that the author
thought would enlighten his or her colleagues. Here's what we
would have replied:

> Hel-l-lo??? The customer is in control. Repeat: We are not in
> control, the customer is. The customer has always been in con-
> trol. Even the "poor people." *Especially* the poor people.

177

Charles Schwab is to twenty-first-century investing what Martin Luther was to sixteenth-century religion. Schwab founded his company on the reformed principle that investing should be demystified and that everyone in America should have the opportunity to invest and share in the bounty that resulted in smart manipulation of capital. From the outset, however, he was also clear that these opportunities must be provided with the utmost integrity. Schwab did not want to build a company on the bones of decimated investors. His company's services were to be discounted, and its advice was to be limited, and its transactions must be above reproach.

In 1971, Chuck Schwab founded First Commander Corporation, whose name was changed to Charles Schwab & Co. in 1973. The business moved along nicely in the new niche of discount brokering, but it was considered nothing more than a faddish blip on the radar screens at the Merrill Lynch and Dean Witter headquarters. Just as Sears failed to see Wal-Mart, so full-service brokers underestimated the power of the Schwab message.

After substantially building the business, Schwab sold the firm to BankAmerica Corporation in 1982 for $55 million and joined the big bank's board. Five years later, he bought the firm back for $280 million when he realized that the then-struggling behemoth was never going to keep up with his desire to rapidly pioneer new approaches to packaging and selling financial services.

Today, Charles Schwab & Co. is one of the premier players in an industry that the company helped reinvent, primarily by creating a carefully targeted, superbly crafted financial services masterbrand. Key to this growth is the diversification of its businesses. In 1988, Schwab made 70 percent of its money on trades; in 1999, the mix was 58 percent on trades and 42 percent on nontrade revenue. (See Figure 8.1 for Schwab assets performance.)

Charles Schwab & Co. ranks in the top five in the United States in custody of household assets, well ahead of many banks. Aggregately, American investors have chosen to place 18 percent of their mutual fund cash flow into Schwab instruments, and mutuals are the primary entry point into equities investing for most of those individuals. In a 1998 national survey, Schwab was the most frequent choice among consumers of financial services as

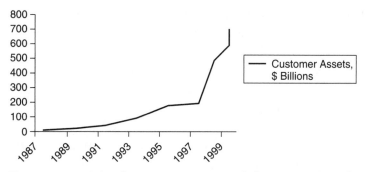

Figure 8.1   *Schwab customer asset growth from 1987 through 1999.*
Source: Company reports.

an alternative to their own banks. The attributes that were most often associated with the Schwab brand: "aggressive to help," "easy to communicate with," and "strong reputation for financial advice." What phrases could better explain why Schwab is winning the hearts of investors?[3]

One of the key reasons for the Schwab masterbrand's phenomenal growth is the company's unerring ability to anticipate what customers want next. Among the changes in financial services in which Schwab beat all or most of the competition to the punch: discount brokering (its flagship business), mutual funds portfolio building (OneSource), ubiquitous online trading (Schwab.com), multiple customer channels (brick-and-mortar, click-and-mortar, telephone), the marriage of discount brokering with referred independent investment advisors (Schwab AdvisorSource), and a new model for serving fee-based investment managers (Services to Investment Managers program).

OneSource Builds the Brand

The OneSource story is particularly telling, in that it demonstrates how the company expanded its masterbrand community, in this case directly toward an arena that was about to explode.

Schwab launched its Mutual Fund Marketplace in 1984 with approximately 100 no-load funds. As mutual funds became more popular, Schwab came up with a way to offer its customers a wider selection of no-load funds without charging them a transaction fee. The company negotiated service fees with the fund companies, which provided Schwab with 25 basis points, plus valuable data on the investing habits of the fund customers.

The company's OneSource was launched in 1992 with 90 funds as the first no-load, no-transaction-fee mutual funds "supermarket." By 1997, it had become the third largest funds brand in the country, just as the mutual funds frenzy hit its full stride. In 1999, OneSource was folded into Schwab's Mutual Fund Investors package, which serves as the entry point for customers into more than 1,500 funds, enabling the company to now hold funds assets exceeding $250 billion. Schwab's own proprietary funds group has also accumulated highly profitable assets of more than $100 billion. During the 1990s, Schwab's total funds assets increased 10-fold to about $600 billion. Profits increased by between 35 and 40 percent per year.

Strategically, OneSource is an expansion of the Schwab brand community, not simply a service extension. It provides Schwab customers with new ways to interact with the firm, and provides the firm new opportunities to learn what their customers need. The funds managers become part of the Schwab brand community, and look upon the firm as an important access point to massive numbers of investors. By working together, the funds companies and Schwab also learn about what is popular and what isn't among investors.

This is certainly spectacular business building, but it also helped construct a masterbrand that expands its arenas of expertise so rapidly that investors begin to believe that Schwab can be their one-stop shop for virtually any financial service they require. This, in turn, enables Schwab management to consider a wider future offering, possibly including traditional core banking services such as checking, savings, and loans.

Another important, but little-known aspect of Schwab's community building is their CEO Speaker Series, in which their high-end Signature Platinum customers are invited to listen in and contribute questions on a conference call with leading corporate CEOs. The series has included enlightening chats with Scott McNealy of Sun Microsystems; Andy Grove, Chairman of Intel; Herb Kelleher, Chairman and CEO of Southwest Airlines; and

Jack Welch, Chairman and CEO of General Electric. The Schwab masterbrand is enhanced by showing its clout as a host for such prestigious guests, and the CEOs get an opportunity to tell important investors why their companies deserve some attention.

How Schwab Employees Fortify Their Masterbrand

One of the reasons that Charles Schwab is a successful masterbrand community is because its employees are trained to be customer service reps first, then marketers, and finally, product specialists. They are taught to understand the needs of the investor and to align the company's programs to fit those needs, but to do so with the objectivity that can only come from a noncommission incentive system. If clients wish to obtain full financial planning, they are referred to a list of independent financial planners.

The Schwab customer is treated differently than in more traditional broker settings because of the unique relationship that Chuck Schwab sought to create when he first founded the firm. That relationship is encapsulated in the *Guidelines for Giving Investment Advice,* which is the commitment literally lived by the employees who advise customers. They read, in part:

> As Schwab employees, we pledge to act as the custodians of our customers' financial dreams. This pledge is both a promise and a commitment, an honor and a responsibility—it defines who we are as a company. Implicit in our pledge is . . . to offer advice that is free from the conflicts of interest found in commission-based broker relationships.

This is brand-focused service at its best, seamlessly fusing the meaning of the masterbrand with a commitment to out-service the competition.

On 13 March 1999, Charles Schwab & Co. celebrated its 25th anniversary by calling together its employees in a day-long meeting in San Francisco (live for 5,000 employees, broadcast live to 13,000 more across the globe). The event celebrated the longevity of the experiment that Wall Street was certain would die in its infancy. More than that, though, it was an opportunity for co-

SCHWAB'S MASTERBRAND MARKET*

Just as sophisticated navigational tools allow pilots to maneuver through the thickest fog, so too can timely market information help investors make savvy and profitable trades. Until recently, only the largest traders and institutional investors had ready access to such critical intelligence.

Continuing its drive to democratize investing, Charles Schwab & Co. is now leveraging the centrifugal force of the Internet to integrate many of its customers' trades, creating an accelerated flow of information and activity for its customers. Via the Internet, customers are able to easily access more and more of the information they need to make the most intelligent possible trading decisions. Using advanced technology, Schwab helps its customers share the benefits of real-time information about who is buying and selling at what volumes within its own computerized trading platform. According to industry sources, significant numbers of investors are migrating to these so-called internal markets where trades can also be less expensive.

Internalization is yet another way Schwab creates value for and loyalty from its brand community. Investors are often the beneficiaries of faster turnaround, stop-order protection, automatic execution guarantees, and other benefits that they often cannot receive from providers that primarily serve larger institutions. In short, although Schwab is certainly not the answer for all investors, their customers do obtain some advantages in leverage and financial managing capabilities that they might not obtain elsewhere.

All of this underlines the power of one of Schwab's central brand messages, specifically, that Schwab gives the individual investor an opportunity to play and win with the big dogs of Wall Street. This is the way a masterbrand grows and prospers . . . by creating a brand community that provides the information, support, and resources that enable its customers to do the same.

*Based on: Sandra Sugawara, "Schwab Shatters the Trading Mold," *The Washington Post*, 16 April 2000, pp. H01.

CEOs Chuck Schwab and David Pottruck to remind their people once again what the company is still all about, and for those "Schwabbies" to interact with one another, and to learn about all that they are and can do for customers.

Early in the program, Schwab and Pottruck told the story of visiting a local YMCA and seeing senior citizens on fixed incomes arrive for lunch and pay $1.60 for the meal. As Schwab pointed out, "That is not where you want to be having lunch when you are a senior citizen." He later commented that his biggest long-term worry is that today's generation of young people won't have the money to retire.

The audience that day responded emotionally to those remarks because its founder was speaking from the heart about social issues, not just financial matters, and they were issues Charles Schwab & Co. was actually doing something about. Later in the program, the audience viewed a video about a California family that invested heavily with Schwab in the 1980s, only to lose virtually all they had in the 1987 market meltdown. Through it all, the Schwab company gave the family time and assistance to work their way out of their problems, financial and otherwise. According to a member of the family, Schwab almost literally saved the clan, including from the vicissitudes of Wall Street. In any other company, such a testimonial might be so much hype, but with this company and this management, it's easy to see why they are on much more than a financial mission. It's more like a holy crusade.

Schwab management believes strongly that it must never stop revitalizing the mission of its employee community, nor must it ever take its people for granted. David Pottruck, who believes caring is a critical management tool, has repeatedly pointed out: "If we don't have good employees, we won't have customers."

Schwab Online: More Profitable Relationships

Once again, online relationships provide even more opportunities for a company to expand and strengthen its brand community. Online investing has proven to be another triumphant channel for Schwab, although not without technical problems from the server crashes that have plagued the e-commerce industry.

An estimated two-thirds of its customers now trade online, which facilitates quick turnaround service for them, as well as lower operating costs for Schwab. By 1999, Schwab's online assets exceeded $260 billion, compared with about 10 percent of that for E*Trade. They are doing it well, according to a 2000 J.D. Powers survey that ranked Schwab's online service as second among 13.[4] As Schwab customers become more comfortable with online transactions, the company can at least investigate opportunities to offer a myriad of other financial services.

Schwab attacks the online world from a different angle than its major competitors. The online "pure-play" companies tend to attract proportionately more day traders, whereas the traditional full-commission brokers are using their online ventures to extend their broker-advice models, supported by their proprietary research products. Schwab, on the other hand, positions online as part of a network of channels (including branches, telephone, and affiliated advisors). This more open-ended environment enables customers to choose when and where they access their investing, and a choice of which sources to use for research purposes. Karen Chang, head of Schwab's retail branch network puts it into a formula: "Schwab.com equals Schwab.future equals Schwab.community."[5]

The Challenges Ahead

Success breeds competition, usually in the form of replication. The company faces a growing army of competitors who have figured out that Schwab's strategies may be the mainstream of the future. On one flank, deep-discount e-brokers like E*Trade and Ameritrade are adding more services to bulk up their value proposition, and spending hundreds of millions of newfound investor capital in advertising and promotional support. On the other side of the battlefield, full-commission brokers like Merrill Lynch have seen the light after years of insisting it was the proverbial gnat not worth swatting. Merrill is also offering a fee-based (versus transaction-based) compensation option as well, to be more closely aligned with Schwab's approach, plus online discount trading.

Yet, what has propelled Schwab in the past, and will likely serve it well in the future, is not simply the individual service features it offers, but the empowering of its individual investors, and the brand community that it has created to support them. Those pillars, regardless of competitive moves, are not likely to weaken any time soon.

Charles Schwab & Co. management has made the decision to focus their business model on one major market, financial services. For those companies with multiple brands and a myriad of targets to entice, masterbrand building can get considerably more challenging. Our next chapter explores how best to unify the diverse company.

Unify the Diverse Community

We must all hang together . . . or assuredly we shall
hang separately.
—Benjamin Franklin, to fellow signers
of The Declaration of Independence

D on't be deceived by neatly boxed organizational charts or well-meaning promises of future cooperation between divisions; today's multibrand company must market all of its brands under a unified strategy, or fall prey to those that do.

Prospects are too distracted, customer loyalty is too fragile, value propositions are too vulnerable, and technological advantages are too fleeting for companies to function with anything less than a fully unified community of brands. Even in those circumstances when sister brands are not compatible in the eyes of end users, they need to be cooperatively integrated in the back room.

Unifying the Original Multibrand Company

There is no shortage of challenges when some multibrand companies attempt to build a single-brand identity throughout the

187

organization. From where should the overarching identity originate? Who should lead a unification of brands once the need is identified? Why should brands that don't market to the same customers be linked in any way? What if the brands' identities can actually harm their siblings?

The welfare of the company-wide masterbrand must be the highest priority in such decisions, if for no other reason than because today's multibrand company is tomorrow's takeover candidate or merger partner. When the company must act as a company-of-the-whole, the value and leverage of individual brands is superceded by the mandate of the entire organization. In other words, the priorities of individual product brands should be subservient to the needs of the masterbrand, except in those rare cases where one or two major brands essentially *are* the company because they generate the lion's share of the revenue and earnings.

Multibranded companies—thanks largely to the brand management system that Procter & Gamble pioneered decades ago—still tend to raise relatively high partitions between brand groups and business units, and between marketing and nonmarketing work teams. The original intent was that different brands needed to be run as different businesses that dealt with their own sets of issues, and might even compete with one another in the marketplace. Unfortunately, such brands were also competing inefficiently for the attention and resources of management and support teams. (That, of course, is why P&G shifted to category management teams that identified the building of the "company share" as their first priority.)

In such circumstances, it behooves management to find a central rallying point for these disparate groups, a strategy in which they can share in the benefits of fighting for the same brand, namely the masterbrand. The key to making that happen is to have a mutual understanding of what the company stands for in terms of customer benefits, regardless of how closely or distantly it is associated by name with its own marketed brands.

Types of Multibranded Companies: What Kind of Decentralized Community Do You Manage?

Multibranded companies and diverse internal environments may be organized in any number of alternative models:

"Banner"-branded companies. These are sometimes referred to as *corporate-dominant,* because they operate with a single enterprise-wide brand, which may or may not be the corporate parent's name, and whose banner brand is applied to most of its products or services. IBM, as one example, uses its banner brand in the vast majority of circumstances, but has created strong, yet narrow support behind its ThinkPad, Aptiva and NetVista brands, with IBM as their parentage branding. (The one major exception is IBM's Lotus subsidiary brand, which carried such pre-takeover equity that it was thought best to leave well enough alone.)

In contrast, the Virgin, Volvo, and Xerox brand names are used for virtually all products and services marketed by those companies.

Individual product/service brands. These are companies in which individual products or services are branded differently and are generally managed as discrete businesses, all within a hidden corporate halo of the company brand. Henkel KGaA, Procter & Gamble, Kao Corporation, and other multinationals with hundreds of brands in complex architectures are examples of this type of discrete branding approach. These may include brands with varying degrees of visible links to their parent, depending upon relevance and natural associations. Sara Lee Corporation now distributes 31 different brands. Some are close in to the Sara Lee food heritage (Sara Lee baked goods and meat products), others are a bit farther out from the corporate center but still in the food category (Hillshire Farms foods and Jimmy Dean products), and others are about as far from food as you can get (Hanes and Playtex apparel, Kiwi shoe care), but may share some common distribution and sales channels.

Tiered-branding architectures. These include *range* brands, which cover a spectrum of products or services under a shared positioning, and *line* brands, which are usually function-linked brands under the aegis of the original brand entry in the category(ies). Nestlé, Gillette, and Sony are companies that employ these more complex branding strategies.[1]

Multiple-business-unit or divisional organizations. These are prevalent in virtually all companies, even those with only one brand in the marketplace. We add this classification to the list because interunit rivalries and independent actions can be just as distracting from the creation of a strong masterbrand as differentiated brands. In many companies, the actions of the heads of business units and divisions—in the name of initiative and friendly competition—frequently consider their own businesses to have priority over company-wide issues. Although that may encourage "intrepreneurialism," it can also cause crippling disunity and dysfunctions, just when the company most needs to rally around its masterbrand identity.

The Balance Dance

General Electric CEO, Jack Welch, once told his managers: "You can't grow long-term if you can't eat short-term. Anybody can manage short. Anybody can manage long. Balancing those two things is what management is."[2] When it comes to managing brand portfolios, the same kind of balancing expertise is a prerequisite for command.

There are inevitable tensions between brand teams and between operating units. It is easy to underestimate the complex relationships that can exist within marketing staffs and other groups throughout a multibrand company. At times, it seems that the brands and their stewards dance around one another, seeking the attention and resources of management, vying for the love of customer and constituency.

The first instinct of individual brand marketeers, of course, is to protect and shepherd their own brands and to give secondary consideration to company-wide brand-building programs. When you're down to the last day to complete the global marketing plan for Duracell batteries, why should you devote even 10 minutes to worrying about the reputation of Gillette when the parent brand is rarely linked to the shelf brand? If you are responsible for the marketing of the Lincoln brand of luxury cars, which is broadly known to be a Ford Motor Company product, you may not be inclined to spend much energy fretting about the brand identity of the Ford masterbrand when you've got hordes of competitors storming over the nearest ridge.

Yet, whether the connection between a parent company's overarching brand and individual brands is explicit or not, the intersecting of those brands will likely have a significant impact on the business. Granted, it is common to share R&D, new product development, sales, and administrative services among divisions for cost reasons. We are talking here, though, about the *brand* reasons to more uniformly unify the work of distinct business units. Customers and investors are usually very conscious of the link between individual and company-wide brands. In addition, it will inevitably become important internally, as the fate of employee-partners working on one brand is affected by the fate of its sister brand.

Some CEOs believe that a diversified portfolio of businesses and brands is an important hedge against risk, assuming that those businesses fall within the company's core competencies. Yet, many ensure that the company-wide brand is given its due as the masterbrand in the portfolio. Jack Welch has run one of the most valuable and diverse corporations in the world, but he is an advocate for a unified General Electric enterprise-wide brand strategy. Michael Eisner insists that Disney's stable of brands work as a team at every turn, because he knows the power of multiple brands working as one. Marriott International is now marketing a wide spectrum of hospitality brands, but they are marketed within the sharply defined parameters of the Marriott masterbrand.

Although organizational branding issues are rarely black or white, the balancing of individual brand or unit freedoms and the company's need for a unifying masterbrand can often be reciprocal. Some companies are in a state of transition from a dominant or banner-brand place in the continuum, to a multibrand stage, particularly as they seek new growth. However, creating semi-autonomous brands or business units can add even more difficulty to the already onerous task of achieving profitable expansion, as lack of unity causes inefficiencies and unnecessary management distractions. (See Figure 9.1 for the relationship of independent versus unified units.)

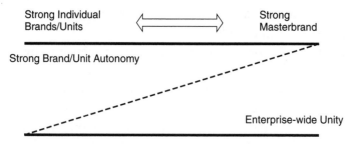

Figure 9.1   *Brand/unit independence versus unified masterbrand.*

Tracking Your MBE: Multibrand Efficiency

In our collective experience, a proactive approach to a unified masterbrand strategy is preferable to avoiding the issue because of a desire for decentralization. However, it does require that egos be checked at the door and candor be the currency of the day. If it is clear in your organization that multiple brands are not sufficiently linked, we recommend the following:

- Conduct a strategic research initiative that explores the relationship between corporate and subsidiary brands. This should include large helpings of internal and brand community attitude research that dissects the overlapping of target perceptions about brand and company.

- Develop and implement short- and long-term external marketing programs that are specifically designed to capitalize upon strengths and to heal vulnerabilities that are the product of the relationship (or lack of same) between the parent and individual brands, and between the individual brands themselves.

- Consider a long-term internal marketing program that aggressively communicates to employee-partners that they work for *one* company with *one* masterbrand and multiple individual brands, all of which are designed to multiply the company's strength in the marketplace.

One analytical approach to look at evaluates the relationship between company and individual brands, in terms of what we call *multibrand efficiency* (or MBE for short, because you can't have too many acronyms in your business). We believe that MBE can be an important tool in determining the most productive ways to manage multiple brands.

In Chapter 2, we noted that a brand community arises when the brand is no longer owned solely by its sponsoring company, and the resulting relationships among and between customers and company generate benefits and loyalty. Multibrand efficiency is a measure of how efficiently multibrand companies are able to create and sustain that community of relationships. The more closely the company and individual brands are in sync—reinforcing one another's strengths, cloaking vulnerabilities, avoiding duplication and cannibalization—the greater the efficiency factor. Importantly, this efficiency can be accumulated in the marketplace and/or internally within the company.

Let's use a hypothetical example of a multiple-brand packaged-goods firm that we'll call Clean Corp., which markets leading household, outdoor, and food brands. If Clean Corp. management wished to determine if their multiple brands were operating in maximum synchronization, they might embark on an MBE study that would measure such key metrics as positive awareness, brand preference, brand performance/importance indices, intent to purchase, and elasticity (the degree to which the brands could be stretched into new markets).

In the case of Clean Corp., the strength of the corporate brand name would likely show significant compatibility with similarly labeled cleaning brands in the same product categories, such as bathroom cleansers or dishwashing liquids. There might be slightly weaker associations with other household products that have less of a cleaning function, such as paper towels. Associations would be still weaker for household products that have nothing to do with hygiene, such as an insecticide. There could potentially be some counterproductive associations for food brands marketed by the company.

The traditional approach to such issues is to simply brand the products according to their proximity to the associations of the corporate or banner brand. For that reason, Clean Corp.'s food brands would carry little or no mention of the parent company on their packaging.

However, is it possible that the brands could work more closely together, without necessarily sharing similar identities with consumers? For example, how might brand teams on the household cleaning brands share potentially valuable information about Americans' need for hygiene with the brand teams on the insecticide brand, since bugs are an indication of some hygiene problems? Couldn't new product research among the food brands be helpful in determining how many Americans are staying at home for meals, which could be leveraged by Clean Corp.'s presentations to the trade about new product opportunities in a wide variety of categories? These synergies might happen spontaneously, but they can be guaranteed by establishing a formal cross-pollination process that established the metrics and measurements of the company's MBE.

Gauging MBE can help companies manage their brand strengths more efficiently and anticipate problems before they arise. However, the ultimate benefit may be that the company—no matter how disparate its brand types and identities—can enhance its leverageability in the marketplace. The result can be a well-coordinated, multifaceted masterbrand community, both in terms of the strong relationships between brand and company and customer, as well as in the way that brands interact and build the masterbrand in its various marketplaces.

Mastering Bi-Level Managing: Marriott and Tricon

One of the most urgent issues that the management of multibrand companies must deal with is how to motivate their people and demonstrate their leadership on two levels at the same time. That is, toward which brand or brands should employee-partners and other stakeholders demonstrate their primary loyalty? Should they show their loyalty toward the individual product or service brand to which they are closest (or, in the case of the corporate staff, the corporate brand)? Or should they direct their resources more toward the brand that is best known among their key target audiences, or among the general public?

Marriott International

Marriott International is an example of a brand-centric, multi-brand company. The company is well on its way to achieving its goal of owning or operating 2,000-plus properties by the end of 2000. Flying such diverse brand flags as Renaissance, Ritz-Carlton, Marriott Vacation Villas, TownePlace Suites, Courtyard by Marriott, Ramada International, Executive Residences, Fairfield Inn, and mainline Marriott, the company now encompasses virtually the entire spectrum of accommodation options, both throughout the United States and abroad. (See Table 9.1 for a listing of the Marriott masterbrand family.)

The Marriott masterbrand value proposition that strategically tethers the properties is the guest benefit of pleasant predictability, based on the sound view that the last thing business and leisure travelers want is surprises.

Management uses the Marriott masterbrand as a reinforcement of quality when needed (such as in the cases of Courtyard and Fairfield Inn), and minimizes its role when it might interfere with a property's reputation (Ritz-Carlton). However, the employee-partners and constituencies of the company are members of the Marriott masterbrand family, regardless of how prominently the Marriott branding is employed in particular properties.

The "By Marriott" parentage branding strategy enables the various chains to tie together their loyalty programs under the Marriott Rewards subbrand. Although this strategy may have appeared risky in terms of over extending the brand, it has brought instead a synergy and a wholeness that is less and less common in the hospitality industry. Marriott is increasingly seen by travelers as an accommodations solution, overarched by a highly regarded masterbrand, common mission, and common commitment to excellence within the value proposition that is offered by each property classification.[3]

Tricon Global Restaurants

Tricon Global Restaurants is another fine example of a multi-branded company with a strong sense of company-wide brand. The company operates more than 30,000 Taco Bell, KFC, and

Table 9.1   *The Marriott Family of Brands*

Hotel Brand	Targets and Role	Marriott Masterbrand Role
Marriott Hotels, Resorts, and Suites	Moderate-upscale, full-service hotels and suites	Flagship brand, serves as parent brand for most company properties
Courtyard by Marriott	Moderate, business-oriented hotels	Endorsing brand
Marriott Residence Inn	Extended-stay, business-oriented hotels	Sponsoring brand
Fairfield Inn by Marriott	Low-end motels/hotels, leisure and business markets	Endorsing brand
TownePlace Suites by Marriott	Moderate extended-stay, leisure, and business markets	Endorsing brand
SpringHill Suites by Marriott	Upper-moderate suites, business and leisure markets, esp. women and families	Endorsing brand
Marriott Executive Apartments	Upscale long-term business apartments	Sponsoring brand
ExecuStay by Marriott	Mid-upscale business all-in-one housing solution	Endorsing brand
Ramada International Hotels and Resorts	Moderate hotels for business and leisure markets	No name brand role, but Marriott Rewards is promoted
The Ritz-Carlton Hotel Company, LLC	Upscale hotels for business and leisure markets	No promoted affiliation to Marriott, but linked at Web site

Pizza Hut stores (McDonald's has about 25,000 outlets), with total sales exceeding $20 billion in 1999. Each chain has strong advertising that keeps the heat on the competition and provides employees with a rallying point. Profit margins and sales have increased considerably since the chains have been united under a single retailing-oriented umbrella (for much of 1999, same-store sales were up between 2 and 12 percent for the three chains). In the past, these brands competed against one another within a larger corporate setting, and not to the benefit of the corporation as a whole. Now, they compete as a strategically more cohesive suite of retail-food powerhouses.

One of the small ways that CEO David Novak and his teams have built the Tricon masterbrand is by employing stupid-smart gimmicks to excite their employee-partners about their respective chains. At Novak's encouragement, internal recognition awards were created and celebrated, including the Pizza Hut Big Cheese and Taco Bell Royal Order of the Pepper awards. Novak has also taken other small but critical steps to ensure that the Tricon units work with one another within their brand community, including the following:

- *Rallying the franchisees.* The most critical sector of the Tricon brand community is its franchisees. In the summer of 1999, Novak held a barbecue for 75 franchisees in what was dubbed "the Big Love-in." One of the reported benefits from that event and others like it, was the increased camaraderie that resulted between corporate and franchisee management.

- *Rallying the employee-partners.* As a consequence of the "Love-in" and other events, each chain's people began to see their counterparts as partners in the brand community, rather than only as rivals for marketing or development dollars. Employees are encouraged to share best practices across brand units to profit from one another's business tactics.

- *Rallying the customer.* Tricon is now opening a series of three-in-one outlets, which help customers to see that the quality and value in one chain can be found in the others. The units were averaging sales of $2 million annually by 1999, compared with $750,000 on average in the industry. A facilities committee ensures that franchises are happy with the treatment of their respective brands. Not only does this multibrand-store strategy reduce operating expenses, it helps create a visible partnership in the customers' eyes that will hopefully lead to greater preference for all three brands. In other words, the Tricon masterbrand that formally existed only in the minds of its stakeholders is hoping to further build on its synergism by going public.

The Tricon teams have demonstrated how a superlative master-brand community can be woven together with disparate parts.

Civilizing the Diversified

Larger, more diversified companies present special brand-building challenges, including:

- Marketing potentially competitive multiple-brand representatives in the same category (e.g., Unilever, Kao Corporation)

- Wrangling with counterproductive rivalries and fiefdoms (e.g., interdivisional bickering at General Motors)

- Balancing the ongoing priorities between headquarters and regional staffs when geographical distance complicates multi-brand managing (e.g., Nestlé, Gillette, and Citigroup)

- Managing one company of brands aimed at a wide spectrum of targets in a widening brand community (all of the above)

Often, the brand stewards from one division or company have a hard time even discussing pancompany brand building to those in sister organizations that appear to be in completely different kinds of businesses.

Management challenges become even more onerous when the unit brand is stronger than the masterbrand in the minds of employees, investors, and others. That can be the case because of the heritage of the company, the stronger attributes of the operating unit, or because no actions have been taken to strengthen the masterbrand. Do viewers care when they are watching a hit NBC program that General Electric owns that network? (GE management certainly cares when declines in advertiser revenue could threaten a less well-funded organization.) When the L.A. Dodgers are losing, does it matter that they are owned by Rupert Murdoch's News Corporation? (It does when Murdoch can use his media clout to rebuild fan enthusiasm for the team.) Is it important that Honda makes Acura? (Yes, if a car buyer is looking for dependability; no, if he or she is looking for luxury expertise.)

Sara Lee Corporation is a born-again masterbrand organization whose management made the decision in 1997 to convert from a traditional manufacturer and distributor to a value-added marketer of major brands, largely by outsourcing a majority of its production. Sara Lee's corporate goal is to build leadership consumer brands in a broad spectrum of food and nonfood categories. That masterbrand objective positively affects the sense of unity among its people, in the recruiting of managers who are interested in using the full synergy of the corporation, and in the way Wall Street gauges the company's strategic direction and sense of purpose.

Yet, despite its clear enterprise-wide masterbrand goals, Sara Lee Corporation is also a highly decentralized organization, with 140,000 employees in 40 countries, who work in what the company describes as "discrete profit centers, each led by an operating executive with a high degree of authority and accountability for the performance of that business."[4]

In verticalizing across horizontal markets, Sara Lee was among the first in its industry to follow the lead of other firms in the computer and apparel industries that contract out much of their manufacturing, often leading to higher returns, and permitting management to focus on new products, managing brands, and building market share. Sara Lee also chose to extend its Sara Lee brand name within the food industry and beyond baked goods, but it has no plans as yet to push its flagship brand into nonfood areas in which it competes, such as pantyhose and fashion accessories.

Sara Lee Corporation is an example of a diversified company that has not let its decentralized approach stand in the way of creating a strong company-wide masterbrand with specific masterbrand objectives that are well known and practiced by its community members.

Johnson & Johnson is another corporate giant that sticks to a diversification strategy, even in the face of periodic criticism of its business strategy. J&J is a $25 billion corporation with three divisions: professional (medical equipment and supplies sold to practitioners), pharmaceutical (proprietary drugs), and consumer (with well-known brands such as Tylenol, Band-Aid, and Neutrogena), each in the $7 to 10 billion revenue range. The corporation operates as 188 companies and 31 principal affiliates, only a dozen of which fly the Johnson & Johnson banner.

Despite its decentralized operating structure, J&J manages to sustain a unified corporate culture. As we mentioned in an earlier chapter, this culture is codified in its famous 50-year old credo, which could be considered the first example of a mission for a masterbrand and its supporting brand community. The credo focuses on its masterbrand community members, as indicated by these excerpts:

> We believe our first responsibility is to the doctors, nurses, and patients, and to mothers and fathers . . .

> . . . Our suppliers and distributors must have an opportunity to make a profit . . .

> We are responsible to our employees . . . everyone must be considered as an individual . . .

> We are responsible to the communities in which we live and work . . .

> Our final responsibility is to our stockholders . . .

J&J builds into its employee-partner training periodic discussions about what the credo means in terms of ethical business behavior. In these "credo challenge" discussions, managers are encouraged to examine the credo in terms of their existing business situations and to suggest how the credo might be made more relevant. By all accounts, the people of these disparate companies, to one degree or another, feel as if they are part of one, value-driven organization, propelled by an over-arching masterbrand.

Gap and Levi Strauss: Different Lanes down the Same Road

Corporate diversification is not a license to de-integrate enterprise-wide sales and marketing programs. CEOs routinely put the company's entire welfare ahead of any single unit's needs, and nowhere is that more important than in establishing a masterbrand management strategy within a multibrand organization. Here are two companies whose histories are interwoven, and which are tackling that challenge in different ways and with varying degrees of success.

The Gap, Inc.

It's easy to forget what some companies were like before they made it to the top. Founder Donald Fisher and his wife opened the first The Gap (named after the famous "generation gap") in San Francisco in 1969, primarily to sell Levi's jeans and records and tapes. When Levi Strauss was ordered by the FTC to release price controls, the Fishers dropped prices and margins suffered. The Gap developed private labels to stay alive, but its outlets and apparel began to lose their appeal.

When he discovered Millard (Mickey) Drexler at Ann Taylor in 1983, Don Fisher found the person who could bridge an even more important "gap," the one between faddish fashion and solid brand building. Drexler's creative insights and energy have transformed The Gap, Inc. from a one-dimensional, second-tier chain into an apparel powerhouse masterbrand that overarches The Gap (and GapKids and babyGap), Old Navy, and Banana Republic retail brands. Drexler is driven to make The Gap brands as ubiquitous as Coke and Nike . . . combined.

The relationship between The Gap and its sister brands is clear (at least internally), yet subtle. The Gap is everyperson's premium outlet for consistent style. Banana Republic and Old Navy are successful flankers whose value propositions bracket above and below The Gap.

Banana Republic has left behind its safari image and has caught the demand wave for haute casual, targeting 25- to 49-year-old busy urban professionals. For several years, the division held back marketing spending until the brand could find its voice. In the fall of 1999, Banana Republic decision makers decided to begin moving away from The Gap image to reinforce its own, more sophisticated imagery. With minimal advertising support, Banana Republic is reportedly holding its own and then some in the highly competitive, premium casual wear sector. The brand has also taken a more singular approach to store merchandising and event promotion, including such events as "Screen on the Green" in Manhattan, an exclusive party on the rooftop of Bryant Park Grill, and a chauffeured ride home for Union Square shoppers in San Francisco.

However, it is Mickey Drexler's Old Navy creation that has stolen the show. (He got the idea from a potential rival who indiscreetly—and prematurely—bragged to the press that he could create a cheap knockoff of The Gap.) Old Navy was designed to be a middle-market fighting flanker that enabled The Gap to compete at lower price points without sacrificing style or endangering The Gap and Banana Republic margins. Old Navy took flanking beyond the flank, though, with arguably the best value proposition in retailing, triggering the "chic cheap" phenomenon that lures Americans who love to talk about how little they paid for their hip look. Its stores boast state-of-the-industry merchandising displays that make shopping fun again, and its pointedly off-center advertising bolsters its hip image.

How far can The Gap, Inc. ride "chic cheap?" As far as it wants. Old Navy pulled down $1 billion in sales from 282 stores, in just the first three years of its existence. Industry analysts now estimate that Old Navy will surpass the flagship The Gap stores in revenue sometime in 2000 and that it will account for more sales than The Gap, babyGap, and Gapkids combined by 2004. Old Navy is a case of the child outgrowing the parent, but without leaving home.

The entire The Gap, Inc. corporation has rediscovered its reason for being as a masterbrand and as a stable of retail brands, despite the fact that most consumers do not likely know that the three chains are owned by the same corporation. Over time, management has learned that every employee benefits from, and that his or her work is enhanced by, a stronger understanding of what The Gap masterbrand is all about. The company runs a rigorous interviewing process to recruit individuals for their management training programs and, once in, those recruits receive continuous indoctrination in what the three brands mean in the marketplace *and* what it means to work for an organization that applies the same metrics and measurement rigors to all of its businesses.

Publicly, The Gap, Banana Republic, and Old Navy are separate retail brands. However, like Procter & Gamble, they are part of a superbly managed masterbrand to employees, strategic providers, investors, and other members of their wider brand community.

Levi Strauss & Co.

In recent years, Levi Strauss & Co. has been attempting to rebound from significant losses in its jeans lines and has embraced segmentation to heal its wounds. No longer content to be "the jeans people," Levi Strauss now hopes to be the "casual apparel authority." In so doing, it is transforming itself into a brand-managing company that now markets multiple brands, in addition to its existing Dockers and Slates lines, with each focused on a different youth audience to compete with the strong branding of Lee, Tommy Hilfiger, and The Gap/Old Navy, as well as strong upstarts such as Mudd, Arizona, Fubu, LEI, Kikwear, and the like.

A central challenge facing Levi Strauss is whether a company that was driven by the ubiquitous acceptance of denim can successfully become a multibrand company without losing the brand soul that has attracted millions to its fold worldwide. That may have been a fairly simple goal to achieve when Dockers and Slates were successfully launched on top of a robust Levi's line, but since the flagship brand sales have been flagging, the challenge becomes considerably more difficult.

Since 1998, the company has been trying new things in a determined effort to recapture its brands' perceived coolness among the right age groups. For example, Levi Strauss introduced the premium-priced Red Line brand of jeans as a completely separate flanker to its main lines, and the Dockers division has also launched the K-1 line to appeal to hipper audiences. One of the key subchallenges in such a case is whether the organization itself can change to accommodate the change in the marketplace.

At Levi Strauss, they reworked their marketing planning and implementation approaches to fit the new marketplace realities. The old organization was reportedly meeting-driven and tended to overprocess decisions, yet such shortcomings didn't have a negative impact on the seemingly endless strength of the jeans brand. In today's hypercompetitive casual apparel marketplace, however, mistakes cost more. A while back, the company missed some key signals, including the surge of wider pant legs among status-conscious young people, the opportunity for wrinkle-free khakis, and the need to de-emphasize distribution among déclassé outlets like Wards. The flagship brand also suffered from a wider trend away from previously dominating brands from the 1980s, a phenomenon that periodically has hit similar brand giants, such as Nike, Microsoft, and McDonald's, among others.

Levi Strauss is a masterbrand whose heritage has always been an enormous asset, but which also creates new challenges for a company seeking to redefine itself in the marketplace and within its own walls. Despite its recent difficulties, a good many onlookers are betting that the company will right its masterbrand, as did its old retailer partner, The Gap, during the 1990s.

Can a Corporate Culture Be a Brand?

A brand has historically been that which is represented to the customer. But what does *represented* mean in a transparent organization where customers can play product designer and influencers of company organizations? Why must a brand be only that which is pointed outward? Why, in fact, can't a brand, or at least a key part of a brand, be what is lived on the inside of the company, and even be the single most influential determinant to what is finally represented to the outside world?

When Durk I. Jager was promoted to handle the helm at Procter & Gamble in 1998, he was described as looking like General Patton arriving with the Third Army. The P&G general certainly didn't slap around any soldiers, but just about everything else has been. Procter & Gamble remains the leading force in packaged goods, with $40 billion in revenue powered by more than 300 brands in 140 countries. What Procter has not yet acquired, however, at least in its current CEO's opinion, is the kind of corporate culture that encourages out-of-the-box thinking. That deficiency, he has publicly declared, could cost the company its goal of reaching $70 billion in revenue by 2005. (The 2005 target date was pushed back from 2003 when it became clear that it was unrealistic, given the plateauing of key brands and maturation of markets.)

Procter & Gamble management has historically resisted any

attempt to create a corporate brand that might overshadow its individual product brands. Yet, the culture and operations of the organization, often referred to as "the P&G way," are so sharply defined and so steeped in tradition that they have been the cause for significant success, as well as for some concern. In fact, author and former P&Ger, Charles Decker, was able to identify 99 P&G principles and practices, which covered whole clusters of behavior from "nothing happens unless it is on paper" to "show what you say, say what you show" to "consumers buy products, but they choose brands." Anyone who has ever worked for, or with, P&G knows that these principles are as real as the brands they support, and nearly as tangible.

Management's aversion to corporate branding notwithstanding, these unwritten rules of the road are crucial components of the Procter & Gamble psyche and of its overarching masterbrand. Yet, isn't the brand that which is sold, and the culture the environment in which it is nurtured? Yes, but an internal environment as solidified and pervasive as at Procter & Gamble *is* part of what the company sells. It sells its disciplined approach to category management to what the company calls its "customers," the retail trade. It sells its rigorous training to potential recruits in much the same way that the U.S. Army sells its educational opportunities to its own recruits. Most important, P&G sells and resells to its own people the need for precision and performance in their work.

Despite being a 30-year P&G veteran himself, Durk Jager openly criticized the organization's culture that "procterizes" people, saying, "At P&G, we tend to put people into a P&G box, a proctoid box, where certain behaviors, and institutionalized ways of acting, are accepted."[5] Even before taking over the company reins in December of 1998, Jager envisioned a more open society within the fortress in Cincinnati: "Great ideas generally come from conflict—a dissatisfaction with the status quo . . . I'd like to have an organization where there are rebels."[6] Management-sanctioned disagreement has never been part of the P&G way, and it will be interesting to see if such a change in culture results in a change in the Procter & Gamble masterbrand.

"The core business is innovation," said Jager. "If we innovate well, we will ultimately win. If we innovate poorly, we won't win."

However, when Durk Jager says "innovate," he is talking about innovating the way that P&Gers *think*, not just what end products they produce. He hopes to significantly expand the company's capacity to out-innovate competition, which will guarantee its future. In fact, Jager has been on a company-wide search for unboxed thinkers who have been squelched in the past, but who hold the key to new growth for the company.

So, how has all this company-wide transformation affected the established brand management system at P&G? In July of 1999, Procter launched two new global products, Dryel home dry-cleaning kit and Swiffer sweeper system, after only 18 months in test market. That may sound like a slow death march in Silicon Valley, but it's warp speed compared with the eight-year testing and rollout of Pampers disposable diapers in the 1960s. In addition, those new brands really are global, carrying the same brand name, packaging, and marketing programs worldwide—a first for P&G. Even the formulized P&G advertising began getting a facelift in recent years.

The organization has also been restructured to fit the new Procter & Gamble masterbrand. The old global bureaucracy with four geographical divisions was apparently not enabling innovation, so Jager has revamped the organization into seven product groups, each of which is global in scope.

Procter & Gamble may not be a consumer brand, but it is most definitely a business-to-business and internal masterbrand of the highest caliber. This may be one of the reasons why former P&G CEO, Ed Artzt, pointed out as early as 1991 that people want to know about the company behind the products. In his view, separating the P&G name from its brands ignored what consumers wanted to know.

Durk Jager is changing the Procter & Gamble *masterbrand*, from the inside out, by changing the way his people think about their businesses. Ironically, the company that created the modern concept of brand may be among the last to recognize that its own masterbrand is undergoing the greatest change of all.[7]

MANAGING YOUR MANDATE

The political slopes are slick, indeed, in multibrand organizations. The product managers, marketing managers, or brand managers all have the same goal: Defend and grow what is theirs. The group managers have larger folds but similar ambitions. Management is often bred from the same strain, torn between the sanctity of individual brands or category management goals, and the needs of the corporation as a whole.

In some companies that market multiple brands, however, there is a growing realization that not all is being done that could be done to make their organization-wide operations as efficient as possible. By rethinking how they have organized their brand-building programs and how they interrelate to one another, management has an opportunity to positively affect such efficiencies.

Questions You Should Be Asking To begin the process of growing healthy unity within multibrand companies, or those with rival business units, first consider these questions:

Is the current brand architecture within the company, intentionally or not, promoting cooperation or less-than-healthy competition? What is the relationship between the company-wide brand and individual product/service brands? Is there a firm but flexible strategic plan for how these two sets of brand should synergistically work with one another to build total company business? How are decisions made about the role that the parent and individual brands should play? How are marketing support funds allocated to each? When a new brand is introduced, what is the process for determining how it will be supported and positioned relative to the overall company-wide brand?

It is a mistake to let the relationship between overarching master brand and individual brands/units develop on its own. The development process and the relationship itself should be carefully managed to derive the maximum impact from the masterbrand, while leaving the individual brands an opportunity to grow and blossom.

To which brand(s) do your company's employee-partners feel closest? Which of the brands in your stable do they understand the best?

(Continued)

To which are they most likely to be loyal, given limited resources and attention time? Does one brand tend to dominate discussions about the company as a whole? Are one or two brands likely to be the ones cited when examples of success or failure are raised? Answers to these questions may indicate how skewed the organization is toward one brand or another, and will help determine how difficult it will be to unite all brands within a single, integrated matrix.

What specific obstacles stand in the way of a closer link between brands in the company? Has the heritage of the company been the most important reason why independent brands have not been more closely linked? Are there real or perceived differences in target markets, brand positionings, and personalities, and other strategic components that are consistently raised as reasons to discourage company-wide brand initiatives? These and other arguments are certainly legitimate, but they do not prevent the multibrand company from finding common strengths to capitalize upon.

What are those commonalities between individual brands and the parent brand that, if capitalized upon, might increase the total company impact in the marketplace? It's not difficult to determine if such common elements exist, and whether they can be leveraged to create greater awareness, positive attitudes, or sales volume for the company as a whole. The difficult part comes in assessing with objectivity the importance of these strengths, and their potential positive or negative effect on total company business.

Actions You Should Be Taking   Company leaders need to identify and act upon opportunities to fully integrate their parent and component brands. Here are some suggestions on how to go about that.

To begin, managers of individual brands or equivalent units should meet repeatedly, informally at first, perhaps over a meal, to discuss collaboratively the need to leverage the strengths of individual brands to create a more unified masterbrand presence. This will likely require evaluating the organization and its people to determine how well aligned they are to strengthen the masterbrand, in addition to meeting functional needs of individual brands.

However, under no circumstances are we suggesting that a successful organization should be completely reorganized overnight to better serve an enterprise-wide brand-building mission. Instead, individual brand managers can begin considering what evolutionary steps can be taken to gradually unify an overly disparate organization, while also maintaining key individual brand identities. As is the case in most of our recommendations, the CEO needs to be actively involved to provide sanction, guidance, and organizational momentum.

The deliberation process might include comparing the benefits and risks involved in closer integration between brands with the use of scenario analysis. This should be a candid assessment of what opportunities are missed because of less integrated planning and actions, and what downsides may occur if, for example, the individual brands are diminished in any way by the strengthening of the masterbrand's presence in the marketplace. The scenario format permits an apples-to-apples comparison of situations that could very well develop if a full masterbrand strategy is pursued.

When those initial discussions are completed, representatives of brand teams should create a pandivisional, multidisciplinary brand council to work with corporate staffs. This should be done to (1) fully analyze and assess the status of the enterprise-wide masterbrand among its customers and constituencies and (2) to determine where key customer needs, drivers of choice, and individual brand priorities might overlap. At the end of this process, the team members should begin to see some advantages to bolstering the masterbrand, assuming that it has not already been extended to its full potential.

The team might also create an empirically based metrics measurement by assessing the existing and potential multibrand efficiency (MBE) described earlier. This can be accomplished by quantitatively profiling how well individual brands work in sync with one another, how well they share resources, and how uniformly they are understood across relevant audiences.

As part of the strategic plan that may emerge from this process, the team should also carefully consider how internal and external online initiatives could help build the company-wide brand. Obviously, that should be a translation that is original and that is suited to the special conditions of online experiences, as opposed to a simple translation of the offline brand experience. In the coming years, the

(Continued)

> success of multibrand companies in multiplying their impact via a masterbrand strategy may very well depend on how efficiently they make use of powerful online channels.

*   *   *

None of this work is meant as a substitute for support of individual brands, but rather as a method of increasing those brands' leverage in the marketplace, through the use of the masterbrand.

Even the most integrated set of brands and operating units will fail to maintain momentum if they are outpositioned by competition. In our next chapter, we discuss the benefits and advantages that a well-constructed masterbrand community enjoys when it competes with more conventional rivals.

PART THREE

The World Outside
Maneuver the Masterbrand

CHAPTER

10

Outbrand the Competition

Get there first with the most men.
—Confederate General Nathan Bedford Forrest[1]

sked the secret of winning battles in the U.S. Civil War, Confederate General Nathan Bedford Forrest is said to have replied: "Get there first with the most men." Translated into today's Netspeak, Forrest's advice would be to "seize and exploit first mover advantage." However, in an age of Internet-based disintermediation, prolific alliances, and transparent organizations, it has become increasingly difficult to determine who—or what—your competition is.

By definition, strategic positioning means continuously adjusting your aim at a moving target. Fortunately, the rapid pace of technical and competitive developments on the Internet creates a virtual laboratory in which to test theories about strategic positioning and the evolution of competition. Whether you're actively engaged in making your masterbrand into an online brand community (brand.comm) or not, the emerging Internet economy offers a fast-forward preview of the forces and conditions that—sooner rather than later—will shape your company's future.

213

Positioning Is in the Eye of the Beholder

Positioning is not what a marketer does *to* a marketplace; it is "what a brand stands for in the minds of customers and prospects, relative to its competition, in terms of benefits and promises." Consequently, marketers can only use *"positioning prompts;"* the actual positioning is "consummated" in the minds of customers and prospects.[2] Nor are other brands the only competition. Rather, the brand must be positioned against the AAAA threat— *any and all alternatives*—that offers the same or improved benefits.

Internet-based disintermediation has created a whole new type of strategic threat to established brands, and given upstart start-ups the opportunity to leverage their first mover advantage. In this environment, outbranding doesn't mean outdoing your competitors at traditional branding. Instead, it means creating a masterbrand and not simply leveling the playing field, but lifting it to a higher plane. When companies find someone who can do a given job cheaper, faster, better, they may decide to outsource. To fully leverage your masterbrand, you must decide to *outbrand* the competition. That is, you must send it out, deploying your masterbrand within its wider brand community, where the whole becomes greater than the sum of its parts.

More than ever, brands today are owned by—and thus must be positioned in terms of—brand communities, which are becoming the staging ground for competition and strategic positioning. It sometimes seems as if the only surviving rule of strategic positioning is that there are *no* rules. There are, however, some guiding principles that can be derived from the experience of several companies that are in different stages of becoming masterbrands, online and off. Before we consider these examples and the lessons learned thus far, let's briefly review how the concept of strategic positioning itself is evolving.

Evolving toward Brand Communities

There are four ways to create value: through product, service, information, or affinity (a.k.a. trust). Although strategic positioning involves all four elements, the *focus* of competition tends to shift over long periods of history and as particular markets evolve.

As mass-manufactured markets mature, improved quality control and the leveling effects of technology create parity in product performance. Expected levels of product quality become table stakes for market entry. The key to differentiation thus shifts to *service* and Ted Levitt's "augmented product," that is, a commodity-plus-service that yields customer benefits (e.g., a PC and technical support).[3] The information and affinity elements of value creation remain latent (implicit in the offer of service and support).

With the service revolution of the last two decades, major competitors in many sectors of the economy are also approaching parity on service. That is, expected levels of *both* product performance and service are now seen as price of entry. As this happens, new ways of differentiating offers are emerging. Interactive technologies of the information revolution allow what we might call *augmented service* (e.g., Amazon.com's mass customization via customer self-service). As both product and service quality become less differentiated, *information* becomes the basis of competitive advantage (e.g., Citibank's enormous database of customer information). Affinity remains latent in the value creation process, but not for long.

With the rise of the knowledge-based economy and mass customization, *affinity* (or a feeling of closeness brought about by trust) becomes increasingly critical because developments such as mass customization or the creation of viable brand communities depend on customers' ability and willingness to share information with providers. Increasingly, providers need customers' *permission* to obtain and use such information. As permission-based marketing becomes the norm, the competitive focus shifts at last to affinity or trust itself (e.g., America Online's total caretaker approach to online management for its customers). (See Table 10.1 for the evolution of positioning focus.)

This shift in the focus of competitive positioning—from product to service and from information to affinity—can also be illustrated through the value propositions and related selling lines of several well-known brands. (Note that this sequence also traces the evolution from company-centric push marketing to the customer-centric *pull* market dynamics of the Internet.)

Table 10.1   *The Evolution of Focus in Competitive Positioning*

Focus of Competition	Stages of Competition			
	Mass Production	Service Revolution	Information Revolution	Knowledge Economy
				Product
Table stakes			Product	Service
		Product	Service	Information
Differentiation	Product	Service	Information	Affinity
	Service	Information	Affinity	
Latent	Information	Affinity		
	Affinity			

- "99 and 44/100's percent pure." (The *company* knows how to make a product.)
- "You're in good hands with Allstate." (The *company* knows how to provide a service.)
- "Have it your way." (The *customer* knows what she or he wants even better than the company does.)
- "Where do you want to go today?" (Let *us*—company and customer—work *together* to learn and meet your needs.)
- "Are you ready?" (The Internet will take us both on a journey to meet your needs.)

Affinity created within brand communities allows the customer intimacy needed to personalize and organize information as *knowledge*, yielding meaningful and relevant customer benefits. Personalized Web pages on Internet portals are one example of this phenomenon. The parallel in corporate structure is the rise of transparent, learning organizations. These thrive based not on any specific functional ability—what they *know* at any given point in time—but rather on their ability to *learn*, to constantly know new things and reinvent themselves accordingly.

In short, in a knowledge economy, companies no longer compete merely to sell customers a product or service. Rather, they compete for the right to get to know customers' needs and to represent their interests. The affinity and trust that are prerequisites for such customer intimacy become the focus of competitive positioning. Increasingly, such affinity and trust are created in the context of brand communities. In this environment, a masterbrand has an inherent advantage over any and all alternatives—including possible disintermediation by customers themselves.

When it comes to strategic positioning, masterbrands have several competitive advantages over other organizations, whether online or not. Specifically, a masterbrand can do the following:

- Create a strong sense of affinity and ownership among brand community members through voluntary actions that demonstrate shared values (sometimes at the risk of alienating "outsiders")

- Continuously reinvent—and even cannibalize—itself to stay a step ahead of the competition and maintain first mover advantage

- Hedge against changes in technology that threaten its very existence

- Make a virtue of necessity by riding the coattails of successful first movers

- Create, maintain, and leverage its most fundamental asset—the brand community in which it operates

- Convert potential liabilities such as disintermediation into assets (new forms of remediation)

- Turn competitors into allies

Let's now consider the strategic positioning advantages of companies that want to become, or remain, masterbrands. Many of these companies are also are in the process of interactivating their brands and becoming online brand communities, or brand.comms.

Building a Community with an Attitude

From motorbikes and cars to coffee and computers, brand communities vary widely in scope and character. In saying that a brand promise must be specific and relevant, we are implicitly saying that no one brand can or should be all things to all people. In contrast, a brand community necessarily includes the ins by excluding the outs (even those who are potential customers). A brand's value proposition may be initially tailored to appeal to and to attract specific types of customers. Once in existence, however, a brand community—like any truly voluntary association—becomes self-defining and self-sustaining. One sign of a robust brand community is that it actively resists heavy-handed direction from any quarter.

Brand communities not only unite, they also divide. Being in or out of a particular brand community is not a one-time given. As brand communities and their members grow and change, tensions can develop and schisms can occur, as they do in any community where citizens are passionate about their beliefs and practices. The vicissitudes of one brand community, American Express, can help us understand how brand communities are created by—and in turn, create—a shared sense of trust, credibility, and relevance for their members.

Several years ago, American Express ran a series of television ads that depicted scenes such as an international traveler receiving his forgotten prescription by helicopter—just one of the small "privileges" of membership that were part of the card's brand promise to its customers. Research conducted by Research International's Max Blackston (then research director of Ogilvy & Mather Advertising) indicated that users did buy into the prestige of the card, and so did nonusers. So, what was the problem?

Blackston did further study and concluded that it was the American Express *brand attitude* that was limiting trial for the brand. Blackston defined brand attitude as the set of "subjective" inferences customers have made about how the company views and acts toward them. In other words, not what customers think of the brand, but *what customers think the brand thinks of them*. This is perhaps best illustrated by Lily Tomlin's infamous Ernestine the Telephone Operator role on NBC's 1960s hit, *Laugh In*. When she was at the receiving end of a customer complaint, Ernestine's favorite rejoinder was: "We're the phone company, sweetie, we don't have to care!" Although it's unlikely that any of us actually heard these words from the phone company, most laughed with recognition at the all-too-familiar feeling we got when interacting with service companies that never quite got the concept of customer service. In brief, we thought that the phone company did not think much of us.

In the case of American Express, card users inferred positive brand attitudes such as "understands my needs," "values me as a customer," and "treats me as a partner." Although some of this was conveyed in and reinforced by advertising, actual experience with the company was also a source of such inferences. By contrast, nonusers had to judge American Express largely by the image it projected through its image advertising. For some, what came across was exclusivity, which came across as: American Express "thinks it's too good for me," "looks down on me," "doesn't want someone like me for a customer," and so on. Not surprisingly, few noncustomers who made these inferences ever gave the company a chance to change them through actual service.

Groucho Marx once quipped that he wouldn't want to join any club that would allow someone like him to be a member. In effect, for some prospective customers, American Express had created a masterbrand image of such a club. Rather than projecting brand attitudes that elicited reciprocity and a sense of shared interests, the company's advertising was creating a defensive reaction in some viewers: They were rejecting the card that had first rejected them. It is critical that a masterbrand not try to be all things to all people, but defining the focus and scope of the brand community is a jointly—and continuously—negotiated effort.

In study after study, Research International has found that customers' perceptions of a company's positive brand attitude (i.e., "listens to me," "respects me," "anticipates my needs") are what drive customer relationships such as loyalty. Negative brand attitudes ("takes me for granted," "doesn't know me") erode customer loyalty.

Figure 10.1 illustrates the role of brand attitudes in creating brand relationships such as loyalty—and, ultimately, brand communities. A brand consists of its brand performance and its brand equity. *Brand performance* meets customers' functional needs (e.g., the mobility that is offered by any car). *Brand equity* meets customers' nonfunctional needs (e.g., the status that is associated with owning a Lexus). Finally, brand relationships depend not only on how customers see the masterbrand (the brand personality they attribute to it), but also on how they believe the masterbrand views them (the brand attitudes they infer from its actions toward them). Brand communities exist when customers sense that the masterbrand treats them with respect, thus eliciting their reciprocal commitment to building the brand.

In short, brand relationship management is inference management (see Figure 10.2). All the things that you do (or fail to do) in the areas of product performance, customer service, communications, and the like, send signals to your customers, some of which over time are seen as negative patterns, such as: "That company doesn't get it," or "They just aren't there when I need them." Just as we come to know the character of our friends and acquaintances through their actions, so also do customers infer whether we value their business and respect them.

Customers especially rely on what they perceive to be *voluntary* actions on a company's part to send brand image inferences that attract their loyalty. Managing your company as a masterbrand in a brand community means acting—and being *seen* to act—voluntarily to create real or virtual occasions for customers and noncustomers to interact with each other and with you.

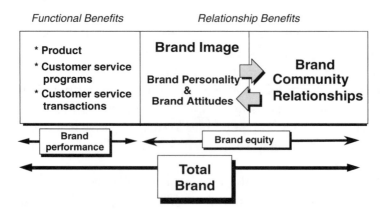

Figure 10.1　*Brand personality and brand attitudes create brand community relationships.*
Source: Adapted with permission from Research International/Cambridge methodologies.

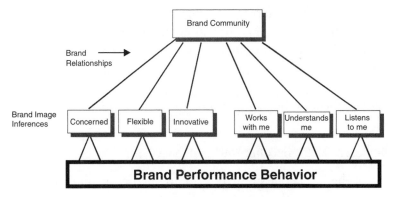

Figure 10.2 *Brand community and brand relationships.*
Source: Adapted with permission from Research International/Cambridge methodologies.

We have all applauded the customer service practices of retailers such as L.L. Bean and its liberal return policy. However, as a Bean spokesperson has pointed out: "We have never actually used the term 'lifetime guarantee' . . . but we do say '100 percent satisfaction guarantee.' We let our customers determine what the satisfaction is . . . we feel that 99 percent of our customers are treating us the way we would think we're treating them."[4]

Behind this deceptively simple policy is a genuine grasp of the dynamics of a brand community—the unspoken trust and credibility that is the fundamental aspect of Bean's brand promise. Interestingly, experience shows that few customers abuse these guarantees. L.L. Bean elicits trust *from* its customers by projecting an attitude of trust *toward* its customers.

It was Mark Twain who observed that the best thing about telling the truth is that you don't have to remember what you said. When it comes to the promise that a brand makes to its brand community, the less *said,* the better. Actions really do speak louder than words—and voluntary actions bespeak the kind of attitudes that make customers *want* to connect with the brand.

Brand communities, then, are voluntary, self-defining, self-governing, and best of all—self-reinforcing. Managing your masterbrand in a brand community means voluntarily creating occasions for current and prospective customers to interact with themselves and you, very much like a New England town meeting. A successful brand community allows input from all quarters, but is not so democratized that decision making becomes impossible. Like any community, a brand community exists through an implicit, unwritten contract. It's not only impossible to write out every implication of your brand promise, it's self-defeating.

The Best Strategy: Become Your Own Successor

One of the most compelling positioning battles under way on the Internet involves the portal brands, and in particular, the masterbrand Yahoo! By continuously reinventing itself in Internet time, Yahoo! demonstrates why managing your entire company as a brand will be the key to successful strategic positioning in years to come.

Some have hailed Yahoo! as a masterful brand, whereas others argue that it is merely a "good idea" that a couple of Netheads were lucky enough to have before anyone else. Time is proving that luck has less and less to do with Yahoo!'s success. There's no doubt that the notion of a user-friendly Internet search engine was and is a good idea—so good in fact, that there have been countless attempts to duplicate it in recent years. However, Yahoo! can continue to defend its position in such a competitive marketplace only by leveraging every possible advantage it wields as a masterbrand portal.

Cofounders Jerry Yang and David Filo have explained that, from its inception in their graduate student days at Stanford to the present, Yahoo! has been about the open and friendly image that the name itself connotes. Within three years of its creation in the spring of 1994, Yahoo! had become the default "place to be" (or at least *start*) on the Internet, used by more than half of those who accessed the Internet from work.

One reason Yahoo! succeeded—even before it knew it was a brand—is that the very concept of a search engine embodies the two key customer benefits of an online brand: (1) It helps users organize preferences, and (2) it offers a source of trust and credibility (see Chapter 1). Once Filo and Yang had decided to offer such a service, they had no choice but to *become* a brand. Because this is and has remained their core value proposition, they were from the outset a masterbrand in the making.

However, as the Red Queen explained to Alice in Wonderland, sometimes you have to run harder and harder just to stay in place—especially *first* place. For Yahoo!, the attempt to remain the default Internet search engine has meant evolving into a full-service portal, adding features and services, in response to—or ahead of—its rivals. For example, when AOL began offering subscribers its ICQ ("I seek you") instant messaging service, Yahoo! responded with a similar feature. Seeking to capitalize on the MP3 challenge to the recorded-music industry, in the third quarter of 1999, the company launched Yahoo! Digital, a multimedia Web site that allows visitors to listen to and download music or watch related videos. This channel is expected to account for less than 10 percent of all music sales in the next few years, but by entering the market now, Yahoo! stays ahead of the curve as the "go to" Internet portal. As David Filo has said, "Whether it's chat or finance or kids or classifieds, we want to get in as early as possible. We want to make sure we don't miss it." (Get there first with the most.)

One lesson that the experience of Yahoo! illustrates is that as a brand community transcends and is something more that its individual members, no one of whom "owns" it. So, too, does a masterbrand transcend and often supersede any specific set of products, services, or features at any specific point in time. Because the masterbrand promise lives above and guides any particular offer, it can constantly reinvent itself to stay the same. Because it harnesses the dynamism and adaptability of the brand community that owns and grows the brand, it can keep pace with the community's changing needs and expectations.

Complicating Yahoo!'s strategy is the fact that the competition is not merely trying to catch up, they are trying to redefine the very grounds of competition. (Get *where* first? With the most of *what*?) For example, Lycos began by describing itself as a "personalized guide" to the Internet. Excite announced that it intended to be "something between what people understand as a search engine and an online service." When San Francisco–based news Web publisher clnet announced the launch of Snap! in 1997, its general manager made a pointed comparison with Yahoo!: Snap! would be "navigation with an editorial perspective."

Predictions that Snap! would be the next Yahoo! in fact understated the challenge. Far from simply attempting to emulate Yahoo!, Snap! and other second-generation search engines helped move the playing field to that higher level, from offering customers simple information to creating affinity-based, customized knowledge streams and products.

Yahoo!'s response? Stick to the game plan of continuously changing the rules. By reinventing itself one step ahead of its competitors, it has continued to become its own successor. Yahoo! has not merely added to its "table of contents," it continually rewrites the book on Internet search engines. As Yang put it: "We are in the business of obsoleting Yahoo."[5]

Yahoo! illustrates one of the major competitive advantages of a masterbrand company: its flexibility and adaptability. Unlike Excite and other search engines that have tried to be—and to own—"cool," Yahoo's brand has remained open and flexible, able to incorporate even financial information and services. Rather than staking out and trying to own a specific, static position in the marketplace, Yahoo! practices positioning as a moveable feast. Rather than trying to own its customers or a share of their wallets, Yahoo! seeks to share them with members of its ever-expanding brand community. In the end, Yahoo! is its brand community. The more Yahoo! reinvents itself, the more it remains true to itself and its original brand promise.

The Severest Form of Competition

If imitation is the sincerest form of flattery, then convergence may be the severest form of competition. The more Yahoo! and its rivals compete, the more they begin to resemble one another. In part, this is inherent in the dynamics of online competition, as search engines become Internet portals and the latter evolve into virtual brand communities. As the stakes increase in proportion to the size of online markets, so too does the field of potential competitors—and allies—expand. These now include not only other search engines and portals, but also alternative online brand communities such as America Online.

Yahoo! continues to metamorphose. In late 1999, the company announced that it is now an e-mall. According to VP of Marketing, Karen Edwards, the move is "merely an extension of our overall brand building." As she elaborated: "We've done a pretty good job communicating to people that Yahoo! is a place to find anything and connect with other people, [but] people still don't necessarily think of Yahoo! as a place to buy things."[6] Yahoo! had forged relationships with numerous online retailers beginning in November 1998. The e-mall merely organizes these retailers by consumer-friendly categories such as kids' clothing or electronics—much as a bricks-and-mortar mall is organized. Although users made $100 million in purchases in October 1999 alone, in number they represented only a fraction of Yahoo!'s 105 million users.

Today, Yahoo! continues to attract Net surfers who want to ride the curl of the latest online wave—whatever and wherever that might be. Like the curl of a wave, Yahoo! maintains its identity, not by occupying a static place in competitive space, but rather by propagating its dynamic throughout the medium of its brand community. One sign that the strategy is working is that Yahoo! spent an estimated $64.5 million on marketing in the fourth quarter of 1999—up from $42.5 million in the fourth quarter of 1998, but considerably less than the $100 million and more that other Internet companies are having to spend to stay afloat.

Although Yahoo! is a literal and perhaps extreme example, it clearly shows that a company's single most valuable asset is the masterbrand itself. More than any specific possessions or ideas, it is the brand promise—and the brand community that this helps create—that constitutes a masterbrand company's *virtual assets*. They are virtual in name only. (See Figure 10.3 for old versus new customer relationships comparison.)

Like Trucks, Search Engines Don't Run on Rails

The "marketing myopia" of the late-nineteenth-century railroads is now legendary. They thought they were in the railroad business

Old View: Company "Owns" Customer

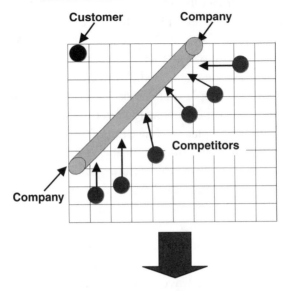

Customer   Company

Competitors

Company

New View: Community Shares Masterbrand

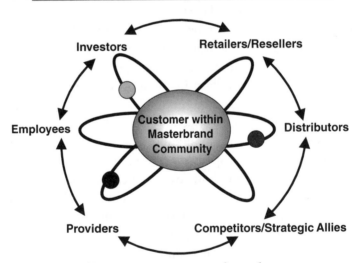

Investors   Retailers/Resellers

Employees   Customer within Masterbrand Community   Distributors

Providers   Competitors/Strategic Allies

Figure 10.3   Old versus new customer relationships.

and focused their technical and marketing efforts accordingly. By the time they realized they were actually in the *transportation* business, trucks had literally and figuratively bypassed railroads on their way to dominating the market. Even as AOL, Yahoo!, and other companies compete to be the ultimate on-ramp to the information highway, there are already signs that the competitive landscape could be changing in ways that will require the creation of true online brand communities and their corresponding companies as brand.comms.

Put simply, Internet portals may soon prove to have been merely transitional devices in terms of customers' online behavior. More radically still, the technology that gave birth to the World Wide Web—the desktop personal computer—may itself soon be supplemented or even supplanted by online "Webtop" computing and wireless remote access, with enormous implications for the creation of online brand communities.

As Netizens gain online savvy, Web site portals may no longer be needed as points of entry to the Internet. Jerry Kaplan, CEO of Internet auction house ONSALE, claims that traffic increasingly comes directly to his site, not through portals. "The next turn of the crank in Internet commerce will be that certain sites will emerge as destinations on their own, thereby eliminating the necessity to buy a broad presence on the portal sites." In fact, Charles Schwab has already discontinued its multimillion-dollar arrangement with AOL, because less than 5 percent of its business came through this link. Even online mortgage provider E-Loan has found that traditional advertising is both cheaper and has a higher conversion rate than online advertising. Says CEO Chris Larsen, "Long-term, we think traditional media are the way to develop the brand. I don't want to be too dependent on portals."[7]

Just as the swiftest dinosaurs evolved into even swifter birds, so too it appears that portals may soon evolve into replacements for the very technology that made them possible and necessary (however temporarily). A generation of workers and consumers raised on office and home desktop PCs may find it hard to imagine going back to centralized, time-sharing computing. However, Web TV, wireless PDAs (personal digital assistants), and the increasing popularity of online calendars and scheduling software (such as

Microsoft's Outlook) are reintroducing the notion that you don't have to have a PC to do personal computing where and when you want to. In retrospect, the PC has been the ultimate experiment in disintermediation, giving all users direct access to their own computer hardware and a chance to be their own MIS support people. We all know how popular that has been.

In the future, portals may point as much to the desktop as to particular sites. Such "Webtop" computers will merely be devices for accessing a Web site where the software and data reside and actual computing occurs. Rather than tech support being a toll-free busy signal, it will be built into the service, along with guarantees about uptime, upgrades, and data integrity and privacy.

The evolution of Internet portals into Webtop computing services illustrates how companies must continuously lap themselves just to stay in place, often reinventing their product or service categories as well. Microsoft has been slow to respond to this development and is facing a serious challenge to its dominance of PC operating system and applications software. PC makers such as eMachines have responded by offering systems capable of supporting Webtop computing for well under $500.

In the end, creating lock-in with a brand community that will grow and change along with your masterbrand may prove to be a better strategy than trying to monopolize a given technology or operating system. As personal computing and telecommunications converge, erasing the boundaries of old empires, the race to provide high-speed Internet access to businesses and consumers is likely to favor those companies that have both the technology and the brand communities to sustain this transition. Among the likely winners? AT&T and (no surprise here) AOL. Don't be surprised, though, if Yahoo! and a select few other Internet portals also morph into Webtop-based brand.comms.

Bringing Good Things to Online

Clearly, we can learn lessons about strategic positioning from masterbrands that had enough foresight to create and exploit their first-mover advantage on the Internet. For the rest of us, however, it may be even more fruitful to look at companies that have achieved masterbrand status *before* going online—and how they are just now beginning to interactivate their brands and associated brand communities. GE provides one such instructive example.

In January of 1999, Chairman Jack Welch challenged every GE business unit to develop a Web site and Internet strategy before the end of the year. To promote Web literacy across GE, internal newsletters and even some of the chairman's memos were henceforth to be available only online at desktop PCs and kiosks placed on factory floors. (Himself a devoted handwritten letter and memo writer, Welch even agreed to begin using e-mail.) Many managers suddenly learned that their e-business acumen would figure largely in their performance reviews and compensation.

In one clear sign of the urgency of the effort, 12 teams were designated "destroyyourbusiness.com." Their mission was to think of ways that competitors might try to do just that—and then decide whether GE needs to adopt these strategies instead. In effect, GE is prepared to destroy the company in order to save it, a strategy that is as risky as it sounds. At the time of this writing, additional teams of "Web fanatics" are in the process of moving existing GE operations to the Internet. Although GE is a Johnny-come-lately to e-commerce, it figures to make a big splash in the cyberpond, not the least by learning from and driving its thousands of smaller suppliers and customers toward e-commerce applications.

The model for GE's move online is the Web site that is operated by its subsidiary Polymerland, which distributes plastics to about 3,000 manufacturing customers. From a mere "curiosity" at its unveiling at a 1997 trade show, the site has grown to become the focal point of an emerging brand community. Customers place and track orders and swap technical advice on bulletin boards. Learning that customers want to know what is happening to their orders, the site now generates outbound e-mail to keep them updated. Polymerland has reduced inbound calls by over 1,000 a week, while cutting back on the number of conventional customer service reps and moving several to e-commerce support.

Like many other companies, Polymerland initially began using the Internet as a way to save on the costs of conventional sales, fulfillment, and customer service by letting customers place and track their own orders. Combined with the GE masterbrand,

Polymerland is poised to become a true brand.comm. Our advice to the new millenium's graduate? In a word: *polymers*.

Because they are already masterbrands, such click-and-brick companies as GE, Gateway, and Charles Schwab are better positioned to take advantage of developments on the Internet, even where they do not enjoy first-mover advantage. Under the direction of strong CEOs acting as masterbrand managers, these companies are able to respond more decisively to emerging online threats and opportunities. Because these masterbrands have long understood and valued customer relationship management, making online interactivity central to their competitive strategy is merely a logical extension of existing practice. Because its value proposition is broadly defined and shared with a loyal brand community, a masterbrand can better survive and drive changes in technology, redefining the marketplace to maintain (or reassert) its leadership.

Better Late than Never—and Maybe Better Late

As the examples of GE and Gillette illustrate, the spoils of victory do not always—or only—go to those with (apparent) first-mover advantage in a given market, whether online or off. In fact, as professional bike racers (and migrating geese) know, it sometimes pays to ride in the "draft" of the leader. More generally, strategic positioning is an unfolding dialectic, with each new position generating the possibility of and need for an alternative.

E-commerce businesses live or die on their fulfillment logis-tics (or those of UPS and FedEx). This is just one reason that bricks-and-mortar retailers are proving to be much more resilient and successful in their online ventures than many pure-play e-commerce companies would like to admit. Just as Bic threatened to render Gillette's R&D assets a competitive drag (see the sidebar), so too does disintermediation appear to devalue physical assets, making them a competitive albatross around the neck of a conventional retailer. As conventional retailers enter e-commerce to supplement rather than supplant their tradition-al marketing and fulfillment activities, some are redefining the competitive environment and disintermediating the disintermediators.

There is emerging evidence that this strategy has brought

SURVIVING A CLOSE SHAVE AND REGAINING THE EDGE OVER YOUR COMPETITION

Examples of masterbrands that have achieved, lost, and regained first-mover advantage can be found offline as well as on. Before personal computing, there was personal shaving—an equally revolutionary idea in its time. By inventing the category, Gillette seemed to have created an insurmountable barrier to competitors. However, such was not the case.

In the 1970s, French challenger Bic had threatened to redefine the personal shaving experience and undercut the advantage that Gillette had created based on its extensive R&D and high-tech approach to shaving. By contrast, Bic had developed an efficient manufacturing and distribution system for inexpensive, disposal products such as pens and cigarette lighters. If it could convince consumers that its cheaper disposable razors were good enough for the job, Gillette's investment in more expensive and complicated cartridge shaving systems would change from a competitive advantage to a liability.

Gillette's management at first doubted that consumers would accept this redefinition. As they began to do so, Gillette saw its market share and margins erode. Although it had missed first-mover advantage in Europe, Gillette quickly developed its Good News disposable razor and captured 60 percent of the U.S. market by 1982. However, lower margins left it with years of financial difficulties and attempted takeovers. Rather than continue to react to Bic and play by its rules, Gillette set out to recreate the market for high-tech, quality shaving.

With the 1989 introduction of its Sensor razor, Gillette did just that, tilting the playing field (once more) to its advantage and seizing the brand and technology high ground of personal shaving. Although it may not have realized that it was doing so, Gillette was also creating at least the potential for a brand community not unlike that of Apple's, although based on less of an emotional bond.

Personal computing is a higher-involvement category than personal shaving, and Apple has done more to cultivate its cult. Both companies, however, have brand communities of dedicated customers defined in part by a shared sense that technology and ease of use (comfort) matter—and that one company (exclusively or more than most) delivers. The success of Gillette's successor products, Sensor Excel and Mach3 razors, suggests that Gillette's leveraging of its brand community to help redefine the category has succeeded and helped it recapture first-mover advantage, much as Apple appears to have rebounded and captured both attention and market share with its iMac, G3/4, and iBook innovations. Even though disposable razors still exist as a significant and profitable part of the market for Gillette, Bic, and others, they no longer define the market as a whole. Gillette has consequently strengthened its market share and margins.

Internet competition full circle, requiring pure-play companies to adjust accordingly. Recently, a new phenomenon has emerged in the online competitive position: the *Not*.com. CEO Sue Levin created Lucy.com to sell women's exercise apparel online. Her latest breakthrough move? She's mailing thousands of paper catalogs to customers and prospects. As irrational exuberance for Internet IPOs has given way to rational foreboding, some would-be "e-tailers" have sensed that the public may have seen one too many ads for yet another something.com. As former Nike brand manager Levin observes: "Our strategy is Lucy *not*-com . . . 'dot-com' is starting to stand for something decidedly negative in consumers' minds: opportunistic twentysomethings, rather than admirable businesses."[8]

For example, BigStar Entertainment—the New York–based pure-play that sells videotapes and DVDs online—paid to have a fleet of 23 delivery trucks carry its logo all over the city. It *didn't* pay to have them carry its products, however. SVP of Marketing, Donna Williams, admits that the ploy was intended to "create a sense of permanence, to give people the impression that BigStar is actually out there in the real world." Even though they are not employees, truck drivers hand out coupons for and are trained to answer questions about BigStar. Initial results prompted BigStar to deploy an additional 200 trucks in cities such as Dallas, Los Angeles, and San Francisco.

As e-commerce competition continues to evolve, the apparent albatross of physical assets may yet again fly high. Why? Because, historically, brand communities have existed in space as well as time, with visible, tangible evidence of shared values and a company's ability to deliver on its brand promise to community members. Precisely because of the enduring need to create trust and credibility within a brand community, online companies will eventually develop new—and perhaps purely virtual—methods of establishing both presence and permanence.[9]

Seeing Green in Blue Mountain

Fats Domino met his thrill on Blueberry Hill. Excite@Home had a similar epiphany when it saw Bluemountain.com, the online offshoot of Blue Mountain Arts Publishing Company. Created in

1994 by two self-described ex-hippies, Stephen Schutz and Susan Polis Schutz, Bluemountain.com was intended to be a "spiritual and emotional center for the Web"—a natural extension of their small business that published poetry and sold paper greeting cards. Less than five years later, solely on the strength of its free greeting card service (used by a million visitors each day) and word-of-mouth referrals, Bluemountain.com had grown to become one of Media Metrix's top 20 Web sites, with over 300 servers and nearly 100 employees.[10]

Deciding that the operation had become too costly and complex to manage on their own, the Schutzes and their son and executive director, Jared, decided to spin it off as a separate company early in 1999. By October, they had agreed to be acquired by Excite@Home (majority owned by AT&T). Wall Street reacted favorably to the announcement, barely blinking at the cost, which with Holiday season performance bonuses, could total nearly $1 billion. With this move, Excite@Home increased its audience by 40 percent (to approximately one-third of all Internet traffic, vaulting ahead of Disney, though still trailing AOL, Yahoo!, and Microsoft).

Sam Walton demonstrated the value of greeters. American Express touts the privileges of card membership. However, it took Bluemountain.com to show that literally giving away a free greeting card service could create a virtual brand community of members that has cash value in the marketplace. At the time of this writing, plans call for Bluemountain.com to capitalize on this value and reward its new owners by selling flowers, chocolates, and gifts as a natural complement to its free greeting card service.

As CEO George Bell explains Excite@Home's strategy, "We recognize the importance of making the narrow-band end of the funnel [Internet over conventional phone lines] as robust as possible explicitly for the purpose of converting those users to broadband [cable Internet access] eventually." If the Bluemountain audience won't (yet) come to broadband, Excite@Home is prepared to come to—or buy—the Bluemountain. As befits its idealistic origins, the Bluemountain.com employees all received stock options when the company was created and will benefit from its sale.

Rounding out this story of doing well by doing good, Jared

Schutz assures onlookers that "the Excite@Home team are understanding about the nature of our community, and we are confident they will continue to be good stewards into the future." We'll see. Yahoo! had similar expectations, but ran into trouble when it acquired and tried to commercialize GeoCities in 1998. Members used to free web-page services revolted when Yahoo! tried to get them to relinquish copyrights on their creations. As the term *brand.comm* is intended to remind us, a company owns its brand in common with the brand community that helps it achieve masterbrand status. The potential rewards of managing your company as part of a brand community are proportional to the difficulty of the task.

As with the debate about brand building via online versus offline media, the idea of creating value by giving something away is still controversial. One venture capital advisor warns: "After you give something away free, it is very difficult to start charging for it, or even for other things." Although that may be true, cofounder of Excite, Joe Kraus, believes that "anything that has the potential for a broad audience will eventually be free."[11]

For example, in 1994, 40 percent of Dow Jones' online revenue came from news headlines and stock quotes—services it and hundreds of other sites now provide for free. As Kraus sees it, the Internet has created (or exacerbated) an "attention economy," in which companies will go to almost any length to get potential customers' attention rather than their money (at least, initially). The result is that ready-made audiences created around free services such as Bluemountain.com's are fast themselves becoming economic assets. (Microsoft paid $400 million for Hotmail's free e-mail service and 11 million customers.) As we have noted elsewhere, brand communities, however virtual and tenuous they may be, are becoming the natural units of value creation and competition.

With Enemies Like These, Who Needs Friends?

The counterpart to, and driver behind, much Internet reintermediation is the new dynamic of strategic alliances within and among masterbrands and their brand communities. Just as the Internet blurs the traditional roles of buyer and seller, so too has it undermined conventional wisdom about competition and positioning, breaching the walls of the company as fortress to make way for the company as brand.

Strategic alliances are generally intended to do three things: (1) share customers, (2) share marketing and promotion costs, and/or (3) improve products and services. Avoiding the time and resource commitments of mergers or acquisitions, such alliances are increasingly informal marriages of convenience. Although this strategy gives both partners flexibility, it also puts a premium on trust and a shared commitment to an overarching vision. Brand communities are the natural unit of such strategic alliances, and masterbrands provide the discipline and vision that are needed to make them work.

Asked how much of Coke's revenues comes from alliances, then-chairman Doug Ivester once quipped: "100 percent." In truth, Coke has risen to masterbrand status in part through informal alliances and agreements with other world-class brands. Importantly, however, Coke's alliance with McDonald's exists not as a written contract, but only, as Ivester put it, in the form of "a common vision and a lot of trust."[12] As in both companies' alliances with Disney, the shared vision focuses on families and the complementary masterbrand promises that each makes to its brand community. (As this book was being completed, Mr. Ivester announced his unexpected decision to retire on the heels of Coke's lackluster performance in 1999, especially overseas. One wag noted that "A Coke CEO couldn't kill the brand if he wanted to."[13] Still another advantage of being a masterbrand.)

In today's Internet-assisted economy, making strategic alliances may appear easier than it is. All the more reason then that masterbrand discipline is needed to guide the formation and maintenance of such alliances. AT&T entered into over 400 alliances (most of them short-lived) in the six years be-fore it finally decided in 1996 to split itself into separate, more tightly focused business units such as Lucent Technologies. Strategic alliances are a means to an end, not ends in themselves.

Understanding and managing your organization as a masterbrand can provide the necessary guidance to identify and pursue an appropriate competitive positioning strategy. By putting the long-term interests of your brand community first, you can find real advantages in making what might appear to be counterintuitive alliances with strange bedfellows.

Nowhere is this better illustrated than in the race to stay or get ahead in e-commerce. And so, we can end our overview of strategic positioning where we began: the fight to become the preferred Internet portal. As we have seen, online auctioneer eBay figures to be one of the Internet's masterbrand survivors—but it faces competition from a linkage of 100 Internet sites. In September 1999, archrivals Microsoft's MSN, Excite@Home, and Lycos, among many others, announced that henceforth they would link their individual Internet auction sites in an effort to overtake eBay and neutralize its first-mover advantage. The mouse that roared in this scenario was Fairmarket, a small company based in Woburn, Massachusetts, that had begun as an online service to help businesses auction off discontinued or returned inventory.

As Excite's SVP, David Tse, explained: "In auctions, scale is really valuable." Scale was what alliance members hoped to achieve overnight by their move. The alliance faces an uphill struggle at best, however. At its inception, the aggregated auction sites had a total of just 60,000 items—compared with some 3 million items available through eBay, which remains (for now) the 800-pound gorilla. According to Lycos' Director of Business Development, Jeffrey Bennett, "We are in the business of aggregating an audience" (a.k.a. building a brand community). Once the various parties agreed to this definition of the alliance's value proposition to customers, they could overcome concerns about maintaining a narrow, proprietary advantage over their rivals-cum-partners. For example, rather than start its own auction site or sell links to eBay, Bennett says Lycos decided that "going with a joint venture would give us more traction" and take less time.[14]

Fairmarket estimates that the aggregated auction sites will encompass three-quarters of all online shoppers and attract a collective total of nearly 50 million visits each month. Importantly, each member of the alliance will maintain the look and feel of its own Web site. The aggregated auction will thus appear transparent to each company's customers as it seeks to strengthen ties to its own brand community and perhaps reach out to others.

The alliance has its doubters, however, including the eBay spokesperson who points out that would-be rivals such as Amazon.com and Yahoo! have found replicating eBay's sense of community much more difficult than they had anticipated. At least one e-commerce analyst agrees, characterizing the alliance's announcement as "an admission that eBay pretty much owns the market. I think it's going to be pretty hard to dislodge them."[15]

Kill the "Killer App"

"Get there first with the most" is looking better all the time: First movers still have an advantage, and size does matter. If there's a single watchword for competitive positioning in today's Internet-assisted economy, however, it may be Yahoo!'s habit of turning the negative adjective *obsolete* into a positive verb. Although not all companies operate in cyberspace and Internet time (yet), increasingly it may be necessary to obsolete your company and its apparent competitive advantages—rather than waiting for your competitors (or customers) to do so. In one way or another, all of the strategies we have reviewed in this chapter follow from this simple, but challenging advice. Whether hedging against or driving changes in technology and regulation, overtaking first movers, or turning competitors into allies, a masterbrand company has advantages and resources that ordinary companies lack.

The example of Yahoo! also illustrates most clearly why a masterbrand is better able than others to act on the obsoleting principle of strategic competition. Yahoo! simply *lives* its brand promise to customers to be *the* trusted source for helping them organize their priorities and find what they need on the Internet. Yahoo! is in a position that few companies enjoy—to literally "kill the killer app" (i.e., to obsolete any particular product, service, or information that appears to give it a competitive advantage at any specific point in time). Yahoo! maintains its first-mover advantage not by attempting to lock in any particular technology or service, but rather by staying *on the move*, continuously reinventing itself and its brand community.

Any specific product, service, or information offering can, should, and will be obsoleted, if not by competitors, then by the company itself. The only thing that can never be obsoleted is the ultimate positioning that these competitive moves are driving toward—the affinity that bonds a masterbrand to its brand community.

This doesn't mean that a brand—even a masterbrand—cannot be outpositioned in the struggle for the hearts and minds of its brand community. It means simply that, increasingly, this is where the battle will be joined. Because, like Yahoo!, a masterbrand fundamentally *is* the brand promise that creates and nurtures a living, dynamic brand community. Masterbrands have an advantage when it comes to changing in order to stay the same, continuously obsoleting various means to achieve the same overarching end of creating customer trust and value.

MANAGING YOUR MANDATE

Because strategic positioning is a dynamic process of constantly adjusting to changing market conditions, there can be few hard and fast rules that apply to all companies in all circumstances for all time. The competitive positioning questions you should ask and the actions you should take will vary accordingly.

Questions You Should Be Asking   Our review of how masterbrands are competing in today's knowledge economy suggests that an essential set of questions and actions can be organized around the notion of obsoleting your apparent competitive advantages at any point in time—be they product, service, or information—in favor of increasing customer affinity and the creation of additional value for your brand community. Accordingly, some questions we recommend you consider are:

What are the products that currently appear to give your company a competitive advantage in specific markets? What are the benefits that customers seek by using these products? How readily can they be replicated by competitors? Can customers obtain these benefits directly for themselves without using your products or those of your competitors? (Remember: Your competition is "any and all alternatives.")

What are the <u>services</u> that currently appear to give your company a competitive advantage in specific markets? Are you in a position to obsolete your own services, or are you a step behind the competition in doing that? Are customers themselves obsoleting specific products in favor of (self-) service? Have you resisted—or assisted—this process? How do (will) customers view your company as a result? Are you managing this inevitable process of obsolescence to enhance customer intimacy and trust and build (or strengthen) your brand community?

What <u>information</u> can you offer customers that currently appears to give your company a competitive advantage in specific markets? What is the value to your customers of this information? Who owns this information and how does it create value for you and your customers? Is it proprietary and valuable only if you maintain exclusive ownership (zero-sum game), or does its value to you and customers alike grow the more it is used and shared by your brand community and others (including competitors)? How was this information created and what value do you add to this process? In what way(s) has this information obsoleted preceding products and services? Who drove this process? How are you viewed by customers, allies, and competitors as a result of your role in this process?

What are your brand community <u>affinity</u> assets, and how is your competitive positioning strategy designed to leverage and, in turn, create such assets? What are specific examples of where your company has obsoleted products, services, or information in favor of creating increased customer affinity and a stronger brand community? Where have you conspicuously *failed* to do this and why? What are the short- and long-term institutional barriers to obsoleting your apparent competitive advantage(s)? Is your competitive strategy of self-obsoleting clearly visible in your value proposition? Does it attract potential customers and allies, to ward off would-be competitors ("No one's gonna out-AOL AOL"), or to convert them into allies (the Fairmarket online auction consortium)?

(Continued)

Actions You Should Be Taking When you've explored and begun to answer these questions (keeping in mind that no answer can be definitive once and for all), there are actions you can take to begin obsoleting your apparent, short-term competitive advantages in favor of a long-term, transparent strategy of building your brand community. Examples of such actions include the following:

Form destroy-your-business teams (à la GE) to formulate plans for doing just that—before your competitors (or customers) can do so. But don't stop there. Be sure that these teams *also* tackle the constructive corollary of this destructive step: Build your masterbrand. It's critical that these teams look at destroying your existing competitive advantages in ways that build the brand community, not just by going online and digitizing bad habits for their own sake.

• Have these teams perform autopsies on selected products, services, or information offers that have (recently) been obsoleted by your competitors or changing market conditions.

• Determine what replaced these products, and why. Note especially how existing or new market entrants used this to move up the competitive positioning ladder to increase their affinity with current or prospective customers.

• Identify products, services, or information offers that have been successfully obsoleted by your company itself. (Alternatively, look for where this process has *failed*.) Determine what prompted this move—and especially how you first became aware of the *need* to do this. Explore the institutional factors (organizational structure, lines of communication and authority, explicit and implicit rewards, etc.) that facilitated or inhibited this reaction.

• Identify products, services, or information that are *at risk* of being obsoleted by your company itself. Focus your destructive/constructive efforts on these areas, drawing on experience that is gained from the autopsies.

• Make sure that individual product lines, revenue streams, and the like are not obsoleted merely piecemeal by individual product managers. Rather, ensure that this process of obsoleting is managed across the entire company as part of its competitive strategy as a masterbrand.

• Based on this analysis, look for ways to institutionalize the obsoleting process (as oxymoronic as that may sound). For example, train, encourage, and reward employees for "working themselves out of a job"—as long as the net result is to increase customer value and affinity, thus strengthening your masterbrand community.

Once you have your own house (reasonably) in order, do a little snooping around others'. Analyze competitors' strategies and actions to determine where they may be able to obsolete your product, service, or information better, cheaper, faster than you yourself can. Where this seems likely to happen, consider ways in which to collaborate in the greater interest of creating value for your brand community and of moving your competitive advantage to new products, services, or information (possibly returning the favor for your competitor-ally).

• Examine your products, services, and information with a critical eye vis-à-vis competitors. Do you have an advantage only as long as customers don't have the kind of near-perfect information that is rapidly becoming the norm online? Do you try to create shareholder value by withholding customer value? If so, can you create a win-win scenario for customers, competitors, yourself, and shareholders by becoming more transparent to all parties concerned?

• Examine your competitive strategy itself. Is it based on locking up customers by locking them into a proprietary offering (with or without their awareness and understanding of alternatives)? Or is your competitive strategy transparent to customers and competitors alike—the promise to provide the best possible value in a given area, whatever it takes or whoever has it (the Yahoo! strategy)?

• Finally, work to align your competitive strategy and day-to-day operations by training, encouraging, and rewarding employees for consorting with customers and intermediaries that make up your brand community, as well as with current competitors who may yet prove to be collaborators. More than ever, it pays to "know your enemy"—and it may even pay to pay him or her, where the net result is a stronger, more diverse masterbrand community.

*   *   *

Now that we have examined in some detail the winning ways of Yahoo!, a self-professed, open-ended masterbrand, our next chapter will take a closer look at what is arguably the largest and most successful *brand.comm* in the world.

Masterbrand: America Online

I don't know one engineer in Silicon Valley who
uses AOL . . . but every one of them has told 20
not-technical people that AOL is the best way to get
on the Internet.

—Milo Medin, chief technical officer
and founder of Excite@home[1]

U nlike Sun Microsystems, the America Online masterbrand is
not about open-endedness. On the contrary, CEO Steve Case
has stated more than once that he expects AOL to be more
powerful than Microsoft. What AOL seeks is to provide its members with freedom that they can find *within a proprietary portal* but
that leads to the open Internet beyond.

Steve Case was working in marketing at Pizza Hut in early
1982, trying to figure out what kind of new pizza America would
want next. He ran across an early online information service
called the Source and was intrigued, especially because he knew it
could be made better by making it more consumer-friendly. A year
later, Case joined Control Video, eventually restaged as Quantum
Computer Services, which created the Q-Link online service.

That, in turn, became America Online in 1989, and Case's chase was on.

With its acquisition of Time Warner early in 2000 (which we'll discuss in more detail later), AOL Time Warner is now the world's largest media company, with revenue of the combined company expected to be about $40 billion and a market capitalization around $300 billion, making it the fourth most valuable company, following in the wake of only Microsoft, Cisco Systems and General Electric. Worldwide membership in AOL was about 22 million souls by mid-2000 in more than 100 countries and 1,500 cities. Close to 40 percent of all time now spent online in the United States takes place within AOL's portal. AOL brands include the AOL masterbrand network and e-mail, the Compu-Serve Internet service, the Netscape browser, and a variety of other online service brands.

The acquisition of Time Warner means that Steve Case may be able to achieve his ultimate dream—namely, to extend his masterbrand out of the computer and into the rest of the lives of his brand community. Case hopes to deliver access and messaging beyond computers to television programming, cellular phones, and other online and offline devices. Case's plans have been compared with those of Bill Gates, who hoped to run the world from the PC. In AOL's case, they are thinking much bigger.

How will he get there? Probably by sticking to the central AOL mission, which is to communicate with people, using irresistible content in a way that is easy to use, regardless of how sophisticated the technology might be. That kind of simple logic is a lot like the straightforward approaches that have driven the success of other habits of the American heart, such as McDonald's, Walt Disney, and network television in the 1950s.

In the process, Case and his team have built what is easily the largest masterbrand community of its kind in the world. With its easy-to-understand access, user interface, and content offerings, AOL is the perfect place for novices to learn what this Net thing is all about. Once in the AOL community, they find a myriad of reasons to stay and make friends. It's also the perfect place for novices to learn about online life in a forgiving environment, filled with other novices with similar fears and hesitation.

Meeting Needs, Using Technology

From the beginning, Steve Case set out to design a superior brand of communications. "We want to offer the most magical service possible," Case says. "We'll use the technology as a means to an end, but we've gotten here because we figure out what the customer wants, not what the technologists think."[2] In essence, Steve Case has been doing nothing different than what he did at Procter & Gamble and PepsiCo, that is, determining consumer needs and filling them. That fact is sometimes overshadowed by the extraordinary scope of the tools he uses, but it is brand building, through and through.

One of the key differences in AOL's consumer strategy versus those of other Internet rivals is that the latter are attempting to provide niched products or services. AOL, in contrast, is building a broad-based masterbrand community, *through which* it can sell products and services. The channel, in other words, becomes the crown jewel, instead of the item that is for sale. AOL's tools for creating its community include such features as:

- *Instant Messenger.* This feature permits a community member to send messages on a whim more quickly than e-mail. Reinforcing this feature is AOL's "buddy list," which indicates that a member's friends are also in the community, and are reachable by instant messaging. By the end of 1999, AOL claimed to have 35 million people using this service.

- *Netscape Netcenter, Netscape Navigator, Communicator browsers.* This is a feature that gives the AOL community the search capacity it needs to satisfy the insatiable hunger for Net crawling.

- *Love @ AOL.* This AOL feature has institutionalized online classified personals.

- *AOL Hometown.* A feature that enables members to create their own home pages and to interact with those from other community folk.

America Online has created a comforting community feeling that helps to offset the reputation for being cold and distant that online life has acquired in recent years. That feeling will only increase as AOL users e-mail one another on their Palm Pilots, a program which became available at the end of 1999.

One reason for the comfort is that AOL refuses to bombard its users with overchoice, which has blighted more than a few consumer markets. AOL provides its members with relatively few decisions to make, under the theory (that is becoming more like a fact) that some control is good, but too much choice is bad. Contrast that with other portals that have a polar opposite philosophy, and which have considerably fewer users.

However, that does not mean that America Online lacks control. AOL offers quick and easy access to the Web, but its bread and butter remain carefully crafted, well-branded pages that make up its proprietary community. Will that close-ended approach ultimately lead to their weakening, as it has with Microsoft? Not likely, because AOL is a community that listens to its inhabitants; if they want more room to roam in the future, they'll get it on AOL.

Although much of the credit for the early successes of AOL has to go to Case, more recent marketing mastery is the handiwork of Bob Pittman, AOL's president and COO. Pittman, the founder of MTV and veteran marketer at various companies, has been the preacher of the AOL sermon: Keep your eye on the consumer, not the competitor. Pittman is given much of the credit for mushrooming AOL's membership, including raising it from 10 million to 17 million in one recent year. One very effective tactic has since become a Net staple: The company spent hundreds of millions in a free sampling program of AOL software and provided free sign-up trial periods.[3]

Even more impressive is the money that AOL is taking in. AOL received $1 billion from advertising and commerce deals during 1998 and 1999. According to some projections, AOL's advertising revenue will exceed ABC and CBS totals by 2003. (See Table 11.1 for AOL advertising compared with other networks.)

There are also features that exist now, and others that are on their way, which will strengthen the America Online masterbrand by providing members more opportunities to invite the community further into their lives, and by protecting AOL's proprietary systems against competitive incursions, including:

Table 11.1   *AOL Advertising Comparisons*

Vehicle	1999 Fiscal Years* ($ Millions)
ABC Network	3,369
CBS Network	2,983
Time Inc. Magazines	1,700
America Online	1,000
ESPN (1 & 2)	937
Warner Bros. Network	409
Yahoo!	240

Source: Marc Gunther, "AOL: The future king of advertising," *Fortune.com*, 11 October 1999.

*All totals are for 12-months, varying periods, ending June, 1999

- *When.com.* Software that provides personalized calendaring
- *MovieFone/MovieLink.* Services that enable members to scan, reserve, and purchase movie tickets online
- *AOL Anywhere.* Suite of online devices (personal digital assistants, screen phones, TV set-top boxes) that will put real credence in its name
- *ICQ.* America Online's small rectangular screen that remains on a user's screen for lengthy periods, and whose start-up position on the screen potentially enables AOL to preempt other browsers

AOL management see their masterbrand as remaining within the mass-market segment of their business. CompuServe, however, is being positioned as a fighting flanker brand that will be able to reduce prices and field discount promotions and keep its bigger brother out of the mud. The ICQ brand will be the cooler version of AOL, whereas the Netscape Netcenter site will be positioned for business users. By segmenting the subbrands in this way, the AOL masterbrand continues to lord over the estate, but it can be protected, demographically and otherwise, by its offspring brands. The cost of creating such brands is relatively small because of the spadework done by the initial AOL marketing.

Another key part of AOL's community strategy is to augment its masterbrand with a partner when it cannot acquire. For example, in August of 1999, the company created a marketing alliance with CompUSA, which agreed to sell computer keyboards with a button that launches users directly into AOL. The computers come with preloaded AOL and (AOL-owned) Compuware software. AOL and CompuServe customers also get discounted CompUSA customer support rates. In November 1999, AOL signed up Intuit for a five-year deal to become the exclusive online bill-management tool for members.[4] That same month, Electronic Arts paid $81 million to be the primary provider of video games to AOL.

In all of these moves, content providers are rushing to get a slice of the action from the largest electronic content aggregator in the world, and Steve Case is moving closer to offering his customers all the online entertainment they could ever need on a computer screen.

As we mentioned in an earlier chapter, one of its most important moves was its agreement with Sun Microsystems. Sun and AOL created a three-year alliance in November 1998, which enables Sun to resell Netscape's software and to provide AOL with its workstations and servers. AOL gets $350 million in marketing and licensing fees. More than that, the two hope that their mutually expansive brand communities will enable each to stretch its influence much deeper into cyberspace. This pact pushes AOL well beyond the content business and into end-to-end solutions. AOL hopes that this will catapult the masterbrand from a consumer-driven organization toward opportunities to serve the online needs of major corporations.

The New AOL Time Warner Masterbrand

As fond as Steve Case is of surprising his critics and friends alike with bold moves, nothing could have prepared observers for his biggest move of all. In January of 2000, America Online and Time Warner agreed to merge, triggering what was not only the largest business transaction to date (valued at $156 billion in stock), but the creation of what may be the most important communications marriage for a generation.

The deal was really a takeover of Time Warner by AOL, made possible by AOL's far-higher market capitalization. The purchase was also heralded as the "new media" taking over the "old media," creating a potentially awesome online/offline juggernaut that has been estimated to include as many as 80 interlocking companies and strategic partners.[5]

As the hype dust was settling when this book went to press, several issues were becoming clearer. First, the primary reason for AOL's courtship was Time Warner's 13-million-subscriber cable system, the second largest in the United States, which will put AOL on a fast track to wider bandwidth to better serve its customers. Second, the merger will provide access for AOL to an extraordinary array of news and entertainment content.

The most fascinating aspect of the deal may be in what new forms of online brand building take place as the result of the combining of some of the most successful groups of communications equities ever assembled. AOL brands (which we just discussed) will be allied with Time Warner's content brands, which are even better known: *Time* magazine, CNN, the Warner Bros. network and features, and others. With its subsequent purchase of EMI Group plc, the music moguls that carry such superstars as Garth Brooks and Smashing Pumpkins, the AOL Time Warner masterbrand community is growing even as it is born.

AOL will be contributing the strongest portal on the Internet, and a rock-solid grip on how to fulfill the typical consumer's online needs. Considering that only about one-half of the population in the world's most advanced country has a computer at home, AOL's potential for influencing the world's future view of communications is startling. That may only be the beginning of its influence, if it can successfully blend the content brands that Time Warner is bringing to the party.

This is not, however, just about combining content with delivery, but in merging and redefining online and offline brands. Traditional branding is communications-driven, meaning that it is about positioning and conveying values in one-way conveyances to recipients, whereas online branding is experiential, involving the immersing of participants in an interactive relationship with the brand. AOL will soon have the ability to merge those disciplines.

For example, the weaving in of CNN's global news gathering may bolster AOL's efforts to expand abroad and, in the process, create a new form of online news brand. Or the use of Warner Bros. properties may enable AOL to lengthen the amount of time the average subscriber stays online with the network, adding new opportunities to reinforce brand loyalties. Or the prudent use of *Time* content might create a new kind of online reader who is trained to read longer and longer text in a medium that doesn't now lend itself to lengthy copy. Most exciting of all, this dance of the brands will take place within an accelerated convergence of TV, music, film, and online. In addition, such a marriage of content and capability could also become the kick-starter for the long-struggling interactive TV movement.

From a brand-building standpoint, this is still another example of bolstering a masterbrand by evolving its surrounding community of supporting entities, enabling it to morph into new shapes and forms, and employ unheard-of communications channels.

Who Says It's Lonely at the Top?

Now that the company has the lion's share of the market, things are a bit more complicated than a few years ago when online competitors dismissed AOL as literally child's play. For one thing, although AOL's rivals are less organized than AOL for share-of-screen-time, they cumulatively represent a formidable set of competitors. Sooner or later, one or more will provide the kind of simple access that AOL offers, with a greater degree of open-ended choices. Choice and control are still the twin towers of power online, so AOL cannot afford to get overconfident about its current dominance.

To that point, dominance is exactly what they don't have outside the United States. In many non-U.S. markets, such as the United Kingdom and continental Europe, AOL is struggling to compete with free Net access from its overseas rivals. Through 1999, the company had signed up fewer than 4 million subscribers, compared with more than 20 million in the United States.

Another even more profound challenge may come from the prediction that portals will soon be replaced by Web-based computing that will have little or no need for portal entries. That is one reason why AOL may be hoping to ensure its future success by diversifying and expanding its communications investments. Steve Case and crew have also invested in TiVO, which will permit it to allow members to store hours of data and video on a hard disk. To expand its brand name beyond the PC, AOL plans to launch AOL TV, which will let users bookmark their favorite channels, access information and merchandise, and chat with other TV fans. AOL TV will be bundled with Hughes Electronics' DIRECTV broadcast satellite service, as well as a pending broadband satellite Internet service, called DirectPC.

Amid a flurry of deals at the end of 1999, AOL also signed an agreement with Wal-Mart, the nation's largest retailer, that will likely extend the Internet to those families that have been underserved to date. Under the agreement, the CompuServe unit of AOL will provide inexpensive Net services under the Wal-Mart brand. Wal-Mart will promote AOL's other services in their stores and TV advertising, and AOL will return the favor among its 20 million subscribers. This so-called bricks-and-clicks form of strategic partnering was also adopted in nearly simultaneous agreements between Yahoo! and Kmart, and Microsoft and Best Buy.[6] In each case, the core masterbrands are allying with each other to expand their own brand communities with the assistance of their partners.

In a *Business Week Online* interview in July of 1999, Steve Case summed up his company's masterbrand strategy for the future:

> ... we are the leading brand with far and away the largest audience ... For people who are comfortable using AOL, they want AOL to be on their TV or pocket device. They don't want to have to create a new E-mail address for that device, a new stock portfolio, or a new tracking service ... People want services available to them pervasively, not just on one device.[7]

Pervasive is exactly what AOL is, and will likely be well into this millennium. It's an impressive case of a master visioneer building an expansive and expanding masterbrand community.

CHAPTER 17

Interglocalize the Masterbrand

*A desk is a dangerous place from which
to view the world.*
—John LeCarré, from
The Honourable Schoolboy

On November 1, 1999, Ford Motor Company took an unprecedented step toward one-world marketing. The global giant simultaneously ran the same two-minute commercial on every major television network in the world, despite time zone differences, in support of its seven global brands. The commercial featured the music that Ford called its "global anthem."[1]

Global Debunked, Global Affirmed

At first glance, globalization looks to be an unstoppable juggernaut. Most of the larger capital markets are inexorably intertwined; cultures bubble up and overflow into one another; travel, news, and online communications slide beneath the walls of totalitarianism as easily as through telephone wires. To advocates of globalism, there is no doubt as to our future: We are and will be in contact with one another anywhere on or off the planet. We are sharing and will share significant elements of our cultures, at least among developed countries. Finally, we are buying and will buy one another's goods and services, seeking out global brands, and learning to love them almost as much as we love our indigenous counterparts.

But then, there are those who believe that it's all an enormous hoax, instigated by Theodore Levitt, the admired/misguided (it depends on your point of view) professor at Harvard Business School, who first proposed the concept in 1983.[2] Most so-called global companies are really just doing business in multiple regions, according to this view, with little or no strategic coordination between their semiautonomous business units. The few global brands that appear in most major markets are aberrations whose experiences are rarely replicated.

For masterbrand builders, this is more than an intriguing debate. A masterbrand works most successfully in a highly integrated environment, and there is literally a world of difference between global and locally networked integration strategies.

Conventional wisdom suggests that companies should go global for several hard business reasons, including expanding revenue by pushing into new markets, and bolstering profitability by achieving greater economies of scale. Procter & Gamble is an example of a company that has committed to an aggressive multiyear revenue goal, and whose only hope of hurdling that goal is to expand into new geographical markets, as well as to enter whole new businesses (e.g., Dryel for dry-cleaning clothes).

Once critical mass is achieved, profitability can be attained more reliably with global operations than with those that depend entirely on domestic sales. However, seeking synergy for its own sake can sometimes prompt unwise decisions. Consultants Michael Gould and Andrew Campbell tell the story of a CEO of a multinational food company who forced the globalizing of brands to drive up profitability and stock price. Unfortunately, one of its U.K. cookie brands died on the shelves in the United States, and a German promotional program failed when it was rolled out into neighboring EU countries. The result was internal divisiveness and resentment rather than leveraged global strengths.

Another common motive for globalizing is to diversify to protect the company against cyclical, regional downturns. During the 1990s, McDonald's weathered a tough series of years in the United States, whereas its non-U.S. operations continued to expand and remain profitable, essentially keeping the company fires burning and funding the eventual turnaround. However, the downturns in certain regions can as easily offset the value of protecting your company from those in your home region. A good example is Citigroup, the financial services giant created from the merger of Citibank and Travelers Insurance. Citigroup was hurt by the failing Asian economy and the Russian defaults in the 1997–1998 period, but it rebounded nicely with record profit when those economies began to stabilize. Numerous U.S. technology firms have also felt the sting of overseas cost run-ups, such as those caused by the 1999 Taiwan earthquake.

There are also forces at work that encourage some companies to resist globalization, including the renewed interest in local communities. There is a resurging interest in local customs and heritage in many parts of the world, and scholars and pundits caution against destroying the specialness of an area for the sake of adopting global brands. The same concern in many U.S. communities about the replacing of local coffee houses with Starbucks outlets is replayed in Europe and elsewhere as that masterbrand expands its reach.

Clearly, the pace of globalization has been overstated because the advance of a few global brands and the cost savings by some major multinationals made it appear as if global was the only way to go. Although going global may not be for all companies, it looks as if globalization will be the logical option for most larger corporations and, thanks to the Internet, a surprising number of small to mid-size firms as well.

In addition, regulatory and ecopolitical alliances are speeding the globalization process or, in some cases, a regionalization process that will lead to global sales and marketing. The NAFTA, EU, and Mercosur agreements have accelerated globalization for fully developed economies and ushered in coming-out parties for less-developed economies, such as those in Mexico and Vietnam, that now operate within regional trading blocks.

From our view, globalization is an inevitable part of many, if not most, corporate futures and a crucial part of masterbrand building. One obvious reason is the Internet, which is becoming a mandatory channel (of knowledge sharing, if not commerce) for virtually all companies, and its globalness will not be fenced in. Technology is to business what science is to society: unaffiliated with any particular country or ideology, and now, easily exportable to all.

Beyond Borders, Beyond Economies

One of the signs that globalization is inevitable is the proliferation of similar consumer and business-to-business target profiles. A 1998 Roper Starch report concluded that, although nationalism remains the primary factor that drives consumer behavior, five kinds of consumers appear to live in virtually every major country. Those five typologies were dubbed: (1) strivers (who value wealth, status, and power), (2) altruists (who seek equality and justice), (3) devouts (who value faith), (4) creatives, and (5) fun seekers. What differentiates populations, according to this research, is not wholly disparate cultural mind-sets, but simply different proportions of these basic five people types. Thus, jewelry retailers do better in high-striver countries such as the United States, and religious booksellers are more likely to prosper in more devout countries such as in the Middle East.

Visa International even created a special marketing effort designed to enhance its masterbrand among what Visa execs call the "borderless segment." These consumer segments often buy as much according to their lifestyle requirements as by regional preferences. They may include rising young business executives in Singapore, Brazil, or Toronto, who share common economic desires and tastes. They might be working mothers in Argentina who have to juggle the same work and family responsibilities as their counterparts in Kuala Lumpur. Increasingly, they are Internet shoppers who use Visa cards to order goods and services from New Zealand and São Paulo.

Visa tends to concentrate its marketing efforts against higher-income globetrotters who share common purchasing needs, regardless of their homeland. Another group of borderless consumers to whom Visa markets are those who are attracted to worldwide happenings. This can include anything from the Olympics or soccer World Cup to an internationally distributed, blockbuster film, such as the 1998 release of *Tomorrow Never Dies*, in which Visa's six regional divisions tailored the global sponsorship of the hit movie to meet their unique needs. Visa purchases were stimulated by James Bond–style BMW promotions, discounts on Bond videotapes, and giveaways of theater tickets or invitations to regional premiers. Visa USA also ran a highly successful Bond tie-in advertising campaign in support of Visa Check Card.

For other brands, cultural differences are overcome by adopting universal attributes or benefits that find a home in every house. The $13 billion L'Oréal company has done so with no fewer than 85 products, many of which are welcomed as global brands, including Redken hair care, Ralph Lauren perfumes, Vichy skin care, and numerous products under the flagship L'Oréal brand. Rather than selling a one-brand-fits-all approach, the masterbrand L'Oréal celebrates different cultures and lifestyles, while maintaining loyalty within its stable of strong brands.

L'Oréal manages this despite the wildly different state of economies in various regions of its marketing world. Asia, Europe, and the Americas have all experienced rocky financial times during the past decade, but the populations of each did not let financial instability prevent them from clamoring after L'Oréal's brands. What do we mean by clamoring? We mean achieving close to $1 billion in earnings and a ninefold increase in stock valuation during the 1990s.

Global marketing does not simply refer to selling in multiple regions, but to a coordinated global marketing structure and approach that raises the value of the brand because it taps common needs and issues of human beings across the globe. Leading global masterbrands, such as IBM, British Airways, Toyota, and Gillette, enjoy strength in dozens of markets because they meet the common needs of human beings better than their competitors. They understand and remain attuned to local customs but also cater to borderless customers.

Global Is Pancultural

McDonald's, Coca-Cola, Michelin, Kodak, and other global masterbrands have learned the cultural art of *bend but don't break*.
Their people research and recruit within local areas, ferreting out
the mores and needs that are key cultural indicators, and creating
products and services that match those needs. At the same time,
they manage to retain a wholeness to their global masterbrands
that both transcends cultures and sends out a set of consistent
brand messages across several continents.

For some companies, cultural differences offer an opportunity
to customize a brand and reinforce the company's commitment to
fit its brand into local mores. However, is it a good idea to be an
American brand, or is it better to be a world brand whose country
of origin is of little importance? That would depend on what's
being marketed. Coca-Cola, Levi's, Nike, Disney, and McDonald's
have long been carriers of American culture to other lands. It
works well for them because those brands represent the freedom
and affluence that many non-U.S. citizens admire.[3]

Globalization is a strategic pillar for a masterbrand like L'Oréal,
because it has built an identity based on cultural sophistication.
The soccer side of Nike's global brand has emphasized almost a
non-U.S. persona, which, in the case of a sport like soccer, can be
a distinct advantage. Sony is embraced as a world brand with its
country of origin of little relevance, other than a faint reminder
that Japanese electronics are reliable. Some brands seek to inter-
mingle their value proposition with the strengths of their countries of origin, as in such cases as Foster's beer (the raw wildness of
Australia), BMW (the precision performance that Germany made
famous), and Omega (the dependability of Swiss watchmaking).
For better or worse the firmly seated masterbrands that are unde-
niably global are often part of the cultures in which they market.

The Global Company as Integrated Masterbrand

Dominant global companies are discovering that the complexity
of operations and marketing on a worldwide scale increasingly
requires an integrated approach. In 1998, Visa International com-

missioned a best-practices study of 35 leading global marketers to discover what common denominators existed among companies that consistently succeed at global marketing. Although the specific results of the research remain confidential, the findings did confirm that integrated brand marketing was becoming a common practice among leading global marketers, and that all companies researched—including those that have been historically decentralized in their marketing organizations—were moving toward more integrated marketing efforts.[4]

Integrated global marketing does not have to mean that local managers lose control of their markets, or that all strategic planning takes place at headquarters. What it does mean is that individuals and teams at local and regional levels set aside their turf issues to work in close synchronization, with one purpose in mind: To build preference for the masterbrand in all markets in which it competes. This is the same dynamic that we witness within domestic organizations that have learned how to create enterprise-wide masterbrands by lowering the walls between departments and business units.

That task admittedly becomes more difficult when cultural differences encourage local managers to insist on local approaches, or when global strategic decisions are made at headquarters with only passing attention paid to the consequences at the local level. These difficulties, however, do not reduce the need for a well-integrated global marketing program that will increase the opportunities for success in the global marketplace.

A business-building approach that has been explored with considerable success during the past decade or two is *transnational team* initiatives. A 1996 organizational study concluded that creating successful transnational teams requires: some sharing of cultural norms among the team members, a certain fluency in a common language, an agreement about communication styles and expectations of what constitutes effective group behavior, an effective management style by the team leader. Successful examples have included the development of the so-called world copier as the result of a joint transnational team from Fuji and Xerox during the mid-1980s, Eastman Kodak's transnational team that handled the simultaneous pan-European launch of their Photo CD, and the IBM transnational selling of personal computers throughout 11 Latin American countries in the early 1990s.

These are all viable approaches to building an integrated team because they work cooperatively and productively to create a worldwide presence for a business and its brand community.

Why Global Companies Must Become "Glocal" Brand Builders

Futurist John Petersen has predicted that, during the next decade, Earth will be surrounded by as many as 1,700 communications satellites. Petersen believes this will create a sort of "global brain," a worldwide consciousness of information that could spawn a new era for our old planet.[5] If Petersen is correct, localized and multinational companies will be at a distinct disadvantage to those organizations that fail to make maximum use of this working world information base. To do so, global companies must market global brands—both their individual product and service brands, as well as their companies as brands. The most efficient of the global brand companies will be the global masterbrands.

A proven method of building global brands is through what has come to be known as "glocalizing." On one level, glocalizing refers simply to the seamless integration of global planning and local implementation. However, strong glocal marketers have a process for determining the optimum mixture of global branding and local/regional customization that convince some local customers that the global brand is almost indigenous. At the same time, those who travel globally, or who are simply subject to global communications, are positively impacted by the stature of the global brand in question. Finally, within the company itself, there is an almost palpable sense of brand which is simultaneously driven through the global, regional, and local channels of the organization.

Coca-Cola, for example, creates advertising and other marketing programs centrally, in addition to what is done at the local and regional levels. Management then permits local bottlers and distributors to make decisions about how (or sometimes *if*) these programs run. The company's Atlanta headquarters staff also run continuous in-market tracking research to ensure that the strategic identities of their global brands—Coke, Fanta, and Sprite—

are maintained to meet the company's high standards. The local decision makers are not forced to follow stringent advertising guidelines, but they tend to do so voluntarily because they share a common vision of how the Coca-Cola masterbrand and its offspring should be positioned in their respective markets.

Despite its mass-global advertising program described at the top of this chapter, Ford Motor Company has been strategically shifting toward more of a glocal approach to marketing. The company's "Ford 2000" global plan, initiated under then-CEO Alexander Trotman in the mid-1990s, is now more vigorously balancing the global goals of the company with opportunities to anticipate and react quickly to local and regional changes in the automobile marketplace. If implemented as planned at the time of this writing, this shift would be less of a rejection of globalism than a recognition that markets are changing too rapidly for headquarters managers to make unilateral decisions.

Global beer brewer, Carlsberg A/S, has gradually evolved to its position as a global category leader through a series of marketing and sales experiments. Carlsberg manages to be seen as Danish in some markets and as an international brand in others. Carlsberg CEO, Fleming Lindelov, has concluded that there are several important characteristics that are necessary for a global masterbrand to succeed, particularly one that is marketed in 125 local areas, as is Carlsberg. These include such masterbrand-oriented guidelines as:

- A religious dedication to quality
- A long-term vision regarding the value of the brand in all kinds of environments
- A mystique about the brand that suggests satisfaction
- The global reach that is necessary to attract millions of loyal customers
- Generational renewal of the brand, enticing younger consumers into the fold[6]

Professors Susan H. C. Tai and Y. H. Wong conducted research in 1998 about the degree of standardization (which implies the degree of headquarters control) in advertising decision making among global companies advertising in the People's Republic of China. They found that 36 percent of such decisions are standardized by headquarters in U.S. firms, compared with 40 percent in European firms, and just 15 percent in Japanese companies. European firms tended to use standardized approaches in tactical decisions. Although the Chinese venue might have had some influence on the degree of standardization that was used, the study indicates that there is a wide variation in approaches of global firms.

Professors Tai and Wong also uncovered a variation on the glocal marketing approach, which they termed "regcal," referring to some companies' use of programs that are designed regionally, but implemented locally. For example, Nestlé's Nescafé operates within a set of worldwide policies for that brand, but they are adapted tactically according to local needs, and implemented region-wide in Asia. In addition, the advertising strategy is a pan-region version, but is adjusted according to the specifications of local market target profiles.[7]

Interglocalize for the Customer's Sake

In an age when the customer should be king, global marketing issues are all too often decided using corporate organizational, logistical, or financial criteria. Are country managers always thinking first of the needs of their customers when they insist on local control? Do global managers demand that the U.K. customer and Hong Kong customer experience brand consistency because it will basically make their lives easier? As we explore what builds great masterbrands, both in the marketplace and within sponsoring companies, the highest priority is the same in every company—to deliver the best value proposition to each customer, regardless of the organizational or political ramifications of such decisions.

Needless to say, there is no one right way to serve the global customer's needs. HSBC Holdings PLC is a merged bank made up of Midland Bank, Hong Kong Bank, and Marine Midland Bank, all of which are brand names that have been eliminated. HSBC

LESSONS LEARNED FROM A GLOBAL BRAND THAT NEVER WAS

One brand that sought to appeal to borderless customers such as busy global executives was Motorola's Iridium. Iridium seemed to have everything going for it . . . a proven CEO, formidable technology, the financial backing of Motorola, and global villagers who claimed to be longing to stay in touch with one another 24/7, no matter where they happened to be.

Some critics claimed that Iridium was just a bad product, supported by a worse system, even if it did cost $5 billion to erect. Weighing in at one pound (in an age when most mobile phones weigh only a few ounces), Iridium required ungainly accessories and adapters, which apparently caused its CEO to once bark at his people: "You really expect business travelers to carry all this s---?" At an introductory cost of $3,000 per unit, and calls that ran as high as $7 per minute, Iridium's value proposition was seriously flawed (prices were eventually lowered to $1,500 per unit and less than U.S. $1 per call). The phones also could not transmit or receive unless they were in direct line of sight with one of the system's 66 satellites.

Reportedly, Edward Staiano, Iridium's tough-as-nails CEO, did not win friends and influence people with his team-building style. The selling organization never really got organized. Plus, the company had a board with 28 members who spoke multiple languages, requiring a UN-style approach to meetings, complete with headsets and translators.

In the field, Iridium depended on regional sales and marketing outlets, called gateways, whose management were responsible for selling the phone to major customers. Apparently, those sellers did a less-than-stellar job of finding and landing buyers. In other words, a masterbrand mentality never really emerged, and turned out to be a case of false hopes and inadequate masterbrand planning.

has chosen to create a single worldwide masterbrand that is being marketed consistently across all product and service target sectors. Accordingly, the brand sponsors rugby in Australia that is broadcast worldwide, part of a program that management believes will lead to a global brand, at a cost estimated to be U.S. $50 million, excluding advertising. A similar approach was taken by insurance and asset management group, AXA, which is reportedly spending U.S. $160 million to create a single global brand. However, rather than eliminating its subsidiary brands in one move, that company is gradually phasing in the new masterbrand over time.

The risk in consolidating former local and regional brands into a single global brand is that customers of the former companies may feel lost and abandoned, particularly because they are generally replaced by megasounding corporate parent names. (If you had felt at home as the customer of Marine Midland Bank, you might have a difficult time cozying up to an outfit called HSBC.) That scenario was likely on the minds of the management of the ING Group, the largest financial services group in Holland. In contrast to HSBC and AXA, ING Group has maintained its multibrand strategy because, as its Chairman, Ruud Polet, has said, "We are convinced that it [should be] the customer's choice to choose a brand and distribution channel."

Consequently, the original members of the Group (National Nederlanden, NMB Bank, and Postbank) have maintained their separate brand identities, as have nine other Group companies in Holland and more than 60 brands worldwide. The individual companies have the option to use the ING endorsement (most do so), but are not forced to follow the corporate approach. ING Group management knows that it costs more to maintain such brands, but they believe that they make more in the long run because of brand decentralization.

Using the Masterbrand to Knit the Network Together

Doctor Jagdish Sheth, professor of marketing at Emory University, proposed in 1998 that many, if not most, so-called global marketers are really *multidomestics* in disguise. That is, such companies start their businesses in their home countries, then gradually export their approach to other countries, adjusting along the way for local and regional cultures or economics. What most of those companies fail to do, according to Dr. Sheth, is to create a truly global system. Dr. Sheth proposes instead what he calls *integrated global marketing*, which, when implemented, encourages a company to adopt a globalized approach to the nurturing of core competencies.

At IBM, management works hard to maintain some independence for on-site managers, while ensuring that the sprawling corporation is united on a single global course. One of the ways that this is accomplished is within the marketing arena, where the head of worldwide corporate marketing reports directly to the CEO, with strong dotted line relationship to the vice presidents of marketing for each of the company's operational divisions. All of those individuals sit on IBM's global marketing board and contribute to corporate brand decisions and how they are implemented in the field.

On the tactical level, the Caribbean and Latin American division of Nortel Networks Corporation has tackled the issue of maintaining company unity, despite the dispersion of its global employees, by creating a live monthly show transmitted via video and data networks, called the *Virtual Leadership Academy*. The show is beamed to Nortel offices in 47 countries in the Caribbean and Latin America. Hosted by the division's vice president of marketing, the show demonstrates Nortel's cultural commitment to cutting-edge technology that elevates and celebrates humanity, rather than replacing it. Included in the shows are messages from the Nortel CEO who throws out business challenges for the employee viewers to consider, as well as a call-in Q&A. After each broadcast, viewers are polled to get reactions that guide the staff in ways to improve the communication. It all amounts to sound efforts to support the global Nortel brand.

At Lucent Technologies, marketing approaches are based on common themes, but are customized to fit individual regions. The work is reviewed by global brand councils that are staffed by representatives from around the globe, and that include representatives from the headquarters corporate marketing office. By focusing on specific targets and employing the most efficient media possible, the company claims to have created significant awareness in the United States among key targets with only about $20 million in marketing support during its initial couple of years of existence. Capitalizing on the Bell Labs reputation and using both advertising and public relations programs, the company reportedly achieved between 30 and 40 percent awareness in Germany, France, England, and parts of Latin America within two years of its relaunch as Lucent.

Global marketing is never a simple matter, but it can be considerably easier on the business-to-business side because companies and customers tend to deal in more uniform product and service criteria, and often, price-performance hurdles tend to be similar. Of course, what happens on the ground level with sales may be strongly influenced by the consistency of brand messaging in the marketplace. In addition, the word of mouth among global business communities will often drive the demand for more sophisticated business-to-business products and services, thus placing less of an onus on the global marketing efforts of the players involved.

Nevertheless, there are nuance differences that can be an important advantage for global business-to-business marketers. Quantel Digital Imaging uses different selling techniques according to business mores of the area in which they are doing business. They look for faster sales, often driven by testimonials in the United States, and longer-term sell-ins in Asia. Their messages may be bolder in Europe than in Asia, where boldness is not considered as appropriate. On the other hand, Nortel Enterprise Networks consider customers in most developed regions of the world to have similar needs and tastes, at least in Nortel's product and service category. Nortel therefore tries for a consistent positioning and marketing message across the globe, then tailors it to local tastes.

At the time of this writing, 3Com Corporation was preparing to launch a new worldwide masterbrand program. The program was designed by the company's Global Marketing group, with important input from representatives of all major divisions, business units, and field sales groups, through the 3Com Executive Marketing Council, whose members ensured that all regional issues and opportunities were addressed as the program was developed.

An example of a business marketer that has managed to extend its brand across new boundaries is Navision Software of Denmark. The company operated solely in Western Europe for many years, but had to extend beyond their traditional marketing areas when saturation appeared imminent. As Navision moved outward to Eastern Europe and eventually to the United States, its brand teams managed to deal with new cultural and business standards by creating task forces made up of veteran Navision executives and local managers who melded the company's approach and masterbrand identity with the necessities of the local marketplace. The company also trains value-added resellers (VARs) through extensive technical and marketing courses that enable them to support key clients.

Navision has enjoyed success in such far-flung locations as Iceland and South Africa. However, when the company stumbled in Australia because of problems with the team that had been assigned to the area, management disbanded the team and started over. Such discipline has enabled Navision to successfully expand beyond their home base, and to extend the Navision masterbrand into new territories by consistently translating its message into varied locales.

The IBM, Nortel, 3Com, Lucent, Quantel, and Navison examples point up the numerous opportunities that most companies have to strengthen their global masterbrands.

How the Internet Is Accelerating Glocalization

Currently, the United States and Canada account for about two-thirds of the Net users in the world, but that is projected to shrink to a minority share by 2002. A 1999 International Data Corporation (IDC) report projects that by 2003, upwards of half a billion surfers will be online. According to IDC, the Net population in the Asia-Pacific region and Japan alone will quadruple, reaching 80 million by 2003. The European region is now expected to spend $430 billion online in 2003—compared with $708 billion forecast for the United States.[8]

Internet brands are global brands by default. Globalness, long thought to be a cosmopolitan state achieved by relatively few prominent brands, is now within the reach of most whose management care to make it happen on the Internet. In fact, it's a safe assumption that virtually all major brands will eventually be global because all will be represented on the global Internet, either as sellers of goods and services, and/or purveyors of information.

Global Internet commerce requires special planning for the

thousands of current and pre-extant start-ups who must ponder how to make the leap from the garage to the world stage without losing strategic focus. Global business-to-business enterprises may face even more complex challenges. At the start-up phase, routine marketing decisions (which are never really routine) take on new ramifications. For example, a common challenge for e-brands is to acquire a name that (1) conveys its value proposition or other naming objectives, while (2) not offending distant foreign ethnic populations. If an online advertising campaign is misconstrued by a community on the other side of the globe, the sponsor is likely to hear about it within the first 24 hours after it is launched. Another slightly frightening aspect of the Internet is that a brand's global messages are all in real time. It is, as some have pointed out, live TV at its riskiest and most disconcerting.

Going global on the Internet will likely trigger a change in the operations of a company. National Semiconductor publishes information for its 30,000 products on the Net, and uses its Web site as a procurement contact point for its distributors worldwide. Its call centers handle 25,000 inquiries a month, but its Web site handles up to 30 times that number in the same amount of time. However, National Semiconductor has also run into problems in those countries in which the Internet infrastructure is not fully developed. The company has installed mirrored servers in key international locales to handle the problems.

Manufacturing has been irrevocably changed by the Internet as R&D accountability moves from being asset-based to intellectually based. Separate internal reviews during the last several years within Microsoft and Du Pont reached the same conclusion: There is no need to invest in brick and mortar in local venues if the locomotive of change and innovation can be located in a more convenient (or less costly) region, then imported to the point of purchase.

Pricing also becomes a matter of urgent priority. The Internet has become a haven for comparison shopping, all of which can be done on a worldwide basis. If you are in search of electronic equipment, you can search for it as easily in Japan as in the United Kingdom. The prices you set are world prices, like it or not. They are subject to the fickleness of prospects and the tinkering of competitors on a 24/7 clock. Business-to-business sellers must offer bids on a global basis; country-to-country adjustments may be fruitless because everyone who does business with your firm may know what everyone else is receiving as offered bids.

On the positive side, the Internet makes it possible to contact clients around the world that haven't heard from you lately. Just as the Net is a global network of virtually unlimited dimensions, it is also a series of endless opportunities to establish one-to-one relationships with customers and prospects who could not previously be on your contact list. With these new communications opportunities, however, come commensurate obligations. Once contacted regularly via the Net, these customers expect to hear from you more frequently than in the past, or more damage than good will be the end product.

MANAGING YOUR MANDATE

In the future, multinational organizations will inevitably give way to glocally integrated organizations, particularly in terms of marketing and sales. To accelerate that process for your company, and to ensure that your move to glocal operations makes the most of your company-wide brand, take the time now to carefully examine your organization's readiness to market such a brand.

Questions You Should Be Asking   As part of the process of evaluating global marketing efforts, we suggest that the following questions be addressed:

Is your company's organization designed to encourage more offshore independence, or more centralized authority? For planning purposes, there is no middle ground here. Organizational compromise leaves no one happy, and it leaves the masterbrand diluted globally. Take an honest look at which group—headquarters or the local/regional managers—has the upper hand in brand management. Do the heads of offshore divisions/units report to the CEO? Is there a primary incentive to build the business with little regard for the effects on the global brand(s), or do they take important

(Continued)

steps to maintain and nourish the global brand, even as they customize to their own region?

Have past efforts at integration of your company's functions been resisted because offshore managers assumed that they were thinly disguised power plays by headquarters? The key to overcoming such biases is to persuasively communicate that: (1) there are key differences between integration (which increases cooperative leverage) and centralization (which shifts authority and power from the field to the headquarters); and (2) no single individual or group would benefit from integration, only the global brand itself. That's not to say that skepticism will disappear when these points are made, but if a global masterbrand is to be built or strengthened, these stakes must be driven in the ground, then backed up with reinforcing action.

Do you have a program that keeps all of your marketing units informed of what others are fielding, and what experiences have been successful or have failed? Often, the best source of experience for any given marketing program is the experience of a fellow manager in another part of the world. However, if the sharing of that perspective is not part of concrete operating procedures of the company, that sharing will not take place. In companies that share successfully, the process is considered part of the regional managers' job description, and the experience of sharing ideas is celebrated as an opportunity to learn, and even be entertained by the work of other units.

Are communications channels between headquarters and offshore offices, and between the offshore offices themselves, frequently employed and with successful results? Without such channels, constructive, coordinated brand building cannot take place. How often are regional operational managers speaking with their counterparts? What are the roles of the marketers in this process, of regional heads, and of the CEO and his/her immediate lieutenants? What channels and formats seem to generate the most communications traffic? With e-mail, intranet, videoconference, fax, and phone networks available, there is no excuse for lack of communication.

Are there customer cultural barriers that have prevented full integration of marketing efforts in the past? Have they been empirically verified, or just presumed to exist? Have those barriers been created from within, or do they appear to exist within the marketplaces where the company does business?

Actions You Should Be Taking   There may be ways to present or to re-present the masterbrand in a way that is reasonably focused and consistent globally, but adaptable to local cultures. To discover such an approach, the company may have to create a pancultural panel of employees and outside experts, who can monitor cultural issues and advise managers on the global implications of their business-building initiatives. Assuming that a groundswell of support exists now, or can be generated, for more integrated global masterbrand marketing, we recommend considering the following actions:

Launch a full best-practices study among global, noncompeting companies with similar issues. The path that your company may walk in global marketing has been walked before. We keep coming back to this approach because it is a relatively painless way of avoiding the mistakes that others have made, and that could be made again because of the intrinsic pitfalls of global marketing. The lessons learned by other companies may not be exactly on target with your issues, but they will likely be enlightening and will probably lead to important new initiatives among your people.

Initiate a series of one-on-one and small group conferences with offshore managers in which the concept of integrated, glocal marketing is thoroughly examined. This needs to be in a "safe" environment, in which candid concerns and doubts can be raised without risk of retribution. It is through this methodical but lasting approach that glocal integration has been born in other companies, rather than through unilateral mandates from management. However, management must be the overall sponsor of these discussions, and the periodic physical presence of the CEO in such conclaves would be very helpful.

If a global brand council does not exist in your organization, create it as soon as possible, and make it directly accountable to the CEO. Use it as a forum to begin studying the core and periphery issues of glocal integration. You might begin with a facilitated discovery retreat, in which issues can be raised as a group in a less-pressurized atmosphere, and in which various contingencies can be fully explored.

(Continued)

That could be followed by a series of reports from participants that provide their individual perspectives on the glocalization prospect, and that spotlight special issues that must first be solved in their regions.

Once a sense of cooperative productivity has been achieved, begin development of a truly integrated glocal marketing plan. Obviously, this needs to be a carefully managed process, one that offers opportunity for full input and discussion from all quarters. The long-term goal of the program would be to create a strategic and tactical modus operandi for marketing one or more brands within a single, integrated, glocal masterbrand structure. Importantly, the plan should specifically address how the organizational structure may have to be refined to accommodate the needs of a glocally integrated company.

Establish metrics and measurements of the glocal integration process. These should be as rigorous as for any marketing program, with a no-holds-barred reporting of what works and what doesn't, with rich explanations of why not. Such benchmarking might best be conducted by a team representing all regions and the global staffs, to ensure that the results will be looked upon as reliable and unbiased. (We'll discuss this in greater detail in our last chapter).

*   *   *

Global marketing is fraught with risks and challenges that sometimes seem to exceed even the most difficult problems encountered in domestic markets. This is precisely why it is so critical that an existing or potential global company learns to build its masterbrand from the inside out, and to translate its brand components to offshore markets, using an integrated approach that combines global strategy with local and regional customizations. And now, in our final chapter, we will recommend how to deal with roadblocks standing between a company and reaching its potential as a masterbrand.

Moving Forward with the Mandate

The product is not simply a seat, but an experience
being orchestrated across the airline.
That orchestration is the brand.
—Sir Colin Marshall, former CEO, British Airways

The cases we have discussed in this book profile companies that have pulled together as one to build their businesses. In each case, they have—purposefully or otherwise—built strong masterbrands. It is those masterbrands that will sustain their companies through difficult times and serve as propellants as they surge into new areas of growth.

Of course, it's never that easy. In fact, there are some very sound reasons why it may never happen in your company . . . that is, if you permit the roadblocks to become permanent obstacles.

How Company Mentalities Stop Innovation Cold

There always seem to be sound reasons why "things just don't happen that way here." Here is some conventional wisdom that makes it difficult for company-wide brand building to ever take place:

- *"Building a strong masterbrand would kill our individual brands."* That is rarely, if ever, the case. There are many different forms of brand-built companies, including those that have successfully managed to build a strong masterbrand and strong individual brands beneath it, including Johnson & Johnson (Tylenol, Band-Aid), The Gap (Old Navy, Banana Republic), and Sara Lee (Hanes, Playtex). If they and dozens of other companies can do it, why not yours?

- *"We don't have the time or resources to invest in building another brand."* This usually comes from a well-meaning individual who discounts the positive business effect of building a strong masterbrand. Numbers speak most persuasively to these folks. Unfortunately, those companies that have not yet built their company-wide programs don't have any numbers to discuss. Instead, a best-practices analysis, both outside the company and among multiple business units within the organization itself, might serve the same function.

- *"Our people don't want to work for a brand, they want to work for a company."* Wrong. They want to work for an organization that will promise to pay them what they deserve, and that will offer a great place to work. Create an exciting brand-based organization and you will see them more excited than when they worked for a conventional company with similar strengths.

- *"None of us is the Herb Kelleher type."* Well, how many are? If you are, or if you have on the senior staff a charismatic leader like Kelleher, then make the most of the opportunity. If yours is like most companies, though, you need to build your masterbrand around the *thinking* of the CEO, not around her or his personality. That means that teams of brand builders will represent the masterbrand, rather than one individual. (And, by the way, *every* CEO has some personality traits that can be used to positively represent the masterbrand.)

- *"We can't afford to take our eye off the earnings ball long enough to launch a multiyear masterbrand campaign."* Again . . . you already have, you just didn't call it a masterbrand campaign. Every move your company makes is contributing to the creation and augmenting of an existing brand. The question is whether you intend to manage it, or to let it manage you.

- *"We could never get our people to agree on what the company as a whole should stand for."* Now, that's a problem. Of course, everyone already has agreed (at least tacitly) about what the company stands for in its mission and vision statements, long-term strategic planning documents, and annual reports. What the company may not have done is transform those agreements into masterbrand value statements and action plans that help its teams think like contributors to a single brand, rather than as employees of a traditional company. In short, that's an eminently fixable problem.

- *"Whomever we selected to lead the masterbrand would be considered an interloper by our other managers."* That's why the CEO must personally endorse and participate in the masterbrand-building process. With that endorsement, initial barriers of this type should begin to slide away. It will then be up to masterbrand champions or coaches to use their skills to retain the respect and cooperation of others.

- *"Masterbrands are easy enough for start-ups to create, but we're too far down the road for that."* According to this excuse, companies like Saturn, Nike, Lucent, Starbucks, and the like were founded by visionaries and their situations are not relevant to mature, traditional companies like yours. It becomes easy to discount these examples as teaching cases because they never had the unhelpful heritage and bad habits that older companies had to deal with. However, the steps that the people of such companies have taken are well within the reach of every company in business today. It undoubtedly will require more energy than starting from scratch, but the same partnerships that visionary masterbrand companies created can change old companies that seem forever set in their ways. Just ask the 20-year veterans at Ford, Apple and IBM, who have seen their companies lose their way, then be reborn as cohesive masterbrands.

- *"We put our company name on everything that leaves this place. What more could we possibly do?"* You can build your master-brand into everything you do, and vice versa. See Chapters 1 through 12 for details.

How to Build Your Masterbrand

Throughout this book, we have suggested specific actions for com-pany leaders to take to begin the process of building a strong com-pany masterbrand and, ultimately, a productive brand community. Let's take a last look at these proposed actions and some added comments.

Action: *Grow a Masterbrand Community*

Building a brand community is the outcome and objective of your efforts to become a masterbrand company. As with other commu-nities, a brand community exists as an ideal that, although never perfectly attained, can be an aspiration and a guide to action. Not all companies can or should try to create full-fledged brand com-munities, but almost all can benefit from moving farther along the continuum toward the trust and customer intimacy that brand communities create. Some additional perspectives to keep in mind:

Ask not what a brand community can do for your company, but rather what a brand community can do for your customers, employees, and strategic partners. As we have seen, giving something away to create value for potential customers is neither as reckless nor as altruistic as it may seem. The point is to focus on creating value for your customers in any way possible, where your efforts should sup-port and multiply the value created by other brand community members. This means being prepared to obsolete any apparent competitive advantage *before* your competitors (or customers) do so, as long as you enhance affinity with your brand community. As your brand community increasingly becomes the natural unit of value creation and strategic positioning, all aspects of your com-pany's organization and activities must revolve around it, stabi-lized and kept on course by a strong and pervasive sense of what it means to be a masterbrand.

Pull together a multidisciplinary team to found or to foster your brand community. Fortunately, mid-to-large-size companies already use multidisciplinary teams to tackle broad policy and work issues. The masterbrand community is, by definition, composed of a large group of individuals who, in turn, reach out in their dealings with customers, suppliers, communications partners, strategic partners, and so on.

Establishing such an organization to help build the masterbrand community may be the easiest part of the task. Far more difficult is sustaining enthusiasm over time for a job whose immediate rewards are difficult to quantify. We recommend that the leaders of the group spend a significant amount of time determining what would most motivate its individual members to stay involved with the process. Those inclined toward empirical analysis might be given the task of reviewing background data on the task, or creating a quantitative metrics system. Those with interests in communications might be the liaison to the communications agencies, and so on.

This group must operate on a consensus management approach. It must have the characteristics of a town hall–type organization, but without so much democratization that it is unmanageable. Thus, the leaders of the group need to be instinctively sensitive to the needs all of the members of the group, but without taking their collective eyes off of the target of creating a strong, interdependent masterbrand community.

In addition, ensure that as many planning representatives as possible get an opportunity to represent the group with management, the employee-partner groups, or to external audiences. This will motivate them to concentrate on the development process, and reward them for their hard work with well-deserved recognition.

Identify key members (customers, employees, intermediaries, investors, etc.) of your existing or prospective brand community, and prioritize the actions that will attract, encourage, and support them in their efforts to create value through mutual association. This step is critical in evaluating your company's capabilities for creating and sustaining a true brand community. It may determine whether (and how far) you pursue this strategy. Audits of communications, training, and other resources must be undertaken, guided by this vision of who will play what role in your brand community, and why.

Determine what aspects of your masterbrand you are willing to co-own with members of your brand community, then demonstrate your largesse with tangible evidence of their ownership. A masterbrand company cannot afford to unilaterally impose strictures or set limits on its brand community in a misguided effort to lock up captive customers. A brand community requires and fosters a sense of trust and credibility that is based on mutual ownership of its masterbrand. Unless you are prepared to operate as a fully transparent organization, sharing customers, resources, and the resulting wealth, you are not yet ready for brand community prime time.

Action: Interactivate the Brand.comm

Brand communities existed before the Internet, and most currently thrive offline more than online. Increasingly, however, intranets and extranets allow companies to literally turn themselves inside out; to forge stronger, more diverse value chains; and to better serve their customers. Often beginning as an effort to improve internal communications and training, or to automate order taking and fulfillment, a company intranet frequently is supplemented with one or more extranets that link suppliers and distributors and streamline logistics for all. Thus, the stage is set to include customers in this process and to create an online brand community, or a brand.comm. As you contemplate this move, consider the following:

Be prepared to change your business practices to fit the Internet, instead of trying to mold part of the Net to serve your business. As GE moves its masterbrand online, it is explicitly trying to avoid merely digitizing bad habits. To which we might add: Don't just digitize *good* habits, either. Instead, look for the qualitatively different ways you can interact with employees, customers, and other members of your brand community via the Internet and other interactive communications technologies. Today's means may become tomorrow's ends, just as FedEx's package-tracking technology evolved into its burgeoning business of logistics support.

Keep in mind the conceptual distinction between e-business and e-commerce even (and especially) as the two converge within a brand community. As Levi Strauss and other companies have discovered, using the Internet to improve business practices doesn't necessarily require or prepare you for selling online. Decide which link or links you want to add to your customers' overall value chain, that is, where and how you can best create value for your brand community. Focus your efforts accordingly and let others do the same. Make sure you're trading *with* your customers and other brand community members within a collaborative environment—not *at* them.

Hire, train, motivate, and reward your employee-partners for their brand community-building skills as much as any others. The only thing certain about your brand community is that it will change in ways that you can guide but cannot control (and don't *want* to). Your masterbrand is there to help you stay the course, remaining the same by changing as you reinvent the company to meet customers' evolving needs. Because you'll be "making it up as you go along," you'd better take along employee-partners who are capable of doing the same.

Create an online ecology that attracts and creates value for a wide range of brand community partners. Because you must specialize in your core area of value creation, you will need creative, aggressive, and willing partners to supplement your efforts. Although a lot of these potential partners might look like—and occasionally be— competitors, you can't define your own success narrowly as the outcome of a zero-sum game. Rather, you must align your success with that of your partners, by creating win-win opportunities for all members of your shared brand community. You must identify—and overcome—all barriers to this transparency and cocreation of value, starting with turf issues within your own company. Not the least of the benefits of this move toward an open, interdependent environment is that Darwinian pressures will force you to become a "learning organization" that knows how to survive in such settings.

Action: Extend the Online Community

Intranets can evolve into extranets and lay the foundation for an online brand community. So, too, do brand communities "grow out of" conventional companies, both logically and chronologically. However, it is critical that, psychologically, you *reverse* these sequences and always keep the brand community first in your thinking. When we extend the masterbrand, there is a very literal sense in which the resulting brand community grows out of the conventional company—the same way that a crab grows out of its shell. More specifically:

Build your brand community around the existing interests and activities of its members. Actually, this should follow logically from always putting the customer—and, thus, the brand community—first. However, it's easy to forget this and to slip into the field-of-(pipe)-dreams mentality: If we build it, they will come. Instead, iVillage and many others are demonstrating that the most successful online communities are those that build on and extend the natural inclinations of particular social groups (e.g., first-time mothers).

Online auctions would seem to be the ultimate example of *dis-intermediation*—bringing buyer and seller into direct contact. A funny thing is happening on the way to the trading floor, though: Auction sites such as eBay are growing into full-fledged online brand communities. This development is less surprising if we remind ourselves that auctions are inherently social occasions, simultaneously bringing together numerous buyers and sellers. Although the Internet has changed their scale and scope, the comparison and haggling at the heart of an auction are among the oldest known social activities.

Far from technology depersonalizing society, then, the Internet has become the medium for socializing technology. Your master-brand will be a rallying point that helps your brand community define its purpose and maintain its identity amid change, but you'll want to leave a lot of the heavy lifting to community members. If you let *them* build it, they won't have to come—they'll already be there.

"Reintermediate" your masterbrand, online or off. Some wit observed that the thing he most dreaded about a classical music concert was not knowing when to clap. We pointed out early in our book the potentially disruptive power of the Internet, but disintermediation is only the first movement of a larger symphony. It's already becoming apparent that the Internet gives more than it takes, and that it's true value is in creating, not breaking, links. There will be a good deal more applause than jeers as the Net's full potential unfolds.

Extending your masterbrand into a brand community means (re)establishing relationships with and among customers, online or otherwise. As Fidelity learned the hard way, it's better to use the pull dynamics of the Internet to attract brand community residents to your Power Street than it is to try to push less attractive customers into online self-service. A brand community is necessarily inclusive of some by being exclusive of others. However, being part of such a community means that you don't make this decision by yourself.

Action: Coach the Customer's Team

Just as Sun Microsystems believes that "The network is the computer," so too is the brand community the masterbrand. That is, the masterbrand exists only in and through the network of interlinked community members who bring the brand to life. Although a true masterbrand is ultimately owned by all community members, you must begin the process of building a masterbrand community by coaching the customer's team, your employee-partners.

Reengineering, TQM, and other tools of modern business management haven't always lived up to their initial promise. Current studies suggest that these approaches don't necessarily correlate with better business performance as measured by ROI and other indicators. In contrast, companies with higher levels of employee commitment simply perform better. This should not be surprising if we're truly living in an information economy. It's even more likely to be true if we're moving to an affinity economy in which brand communities as the natural units of value creation and competition. If you want the highest ROI in your employee-partners, you need to see and cultivate them as what they are—your fundamental masterbrand assets. Consequently, we strongly recommend the following:

Conduct a brand diagnostic. Company marketers and salespeople sometimes feel as if they have got to "get something into the field" before they have got a firm understanding of what is actually happening out in the field or, for that matter, within their own companies. A brand diagnostic is not a consultant's invention to generate fees; it is a necessary step that enables all decisions made after it is completed to be as accurate as possible—whether a consultant is hired or not. Don't skip this phase. You'll regret it in the morning.

Plan and implement a comprehensive internal marketing program, with at least as much energy and enthusiasm as those programs aimed at outside audiences. There is an understandable tendency to spend marketing research resources surveying the marketplace, and a similar tendency to believe that we already know what our organization's people are thinking. What we forget is that working for a company does not preclude employees from acting in unpredictable ways. The company-wide masterbrand requires clear and frequent communications, or it will surely wane and decline. It's a cliché to say that communications is the most important issue in corporate life, largely because it is true.

Depending upon your business, the people in your organization may be the single most important target in your marketing program, because if they do not believe in your value proposition, then sooner or later, the customer will come around to their point of view. Thus, internal research among employee-partners is *at least* as important as external surveying. A well-thought-through internal marketing plan is the only way to win and secure commitment of another kind—the commitment from management and the rank-and-file that employee-partners can, in fact, help the external marketing process.

As we have written repeatedly throughout this book, employee-partners need to be wooed by the company they work for, and what it stands for in the marketplace. Generally speaking, they should be treated as the single most important recipients of marketing efforts that a company deploys. With their full support and commitment to the masterbrand, anything is possible. Without it, success will be a limited triumph.

Identify the strategic parameters of the masterbrand. In other words, exactly what *is* the company's masterbrand? Where can it go? What other brands can it enhance? How elastic is it? What happens to it when it is merged with the brands of strategic partners?

One technique that we have successfully employed to help determine the answer to these questions is called Brandstorming™, which includes a focused exploratory of what a masterbrand is, and what it could be. Elements include:

- A review of the fundamentals of brand building, particularly as they apply to a particular market (see "brand training" later)

- An interactive exchange of ideas about the key drivers of choice and points of leverage for the market under consideration

- A dimensionalizing of the masterbrand in question, bringing it to life in new and different ways to help examine its strengths and weaknesses versus real and perceived competition

- A reconstructing of the brand in strategic and tactical makeover that stretches the masterbrand into new places

- Assigning specific tasks to all participants that give them an opportunity to take immediate action, as well as to learn more for future initiatives

- A follow-up program via e-mail and/or intranet to gauge and guide the masterbrand development process

Create a team of multidisciplinary senior executives who will spear-head (indefinitely) the masterbrand-building process and its role in the greater community. A good many companies have midlevel groups, some of them charged with steering brand direction, that sooner or later become dysfunctional because they do not have the authority and/or power to make their decisions stick. The head of the team we are recommending must report to the chief branding officer, and that is none other than the CEO. In fact, the CEO should officially or otherwise participate in this group, which is one of the few ways that it will have a fighting chance to survive long-term.

Turn everyone into a trainer. This is a form of viral marketing, in which the employee-partners become masterbrand advocates and spread the word. An important part of the process, though, is the channeling of the information and insights through a brand-building discipline, not just a well-intentioned, but less-effective enthusiasm for the masterbrand.

Our advice here is to integrate the brand training into the instruction or orientations that the employee-partners receive for other purposes, in addition to special brand-training programs. New employee-partner orientations, ongoing and upgrading skill

training, and team-building sessions are all good forums for introducing brand-building subjects. In-depth profiling of customers
and other members of the masterbrand community, as well as key
competitors, should also be part of these programs. The advent of
online training and sophisticated but affordable training software
should make these goals relatively simple to achieve.

Fortunately, we all live with brands every day of our lives, and
it's not difficult for marketing laypersons to understand and buy
into the general idea of supporting a brand. Beyond the basics,
however, there may need to be some in-depth orienting, and even
indoctrinating, about the myriad opportunities offered by a stal-
wart company-wide masterbrand.

Conduct carefully orchestrated off-campus meetings. For the past 20
years or so, some of the finest minds at several think tanks have
been trying to come up with a viable substitute for the conventional
business meeting. Videoconferences and intranets notwithstanding,
there is still no substitute for over-the-table conversation. Similarly,
when it comes to marketing planning, there is still no substitute for
carefully planned off-campus exploratories. In our more horizon-
tally stretched, matrixed organizations, such meetings bring clarity
and constructive consensus decisions, assuming that they have been
carefully prepared and facilitated.

There is also an opportunity to include other masterbrand community members in the off-sites. Bringing in strategic partners,
suppliers, and customers, can add critical realism and street-level
impact to the sessions.

Action: Organize to Brand-Build

In the 1972 movie, *The Candidate*, Robert Redford portrays a
rookie politician whose professionally cynical handlers will stop at
nothing until he is elected the junior senator from California. In
the final scene, victorious and exhausted, he turns to his manager
and asks: "What do we do *now?*" It sometimes seems that we focus
so hard on the process of getting there that we forget where we're
going—or why we started out in the first place.

Total quality management and other tools of the modern corporation are at once the highest achievement and the deepest pit-
fall of conventional business management. As we noted in

Chapter 6, it's hard to be customer-centric when our very tools for managing and evaluating our activities force us to be process-centric. Once we pick up that hammer, everything starts to look like a nail. That's why, when we organize to build a brand community around our employee-partners, we need the masterbrand toolbox. Here are some good places to start hammering:

Help your people understand how important they are to the masterbrand-building process. When a worker is an employee, he or she is seen as a cog in a wheel, albeit an important cog. When the person is called and considered to be a partner, associate, member, or colleague, the feeling of cooperative interaction is introduced. When all such employee-partners feel as if they are contributing to the creation of something important that will change lives, such as in a masterbrand environment, their role is that much more enhanced in their eyes and in the eyes of those whose respect they seek. When all of that is happening within the larger context of a brand community, then all that can be done is being done to offer that person the most rewarding possible work.

Make the masterbrand part of the daily work of the company. The simplest and most direct method of keeping the focus on the masterbrand is to weave brand-building vernacular, strategy and tactics, and initiatives into daily work. Devising a brand-oriented sales development plan is not just to generate short-term sales, but to build the masterbrand's presence to yield longer-term growth. Developing a new way to organize the customer service function according to brand needs will make CS more productive, and it will have a demonstrably positive effect on how the masterbrand is viewed by customers.

As the U.S. economy has burned bright and hot for the past few years, workers in many industries have found that they can make more at the outfit down the street. If salary hikes and signing bonuses are all that they are looking for, nothing will keep them down on the farm. However, if a company has done everything possible to respect the rights of, and provide opportunities for, valued employee-partners, then compensation obsessions will at least be tempered. Rallying employee-partners around a masterbrand that makes a difference will make a difference in the way they look at how they make a living.

Create a dynamic masterbrand infrastructure. The best of intentions remain just that unless translated into workable organizational approaches. Every important company initiative must have a champion or a group of fervent sponsors who birth, grow, and protect the *idea* of a masterbrand, in addition to the physical trappings of the same. This requires a formal commitment to an organization within an organization, with its own sense of vitality and purpose.

Over time, the brand champion, brand council, and brand coach must become more and more central to the operation of the company as a whole, because they are responsible for nurturing the strategic essence of the organization.

Action: Unify the Diverse Community

Whether deployed in a small, local brand community or spanning large, diverse, or global organizations, a masterbrand is the enduring point of reference that unites and energizes the whole, multiplying value for customers and shareholders alike. Diverse companies should consider the following:

Tackle the common challenges of multiple brands and autonomous business units. Most of the companies discussed in our book have not been multibrand organizations, and readers may wonder how relevant the lessons described from those companies are to their businesses. As we pointed out in Chapter 9, though, the lessons learned from multibrand companies can also be applied to multiunit companies—in other words, almost all companies you could name. Do not be discouraged by diversity; use it to build a richer masterbrand.

Concentrate commitment. Companies with strong semi-independent business units, divisions, and/or brands, have a much tougher time determining what their masterbrand should be, and what it should represent, not to mention who in the organization should be responsible for it. The lesson from such experiences is simply this: What's difficult about building a masterbrand does not necessarily have to do with the diversity of the company's businesses. It is more a function of the determination of management and the people of the company that determines if that company will become more unified and powerful in the markets in which it competes.

Turn the tables. The key will be convincing the players: (1) that their individual brands or units will be strengthened, not diluted, by a masterbrand strategy; and (2) that future opportunities for innovation and growth will, likewise, be improved with a masterbrand approach. Companies like Gillette, Johnson & Johnson, Sara Lee, and Tricon are managing to maintain a feeling of unity, around central brand-driven beliefs, despite the diverse set of brands that they must market. And therein is the message: If they can do it, so can your company, no matter how diverse it may be.

Aciton: Outbrand the Competition

The oft-quoted Pogoism, "We have met the enemy, and he is us" is turning out to be pretty good strategic advice, because you frequently need to become your enemy to beat your enemy. Every organization today faces the same AAAA threat—*any and all alternatives* to the specific ways it creates value for its customers. As Yahoo! has shown most clearly, you need to be prepared—and be able—to obsolete yourself before your competitors (or customers) do this for you. As this process drives the focus of competitive positioning from products to services to information and finally affinity, it takes a masterbrand community to remain the same across continuous change. Some additional thoughts:

Kill the "killer app." Although "planned obsolescence" may have existed only in the fevered imagination of critics of the throw-away consumer society, it may finally be an idea whose time has come—not to the products, but to the *processes* of today's even more affluent society. If, as Lycos and other Internet-based companies believe, anything with broad appeal will eventually be given away free, then the new dynamics of value creation will drive an equally radical rethinking of competitive strategy.

Brand communities are built on and foster credibility and trust, largely via the brand attitudes projected by a company's actions to its customers, employees, and other community members. Thus, Yahoo! simply *is* its masterbrand promise to be the trusted source of anything its customers want on or over the Web—and it will link to friend and foe alike to deliver on this. Nothing demonstrates masterbrand attitude like a willingness to turn your transparent organization inside out to serve customers, integrating them into your value chain, partnering with competitors, and generally doing whatever it takes to serve them.

Don't let your products stand in the way of the services you could provide—and don't base those services on providing information that customers can get better, cheaper, faster elsewhere. Examine every link in your value chain, every switchpoint in your brand community network to determine how you can obsolete old means in favor of the enduring end of increased affinity with customers, employees, and other community members.

Don't destroy your business, maneuver your masterbrand. Many successful companies outsource peripheral aspects of their business to others who can do a better job, allowing them to focus on core activities. A masterbrand company takes this one step further, outbranding the competition by performing the core function of brand building where it's done best—out among members of its brand community. By, in effect, outsourcing brand building, a masterbrand company inspires its brand community members to "in-source" their creativity and enthusiasm for the brand. Although the company's financial, technical, and other resources will still be needed to harness this inspiration and convert it to customer benefits, a masterbrand is less likely than other types of companies to fall into the trap of the "killer app."

Action: Interglocalize the Masterbrand

Being a masterbrand does not mean mastering others with your brand. Nor does it mean becoming a global company by imposing your vision and version of the world on unsuspecting prospects. Just as the openness and collaboration that are intrinsic to the Internet undermines traditional hierarchy and notions of center and periphery, so too does a masterbrand allow companies to be both global and local, in part by being online and interactive. Put this potential together, and you can "interglocalize," a brand anywhere in the world. Some steps to consider:

Clarify the scope and depth of your company's commitment to global commerce. In the offline, or online, marketplace, if you are committed to operating globally, it will require special considerations about how to build and maintain a synchronized masterbrand strategy. If your company is already operating globally, it may make sense to conduct a thorough analysis of current global marketing conditions, within the scope of erecting a carefully orchestrated masterbrand.

Even if your company is not planning to sell abroad, there are still lessons to be learned from global brand building. For one, the skills that are needed to "glocalize" your brand efforts can be applied to domestic vertical markets or regional U.S. initiatives. Broadly speaking, glocalizing is simply the concept that both central planners and field representatives must have appropriate input into the ultimate sale to the customer.

Finally, intelligent integration is a paradigm that should be applied to all marketing endeavors, and it is in the glocal programs that the most can be learned about how to implement those most productively. So, even if your company is not involved in glocal marketing or sales development, it can learn valuable lessons from those that are.

The Matter of Metrics

It's a well-established principle that if you can't measure it, you can't manage it. Unfortunately, in practice, this often means that we manage only those processes and outcomes that can be easily quantified. For example, customer service gets operationalized into slogans such as "80/20"—picking up 80 percent of customer calls within 20 seconds. We fail to measure (and thus implicitly denigrate) allegedly softer, qualitative aspects of our performance. We do so at our peril, however, because it is precisely these subjective customer perceptions—especially inferences about our brand attitudes—that drive customer loyalty and build brand communities.

Managing your organization requires metrics of brand community cohesion that are the key to, and that must be linked with, conventional measures of business performance. Although this could easily be the subject of an entire book, we can briefly review a few points that you should consider in developing such metrics.

If your strategy is to manage your masterbrand within a brand community, you'll need to supplement your existing financial measures of business performance with additional metrics in some or all of the following areas. Use diagnostic research to determine how these measures interrelate and to establish baseline levels and realistic goals for each. Monitor and report key metrics as continuously and widely as possible.

Brand Community Cohesion

Establish parallel tracking systems to monitor "relationship barometers" among employee-partners, brand community allies (suppliers, distributors, strategic alliance partners, etc.), and customers. (With appropriate modifications, you should also track some of these key measures among financial analysts, regulators, employment services, or other third parties.)

Attitudinal measures. Ask yourself these questions:

- How well do [employees/allies/customers] *understand* the masterbrand? Can they identify—and identify *with*—its core attributes (e.g., "innovative" for 3M)?

- How *committed* are they to your organization and to the masterbrand?

- In what ways do they feel they *own* the masterbrand, jointly with other community members and uniquely as a function of their specific role in the brand community?

- What do they feel *they* do for the masterbrand?

- What do they feel the masterbrand does for *them?*

- Is the masterbrand and its promise perceived to be unique (non-replicable) and preferred? If so, in what way(s)?

Behavioral measures. Ask yourself these questions:

- How often, where, when, and how do brand community members interact? For example, how often do employees meet to discuss brand community building? How often do employees interact with allies? How often do customers interact with your organization (e.g., visit a Web site)? With other brand community allies? With each other?

- How many active or potential links are there in your brand community network? Which of these are active or latent for specific members and why? Is this growing or otherwise improving over time? Why or why not? In what sense more (quantity, quality) is better will depend on the nature of your business and brand community. With a little imagination and work, however, this can be a useful, quantifiable metric.

Brand Community Range and Extendability

Consider both the potential and actual range of your brand community.

Develop and monitor attitudinal metrics of the potential range and extendability of your brand community. What products or services would various members consider appropriate additions to your brand community? How (and for whom) is this changing over time as your brand community matures? What other organizations or brand communities might appropriately join yours, and what is the basis of this potential overlap? Again, how is this changing as your brand community evolves?

Develop and monitor behavioral metrics of the actual range and extendability of your brand community. Quantify the actual extension of products or services to existing brand community members and the relationships that are formed with other organizations and brand community. Note especially the rate of change in these metrics: Is your brand community developing the kind of critical mass that sets off a self-sustaining value chain reaction? Or are you still operating as a conventional marketing organization, pushing incrementally more or different products at captive customers?

Technology and Innovation Measures

These should be developed not for their own sake, but as leading indicators of the capacity to engage in effective brand community building within and beyond your organization. Candidate metrics could include those described in the following paragraphs:

Attitudinal and behavioral measures of your employee-partners' Internet savvy (and receptivity to the appropriate use of technology more broadly). How do they view the importance of IT to the organization in general and to themselves in particular? Is IT seen as a separate function within the organization, or as an aspect of doing their daily work? How receptive are they to using the Internet and other technologies to enhance the brand community? How confident are they of their own abilities to do this, and are they willing to seek out training to improve their skills? Do they see the current training for and use of IT as being valuable or a waste of time?

Quantifiable measures of the cost and time savings that result from use of the Internet and other information technologies. Wherever possible, link these metrics explicitly to improvements in community brand-building efforts. For example, document and monitor how an interactive database of customer information reduces time needed for repetitive data entry or recovery, freeing customer service reps to provide more customized or proactive service. (Monitor and correlate the changes in customer satisfaction, brand equity, and brand community cohesion that should result from these internal improvements.)

Here, you could also include qualitative and quantitative measures of how well your organization obsoletes its own products and services to enhance customer affinity. Consider also the *rate* at which this is happening vis-à-vis competitors and changing market conditions.

Quantifiable measures of the extent to which your company is becoming a transparent, learning organization, where the experiences of a few are rapidly disseminated to benefit all. This may be the direct result of increased use of company-wide training and use of intranets and extranets. Do not limit the measures to savings of time and money only, however. Also, try as best you can to quantify the upside value of applying best practices to brand community building—and link this as closely as possible to bottom-line outcomes (employee and customer retention, cross-selling, reduced customer complaints, regulatory treatment, etc.).

The Easy Wisdom of Best Practices

By now, you've gotten the idea of how committed we are to best practice research and analysis. There simply is no better (and, by the way, no less expensive) way to determine what has worked and is likely to work in a market. Just as important, the information relationships that a company establishes with noncompeting best-practice partners can lead to new and better ways to expand the masterbrand community.

Best-practice analysis may not appear to be helpful because most markets are changing so rapidly that there may not be much to learn from the past. The reality, however, is that although information technology is changing how we do business, we are still subject to the same kinds of marketing and sales mistakes of the past, just applied to new venues, and at accelerating speeds. What other companies have learned from past experiences can still be very valuable to planning, even in a time-blurred world.

If you have not participated in a best-practices sharing with other companies, you may be surprised how simple and easy it is to establish. It turns out that many companies want to learn from the experiences of others. We have also observed that company managers are more open to discussing their work with noncompeting companies, because of the increasing importance of strategic alliances, which require a certain amount of sharing. We strongly recommend that you create a permanent, high-level group to continuously explore best-practice sharing, employing secondary research and ongoing sharing among other appropriate companies.

Finally, the best of best practices can take place within the organization itself. Too many quasi-independent business units, divisions, and subsidiaries keep their successes (and especially their failures) to themselves. If, on the other hand, they are asked to share those experiences on a regular basis, the company is generally saved much time and trouble by concentrating on proven successes and avoiding frustrating dead ends. A formal, carefully monitored, and strategically managed internal best-practices program will reap rewards far exceeding costs.

The value of best practices is a direct function of the maturity of the markets being studied. The younger the market, the more its participants can use the information gleaned from best-practices sharing. However, the less mature the market, the fewer time-proven solutions are available. In any case, the more experience a masterbrand team has in best-practice analysis, the more likely that valuable insights will be available.

Epilogue

It was the best decision I ever made.
—Akio Morita, former chairman, Sony Corp.[1]

Not long after Masaru Ibuka and Akio Morita founded Tokyo Telecommunications Engineering in 1946, they received an enormous order of 100,000 radios from Bulova Watch Company. But Bulova wanted to sell the radios under its own brand, and marketeer Morita turned down the order. "I said then and I have said it often since," Morita wrote in his autobiography, "It was the best decision I ever made."[2]

Morita and his colleagues were determined that their company would be built on the shoulders of a global masterbrand, not by selling its technology or products through other companies. In 1958, Morita changed the name of the company to Sony Corporation (from the Latin *sonus*, meaning sound, and *sonny boy*, which conveyed a young, American-style imagery). Morita once explained his approach to innovation, which was astonishingly antithetical to modern marketing orthodoxy: "Our plan is to lead the public with new products rather than ask them what kind of products they want . . . The public does not know what is possible, but we do."[3]

The company went on to become one of the most valuable masterbrands in the world by rallying its people around its irrepressible innovativeness. In so doing, Sony created and marketed such breakthroughs as the first commercially successful transistor radio, the Trinitron TV, and the legendary Walkman line of electronic portables.

Sony has also had its share of product failures, financial disappointments, and political in-fighting. But its people have always understood and acted upon what is the premise of our book: Whatever tangible assets a company holds, whatever leverage it enjoys in the marketplace, whatever value it has been accorded by its customers and investors, they can all be multiplied by the unifying force behind a strategically nurtured masterbrand.

Your company may never market global brands with the stature of Sony's, or be as persistently profitable as General Electric, or as highly capitalized as Yahoo!. Yet, your company can be much, much more than it is today if it consolidates and redistributes its energies through a central masterbrand.

It comes down to this: Either you treat your company as a company, or you transform it into a masterbrand. If you choose the masterbrand course, it may very well be the best decision *you* ever make.

We wish you the best of luck on your journey.

ENDNOTES

Chapter 1

1. From: Ted Goodman (ed.), *The Forbes Book of Business Quotations* (Black Dog & Leventhal, 1997, p. 112).

2. Global Most Admired from Jeremy Kahn, *Fortune*, 11 October 1999: (1) General Electric, (2) Microsoft, (3) Coca-Cola, (4) Intel, (5) Berkshire Hathaway, (6) IBM, (7) Wal-Mart, (8) Cisco Systems, (9) Dell Computer, and (10) Merck. Corporate reputation survey as reported by Ronald Alsop, "Corporate Reputations Are Earned With Trust and Reliability," *Wall Street Journal Interactive Edition*, 23 September 1999.

3. James C. Collins and Jerry I. Porras, *Built to Last* (HarperBusiness, 1997, p. 30). *Built to Last* is a superb summary of what has worked in the past, but the rules that created historical longevity appear to be changing.

4. In the past, the term *masterbrand* has been used periodically to refer to family brands that umbrella over a line of individual product/service brands. Our purpose here is to upgrade the meaning of the term to apply across the company as a whole.

5. Peter Haapaneimi, "Corporation 2010," *Chief Executive (US)*, 1 January 1998, p. S2.

6. Study conducted by Gallup Organization and Institute for the Future, 1998, and Don Clark, "Managing the mountain," *The Wall Street Journal Interactive Edition*, 21 June 1999.

7. Janelle Brown, "Is technology unplugging our minds," *Salon.com*, 7 October 1999.

8. ———, "The science of alliance," *The Economist*, 4 April 1998, p. 69.

9. ———, "Faites vos jeux," *The Economist*, 4 December 1999.

10. Daniel Grebler, "Putting your customers second," *Reuters Business Report*, 14 May 1997.

11. Jonathan Littman, "Driven to succeed: The Yahoo story." *Upside* 10, no. 9 (September 1998).

12. Peter M. Senge, "Communities of leaders and learners," *Harvard Business Review*, September–October 1997, p. 31.

Chapter 2

1. Robert D. Hof and Linda Himelstein, "eBay vs. Amazon.com," *Business Week*, 31 May 1999, p. 134.

2. Michael Kiely, "Keep it in the family," *Marketing*, 12 June 1997, p. 36.

3. These claims are extensively documented in numerous studies commissioned

by and available from the Marketing Science Institute, 1000 Massachusetts Avenue, Cambridge, MA 02139.

4. ———, "Unfolding a success story," *The Portland Oregonian*, 10 November 1996, p. G1.

5. Based on interviews with Tim Leatherman and Mark Baker of Leatherman Tool Group, July and October, 1999.

6. David Hoye, "Praise the Mac," *Arizona Republic*, 19 February 1997.

7. Erika Rasmussen, "Snapping back into action," *Sales & Marketing Management*, October 1997, p. 24; and Bruce Horovitz, "New owner is whipping Snapple back into shape," *USA Today*, 9 March 1998, p. 01B.

8. Based on interviews with Robert Solomon and Bill Brown, VP—Human Resources, Outrigger Hotels & Resorts, in June 1999.

9. Based on internal corporate documents of Outrigger Hotels & Resorts.

10. David P. Hamilton, "Hewlett-Packard plans to relaunch its brand and adopt a new logo," *The Wall Street Journal, Interactive Edition*, 16 November 1999.

Chapter 3

1. Lauren Gibbons Paul, "Linking up (extranets)," *PC Week*, 1 March 1999.

2. Gary Hamel and Jeff Sampler, "The e-corporation: More than just Web-based, it's building a new industrial order," *Fortune*, 12 December 1998, p. 80.

3. Our "brand.comm" term is not related to, nor affiliated with, the website brand.com.

4. According to a Cyber Dialogue study reported in Maryann Jones Thompson, "Tracking the Internet economy: 100 numbers you need to know," *The Industry Standard*, 13 September 1999.

5. Joshua Macht, "The Internet is a great place to find new customers. It's an even better place to serve existing ones," Special Issue of *Technology '98* (*Using Internet in Business-to-Business Transactions*), 15 September 1998, pp. 42ff.

6. Nick Wreden, "Good deal for Michelin dealers," *Information Week*, no. 653 (20 October 1997): 98–100.

7. Quoted in Sharon Smith, "Internal affairs (corporate investment into intranets)," *Marketing*, 7 August 1997, p. 24.

8. Michael Schrage, "Procter & Gamble explains why the Web will be the biggest medium since TV" (interview with Denis Beausejour), *Adweek*, 20 July 1998, p. IQ16.

9. Wayne Wilhelm and Bill Rossello, "The care and feeding of customers," *Management Review*, 1 March 1997, p. 19.

10. Quoted in Chris Reidy, "Connecting the dots," *Boston Globe*, 13 October 1999, pp. F1–F2.

11. Forrester Research study cited in Donna J. Abernathy, "Intranets: Are we there yet?" *Training & Development*, 1 November 1998.

12. Studies cited in Peter Haapaneimi, "Corporation 2010," *Chief Executive (US)*, 1 January 1998, p. S2.

Chapter 4

1. As quoted in George Donnelly, "Acquiring minds," *CFO*, September 1999.

2. Quoted in Leslie Walker, "Looking beyond books: Amazon's Bezos sees personalization as key to cyber-stores' future," *Washington Post*, 8 November 1998.

3. Aaron Elstein, "Had enough with advertisements for online firms? Brace yourself," *The Wall Street Journal Interactive Edition*, 20 October 1999.

4. Michael Schrage, "Procter & Gamble explains why the Web will be the biggest medium since TV (interview with Denis Beausejour)," *Adweek*, 20 July 1998, p. IQ16.

5. These observations have also been made and elaborated on by Lynn Upshaw in *The eBrand Letter*, a monthly closed-circulation online analysis coauthored by Upshaw (with Robert Liljenwald), which describes and analyzes late-breaking events and trends in e-business.

6. Susan Karlin, "It takes an evillage," *Upside*, 1 January 1999.

7. Cited in David Sumner Smith, "Wake up to Web brands," *Marketing*, 16 October 1997, p. 28.

8. Jonathan Littman, op. cit.

9. Ibid.

10. John Dodge, "Vital organs, kidnapped fairies go up for sale on auction sites," *The Wall Street Journal Interactive Edition*, 24 August 1999.

11. Neal E. Boudette, "EBay offers entire companies online in germany," *The Wall Street Journal Interactive Edition*, 27 December 1999.

12. Gregory L. White, "How GM, Ford Think the Internet Can Make Splash In Their Factories," *The Wall Street Journal Interactive Edition*, 3 December 1999.

Chapter 5

1. Robert D. Hof, "Is the center of the computing universe shifting?" *Business Week* 18 January 1999, p. 64.

2. From a conference call with Scott McNealy via Charles Schwab Signature Services CEO Speaker Series, 26 May 1999.

3. From Sun Microsystems Web site, September 1999.

4. From Sun Microsystems Web site, accessed November 1999.

5. Patricia Nakache, "Smart managing/Best practices: Secrets of the new brand builders AOL, Yahoo, Palm Computing—a few innovative infotech stars have built powerhouse consumer brands in very little time. You may be able," *Fortune*, 22 June 1998, p. 167.

6. John Markoff, "Microsoft sets shifts in Internet strategy," *New York Times on the Web*, 24 September 1999.

Chapter 6

1. From a speech delivered at the 1998 Build Brand Value Conference, San Francisco, CA, 23 March 1998.

2. G. William Dauphinais and Colin Price, "The CEO as psychologist," *Management Review*, September 1998, pp. 10–15.

3. From "America @ Work—The 1999 Workforce Commitment Index," AON Consulting, p. 8.

4. Kenneth Labich and Patty de Llosa, "Why companies fail," *Fortune*, 14 November 1994, p. 52.

5. We first heard the phrase *sense of brand* from Beth Tilney, Senior Vice President of Marketing and Communications of Enron Corporation in May of 1997. Since that time, Enron has proven to be a prime example of a tradition-bound company that was transformed into a leading competitor in the deregulated energy field, at least in part by instilling in its people a strong sense of brand.

6. An important part of Branson's mystique is his professed naivete about a business he is about to enter. That began on the company's first day of existence when an employee threw out an idea about the company brand name: "What about Virgin? We're complete virgins at business."

7. Martha Groves, "The soul at work," *Los Angeles Times*, 6 April 1998, p. D2.

8. Carol J. Williams, "A retail revolution built on furniture for the masses," *Los Angeles Times*, 8 November 1998, p. C-1.

9. Based on interviews with Elizabeth A. Tilney, SVP—Marketing Communications and HR. Enron Energy Services (Retail). Formerly SVP—Advertising, Communications, and Organization Development, Enron Corp., June 1999.

10. James Harkness, "Brands—the internal dimension," *Brand Strategy*, 23 January 1998.

11. For more on the subject of employees as brand/company ambassadors, see Jan Carlzon, *Moments of Truth* (New York: HarperCollins, 1987).

12. Michael Krantz, "Cruising inside Amazon," *Time*, 27 December 1999, Section: "Inside the Amazon Culture." p. 68+.

13. Daniel Roth, "This Ain't No Pizza Party Pizza Hut and Papa John's are engaged in a Kentucky blood feud. At stake: The future of pizza pies," *Fortune*, 9 November 1998, p. 158; and John Greenwald et al., "Slice, Dice and Devour Papa John's uses sweet-tasting sauce and tangy ads to win market share in the pizza wars. Can anyone stop the Papa?" *Time*, 26 October 1998, p. 64.

14. Joseph Alsop, "Johnson & Johnson turns up tops thanks to its credo, and to babies," *The Wall Street Journal Interactive Edition*, 23 September 1999.

15. Michael D. Eisner, "Letter to shareholders," *The Walt Disney Company 1997 Annual Report*, p. 4.

16. Rekha Balu, "Whirlpool gets real with customers," *Fast Company*, December 1999, p. 74.

17. Jared Sandberg, "The friendly virus," *Newsweek*, 12 April 1999, p. 65.

18. Based on interviews with Kathy Fitzgerald, Senior Vice President, and Directors Kent Miller and Joyce Faucette Farmer, from Lucent Technologies in May and November 1999 and January 2000.

19. Brian Leavy and Michael Gannon, "Competing for hearts and minds: A corporate cultural perspective on marketing," *Irish Marketing Review*, 1 January 1998, p. 39.

Chapter 7

1. From a panel discussion held at the 1998 Build Brand Value Conference, San Francisco, CA, 23 March 1998.

2. David Leonhardt, "A leaderless orchestra offers lessons for business," *New York Times on the Web*, 10 November 1999.

3. Peter F. Drucker, "Management's new paradigms," *Forbes*, 5 October 1998, p. 152. Brackets ours.

4. Kotler, op. cit.

5. For a more thorough discussion of this and related issues, see Stan Maklan and Simon Knox, *Competing On Value—Bridging the Gap Between Brand and Customer Value*, Alexandria, VA: Financial Times Management, 1998, p. 214.

6. Based on (1) interviews with Charles Harstad, 3M Corporate Marketing Staff Vice President, and Dean Adams, 3M Corporate Brand Manager, in July and August 1999; and (2) Tom Andel, "Brand yourself," *Transportation & Distribution*, August 1998, p. 108.

7. Michael Hartnett, "Team leaders and team players . . . ," *Food & Beverage Marketing*, 1 January 1998, p. 13.

8. Nina Munk, "Finished at forty in the new economy, the skills that come with age count for less and less. Suddenly, 40 is starting to look and feel old," *Fortune*, 1 February 1999, p. 50.

9. Based on interview with Dawn Hudson, Senior Vice President—Strategy and Marketing, Pepsi-Cola North America, June 1999.

10. Chris Macrae (and coworkers of the World Class Branding Network), *The Brand Chartering Handbook*, (Harlow, England: Addison-Wesley, 1996, p. 29). Also, many thanks to Chris Macrae for additional insights provided to the authors.

Chapter 8

1. As quoted in Rebecca McReynolds, "Doing it the Schwab way," *U.S. Banker*, 1 July 1998, p. 46.

2. As quoted in Charles Gasparino, "Wall Street has less and less time for small investors," *The Wall Street Journal*, 5 October 1999, p. C1.

3. Rebecca McReynolds, op. cit.

4. Sam Zuckerman, "Fidelity, Schwab score with traders," *San Francisco Chronicle*, 29 April 2000, p. A1.

5. Based on interviews with Edward M. Rodden, Senior Vice President—Retail Brokerages, Charles Schwab & Co., August and October 1999.

Chapter 9

1. For a detailed discussion of brand architecture types, see Jean-Noël Kapferer, *Strategic Brand Management—New Approaches to Creating and Evaluating Brand Equity*. (New York: Free Press, 1992, p. 147) and Kevin Lane Keller, *Strategic Brand Management—Building, Measuring, and Managing Brand Equity* (Upper Saddle River, NJ: Prentice-Hall, 1998, p. 428).

2. John A. Byrne, "Jack: A close-up look at how America's #1 manager runs GE," *Business Week*, 8 June 1998, p. 90.

3. Shannon Stevens, "Brand builders," *Brandweek*, 16 March 1998, p. 19.

4. Robert L. Rose and Carl Quintanilla, "Sara Lee's plan to contract out work is trend among U.S. firms," *Dow Jones Online News*, 17 September 1997.

5. Andrew Marshall, "Corporate profile: Procter takes a gamble to go truly global," *The Independent—London*, 26 May 1999, p. 3.

6. Tara Parker-Pope, "New CEO preaches rebellion for Procter & Gamble's 'cult'," *The Wall Street Journal Interactive Edition*, 11 December 1998.

7. As this book was going to press in June 2000, Procter & Gamble announced Durk Jager's resignation. While Jager was widely praised for his vision, the rapid pace of restructuring took its toll on earnings, and P&G's stock price had fallen by half from a 52-week high in January. Time will tell if Jager's infusion of outside-the-Proctoid box thinking will help P&G create longer-term value, even though he failed to deliver short-term profitability.

Chapter 10

1. Emily Maison Beck, Editor, *Barletts Familiar Quotations,* 14th edition (Boston: Little Brown and Company, 1968).

2. Lynn B. Upshaw, *Building Brand Identity—A Strategy for Success in a Hostile Marketplace* (New York: John Wiley & Sons, 1995, p. 14, 121ff).

3. See Ted Levitt, *The Marketing Imagination* (New York: The Free Press, 1986).

4. L. L. Bean spokesperson cited in: Vivian Marino, "Lifetime guarantee—What does it mean?" Associated Press newswire, 13 January 1997.

5. Linda Himelstein (with Heather Green, Richard Siklos, and Catherine Yang), "Yahoo! The company, the strategy, the stock," *Business Week Online,* September 1998.

6. Suein L. Hwang, "Yahoo! informs the world it has become an e-mall," *Wall Street Journal* (Online edition) 29 October 1999.

7. Both quoted in Himelstein, et al., op. cit.

8. Quoted in Suein L. Hwang, "A new spin for Web firms: Not.com." *The Wall Street Journal* 11 November 1999, pp. B1, B4.

9. David S. Pottruck and Terry Pearce, *Clicks and Mortar—Passion-driven Growth in an Internet-Driven World* (San Francisco: Jossey-Bass, 2000, p. 159).

10. Leslie Kaufman, "Excite@Home to Acquire Bluemountain," *The New York Times* 26 October 1999, pp. C1, C10.

11. Both cited in Saul Hansell, "In the wired world, much is now free at click of a mouse," *The New York Times* 14 October 1999, pp. C1, C21.

12. Ibid.

13. Cited in Mark Pendergrast, "Is Coke still the real thing?" *The Wall Street Journal* 7 December 1999, p. A26.

14. Both cited in Saul Hansell, "Big Internet sites joining auction network," *The New York Times,* 17 September, 1999, p. C2.

15. Hiawatha Bray, "Tiny Woburn firm to battle giant auction service eBay," *The Boston Globe,* 8 September 1999, pp. F1, F2.

Chapter 11

1. Saul Hansell, "Now, AOL everywhere," *The New York Times on the Web,* 4 July 1999.

2. Josh McHugh, "Web warrior," *Forbes,* 11 January 1999, p. 152.

3. Bernhard Warner, "You've got clout," *Industry Standard,* 21 June 1999.

4. Dow Jones Newswires—23 November 1999.

5. Based on an explanatory graphic from: "The (World Wide) Web They Weave," *The Wall Street Journal,* 3 April 2000, p. B12.

6. Kara Swisher and Nick Wingfield, "Behind the recent wedding of bricks and clicks: Need to woo customers," *The Wall Street Journal Interactive Edition*, 17 December 1999.

7. ———, "AOL's case: 'Consistent and unwavering . . . Nimble and flexible'," *Business Week Online*, 12 July 1999.

Chapter 12

1. Robert L. Simison, "Ford to debut ad at same time globally," *The Wall Street Journal*, 27 October 1999, p. B8.

2. Theodore Levitt, "The globalization of markets," *Harvard Business Review*, May–June 1983, p. 92.

3. To a small minority of consumers, these brands represent "economic colonialism," as punctuated by the demonstrations at the December 1999 World Trade Organization meeting in Seattle. Those views have not been a major sales factor in the past, but could sway public opinion in the future.

4. The research in question was conducted by Upshaw & Associates on behalf of Visa International during December 1997 through August 1998. By agreement with cooperating respondent companies, specific findings were not released to the public.

5. John L. Petersen, "Getting ready for the 21st century," *USA Today Magazine*, 1 May 1999.

6. Joanne Cole, "Beyond global: The best multinationals go 'glocal'," *Leadership*, 1 December 1998.

7. Susan H. C. Tai and Y. H. Wong, "Advertising decision making in Asia: 'Glocal' versus 'regcal' approach," *Journal of Managerial Issues*, 1 October 1998, p. 318.

8. As reported online by *Industry Standard*, accessed 7 September 1999.

Epilogue

1. Andrew Pollack, "Akio Morita, Key to Japan's Rise as Co-Founder of Sony, Dies at 78," *New York Times On The Web*, 3 October 1999.

2. Edwin M. Reingold and Mitsuko Shimomura, *Made in Japan* (New York: E. P. Dutton, 1986).

3. Ibid.

ADDITIONAL SOURCES

Abernathy, Donna J. "Intranets: Are we there yet?" *Training & Development* (1 November 1998).

Anthony, J., Steven P. Kim, and Richard T. Quinn. "The employee-customer-profit chain at Sears." *Harvard Business Review* (1 January 1998): 82.

———. "Apple infuriates customers by raising prices retroactively." *The Wall Street Journal Interactive Edition* (15 October 1999).

Aveni, Richard A. D. "Strategic supremacy through disruption and dominance." *Sloan Management Review* (1 April 1999).

Batstone, David. "Direct from Dell." *Iconocast* (11 November 1999).

———. "Behind Branson." *The Economist* (21 February 1998).

Branch, Shelly, "Managers find happy staff leads to happy customers," *The Wall Street Journal Interactive Edition* (23 December 1998).

Brooker, Katrina. "Can Procter & Gamble change its culture, protect its market share, and find the next tide?" *Fortune* (26 April 1999): 146.

Bruce, Anne. "Southwest: Back to the fundamentals." *HR Focus* (1 March 1997).

Bunish, Christine. "Global roundtable: Marketers talk about their challenges, goals." *Business Marketing* (1 January 1998): 3.

Casey, Michael. "Power of Internet changes supply and demand forever." *The Wall Street Journal Interactive Edition* (18 October 1999).

Court, David C., Anthony Freeling, Mark G. Leiter, and Andrew J. Parsons. "If Nike can 'just do it,' why can't we?" *The McKinsey Quarterly* (Summer 1997).

Cronin, Mary J. "Nets at work: Bye-bye, wild Web when your Intranet becomes mission critical, it's time to rein in the cowboys. That's what's happening at HP." *Fortune* (27 October 1997): 264+.

Decker, Charles L. *Winning With the P&G 99—99 Principles and Practices of Procter & Gamble's Success.* New York: Pocket Books, 1998.

Deutsch, Claudia H. "The handwriting on the Post-it Note: Image and returns suffer at 3M." *New York Times on the Web* (6 July 1999).

Ebenkamp, Becky. "Republican candidate," *Brandweek* (11 October 1999): M18.

Edmondson, Gail, et al. "L'Oréal: The beauty of global branding." *Business Week (International Edition)* (28 June 1999).

Emert, Carol. "Old Navy's model plan." *San Francisco Chronicle* (20 October 1999): C1.

———, "Fed reluctantly embraces a 'New Economy'." *New York Times on the Web (Reuters)* (13 November 1999).

Flanigan, James. "Can Procter & Gamble make the tide turn?" *Los Angeles Times* (13 June 1999): C-1.

Galuszka, Peter, and Kathleen Morris. "Spin-offs: Tricon: With all this fizz, who needs Pepsi?" *Business Week* (19 October 1998): 72.

Glassman, Andrew. "Cisco study sees huge Web economy." *CNBC* (10 June 1999).

———, "Global reach, virtual leadership." *Fast Company* (September 1999): 80.

Godin, Seth. *Permission Marketing.* (New York: Simon & Shuster, 1999).

Goldman, Debra. "The Disney Channel is tuning into what you want before you know you want it. All you, all the time." *Mother Jones* (15 May 1998).

Graves, Lucas. "In search of the next Yahoo!" *MC Technology Marketing Intelligence* 17, no. 9 (October 1997): 40–48.

Greco, JoAnn. "Knowledge is power." *Journal of Business Strategy* (19 March 1999).

Gould, Michael, and Andrew Campbell. "Desperately seeking synergy." *Harvard Business Review* (1 September 1998): 131.

Haapaneimi, Peter. "Corporation 2010: Business in the 21st century." *Chief Executive (U.S.)* (1 January 1999).

Hansell, Saul. "Toys 'R' Us falls behind on shipping." *The New York Times on the Web* (23 December 1999).

Higley, Jeff. "Marriott's growth machine adding parts." *Hotel & Motel Management* (1 June 1998): 4.

———, "How Lexus created the brand value, from design to ads to ownership, that every car company is looking for." *Brandweek* (27 July 1998).

Hof, Robert P. and Linda Himelstein. "eBay vs. Amazon.com." *Business Week* (31 May 1999): 134.

Hunter, Victor L., and David Tietyen. "Business-to-business marketing: Creating a community of customers." *Direct Marketing* (1 October 1998): 24.

Hymowitz, Carol, "Amazon.com digs deep for answers when hiring," *Minneapolis Star Tribune* (10 May 1999): 11D.

Janah, Manua, and Clinton Wilder. "Fed-X special delivery." *Information Week* no. 654 (27 October 1997): 42–60.

Kahn, Jeremy. "The world's most admired companies getting to the top is hard. So is staying there." *Fortune* (26 October 1998): 206.

Karlin, Susan. "It takes an evillage." *Upside* (1 January 1999).

Kaufman, Leslie. "Amazon to remake itself into a bazaar on the Internet." *New York Times on the Web* (30 September 1999).

Kim, Chan W., and Renee Mauborgne. "Creating new market space." *Harvard Business Review* (1 January 1999): 83.

Landry, Julie. "Offline auctioneer makes Net bid." *Redherring.com* (18 October 1999).

Landry, Julie. "Participate.com hopes to profit from Web communities." *Redherring.com* (23 September 1999).

Langer, Judith. "What consumers wish brand managers knew." *Journal of Advertising Research* 37, no. 6 (November/December 1997): 60.

Larson, Erik. "Free money: The Internet I.P.O. that made two women rich, and a lot of people furious." *The New Yorker* (11 October 1999): 76ff.

Lester, Richard K. "Companies that listen to their inner voices." *Technology Review* (May–June 1998): 54.

Levering, Robert, and Milton Moskowitz. *The 100 Best Companies to Work for in America.* (New York: Plume, 1994).

Lieber, Ronald B. "Selling the sizzle: Harley-Davidson motorcycles mean freedom to all types of buyers." *Fortune* (23 June 1997): 80.

Lynch, John G., Jr., and Dan Ariely. "Electronic shopping for wine: How search costs affect consumer price sensitivity, satisfaction with merchandise and retention." *Marketing Science Institute*, Report Summary No. 99–104 (1999).

Maklan, Stan, and Simon Knox. *Competing on Value* (London: Financial Times Management, 1998).

———, "Mall loses its e-retailing battle as tenants choose to fight back." *The Wall Street Journal Interactive Edition* (1 December 1999).

McGeehan, Patrick. "Schwab counters a pincers movement." *New York Times on the Web* (17 October 1999).

McFarlane, John, of Sun Microsystems. Speech to eBusiness World Internet Expo (September 1998).

McWilliams, Gary, and Joseph B. White. "Others want to figure out how to adopt Dell model." *The Wall Street Journal Interactive Edition* (1 December 1999).

Muller, Joann. "For the next 'Net Generation,' commerce is where it's @." *Boston Globe* (13 September 1998): Business Section, K1, K4.

Munk, Nina. "How Levi's trashed a great American brand while Bob Haas pioneered benevolent management, his company came apart at the seams." *Fortune* (12 April 1999): 82.

Murphy, Kate. "Can Blue Bell go national without losing local mystique?" *New York Times on the Web* (7 February 1998).

Narisetti, Raju. "Gerstner will stay at IBM for at least five more years." *The Wall Street Journal* (21 November 1997).

Nee, Eric. "Interview with Lew Platt: Why I dismembered HP." *Fortune.com* (11 March 1999).

Norr, Henry. "PC could be next standard appliance." *San Francisco Chronicle* (5 February 2000): A1.

Paul, Lauren Gibbons. "Linking up (extranets)." *PC Week* (1 March 1999).

Peppers, Don, and Martha Rogers. "When extreme isn't enough." *Sales & Marketing Management* (1 February 1999): 26.

Piturro, Marlene. "About the new GLOBAL REALITIES (Successful business in a fluctuating economic environment). *Management Review* (1 March 1999).

Pollack, Andrew. "Akio Morita, key to Japan's rise as co-founder of Sony, Dies at 78." *New York Times on the Web* (3 October 1999).

Pope-Parker, Tara. "P&G puts two cleaning products on its new marketing fast track." *The Wall Street Journal Interactive Edition* (18 May 1999).

Power, Denise. "Levi's extranet links shops." *Women's Wear Daily* (3 March 1999).

Prince, Greg W. "The Snapple decade." *Beverage World* 116, no. 1633 (15 February 1997): 28.

Rebello, Stephen. "Visionaries." *Success* (February 1998): 109.

Reese, Jennifer. "Starbucks: Inside the coffee cult." *Fortune* (9 December 1996): 190.

Reichheld, Frederick F. *The Loyalty Effect—The Hidden Force Behind Growth, Profits, and Lasting Value* (Boston: Harvard Business Press, 1996, pp. 289–293).

Reiman, Jim. "In Web we trust.(electronic commerce)." *Direct* (1 April 1999).

Ross, Sherwood. "Employee involvement key to better returns," *Reuters News Service* (8 September 1998).

Rupley, Sebastian. "Kissing cousins." *PC Magazine Online* (24 November 1998).

Sandberg, Jared. "Users are choosing information over entertainment on the Web." *Wall Street Journal* (20 July 1998).

Schlender, Brent. "The three faces of Steve." *Fortune* (9 November 1998).

Schonfeld, Erick. "10 companies that get it." *Fortune.com* (22 October 1999).

Schuch, Beverly, and Donald Van De Mark. "Continental's comeback." (Report broadcast on CNNfn in "Business Unusual.")

Schultz, Don E. " 'Integrated global marketing' will be new name of the game." *Marketing News* (26 October 1998): 5.

Selwitz, Robert. "Multi-branding opportunities need special strategies." *Hotel & Motel Management* (May 1998): 34–36.

Sharkey, Betsy, and T. L. Stanley. "Marketer of the year: Michael Eisner." *Mediaweek* (9 October 1995).

———. "Single vs multibrand." *Bank Marketing International* (1 June 1999): 8.

Snow, Charles C., Sue Canney Davison, Scott A. Snell, and Donald C. Hambrick. "Use transnational teams to globalize your company." *Organizational Dynamics* (1 March 1996): 50.

Southwick, Karen. High Noon—The Inside Story of Scott McNealy and the Rise of Sun Microsystems. (New York: John Wiley & Sons, 1999).

Sun Microsystems Company Profile. *The Wall Street Journal Interactive Edition* (accessed 8 August 1999).

Thomas, Susan Gregory. "Getting To Know You.com." *U.S. News & World Report* (15 November 1999): 102.

Tolbert, Kathryn. "Rules change as Japan Inc. downsizes jobs for life and seniority traditions are dropped for Western models." *International Herald Tribune* (4 June 1999): 13.

Walker, Leslie. "Looking beyond books. Amazon's Bezos sees personalization as key to cyber stories' future." *Washington Post* (8 November 1998): H01.

Warner, Bernhard. "Digitizing dinner." *Adweek* (16 February 1998): 40–42.

———. "You've got clout." *Industry Standard* (21 June 1999).

Weber, Thomas E. "Going after the desktop: All AOL, all the time?" *The Wall Street Journal Online Edition* (19 March 1999).

———. "The man in the middle." *The Wall Street Journal Online Edition* (21 June 1999).

White, Joseph B. "Ford's CEO Nasser ponders giving more authority to regional units." *The Wall Street Journal Interactive Edition* (17 September 1998).

Whitely, Richard, and Diane Hessan. *Customer-Centered Growth: Five Proven Strategies for Building Competitive Advantage*. Reading, MA: The Forum Corporation, Addison-Wesley Publishing Company, 1996.

Wingfield, Nick, and Joanne S. Lublin. "America Online is quietly hunting for president of international unit." *The Wall Street Journal Interactive Edition* (28 October 1999).

Wreden, Nick. "Internet opens markets abroad—Global companies still need to overcome cultural obstacles." *Information Week* (16 November 1998): 94.

ACKNOWLEDGMENTS

We'd first like to thank our agent, Michael Snell, for his help and advice. Special thanks to our talented editor, Ruth Mills at John Wiley & Sons (now heading Ruth Mills Literary Services), for her wise guidance and support. Thanks, as well, to Airié Dekidjiev and Chris Mindnich, of John Wiley & Sons, and Tom Laughman who assisted us near the end of our publishing process.

We are very grateful for the fine research assistance of Nathalie Vidamour in the early stages of our work, and the later research and exceptional copyediting provided by a most talented book widow, Susan Upshaw. Thanks also to Paula Soffronoff for graphic assistance. We also owe great thanks to our insightful readers whose comments helped sculpt our work, including: Virginia Vann, Dianne Snedaker, Jan Soderstrom, Caroline McNally, and most especially, John Faville.

And, many thanks to those individuals in many successful masterbrand companies, without whose cooperation this book would not have been possible. They include: Tim Leatherman and Mark Baker at Leatherman Tool Group; Robert Solomon and Bill Brown of Outrigger Hotels & Resorts, Brian Swette of eBay; Kathy Fitzgerald, Kent Miller, and Judy Shapiro of Lucent Technologies; Jan Soderstrom of 3Com, John Loiacono and Marge Breya of Sun Microsystems, Elizabeth Tilney of Enron, Dawn Hudson and Dave Dececco of PepsiCo, Charles Harstad and Dean Adams of 3M, Edward Rodden and Len Short of Charles Schwab & Co., Maureen Hurley of Rich Products, Ken Stickevers of Gateway Computer, J. D. Weir of Esurance, and Michael Howse of Abilizer.

Earl Taylor would also like to thank his supportive colleagues at

Research International, especially Gene Pokorny, and the many clients who have supported his work, particularly Charles Hibler of Kansas City Power & Light.

To one and all, we sincerely thank you for your wise and practical counsel when we needed it most.

INDEX

ABOUT THE AUTHORS

Lynn B. Upshaw is a leading independent brand strategist and corporate advisor, and senior consultant to Interbrand Group and Bridge Strategy Group. His clients have included 3Com Corp.; Bayer Corp.; Visa International; Bell Atlantic; WellPoint Health Networks; Esurance, Inc.; NEC Corp.; Noosh, Inc.; Pacific Telesis; Bank of America; ConAgra; and other Fortune 500 and Internet companies. He is the authorof *Building Brand Identity* (John Wiley & Sons) and numerous articles, and is coauthor of the monthly online analysis, *The eBrand Letter*. He is a frequent speaker at industry conferences, universities, and corporate workshops.

Earl L. Taylor, Ph.D., Senior Vice President and Head of Consulting Services at Research International/Cambridge, has provided consultation and research for dozens of clients in the telecommunications, financial services, entertainment, and energy industries, including Bell Atlantic, Shell Oil, Massachusetts Financial Services, Walt Disney, and most of the larger energy companies in North America. Over the last two decades, Dr. Taylor has published articles and conducted seminars in his areas of expertise under the auspices of the American Marketing Association and numerous industry trade associations.